Chan and Enlightenment

Chan and Enlightenment

Chan Master Sheng Yen

Dharma Drum

Dharma Drum Publishing Corp.
New York & Taipei
2014

DHARMA DRUM PUBLISHING CORPORATION

5F, NO.186, Gongguan Road

Beitou District, Taipei 11244, Taiwan (R.O.C.)

www.ddc.com.tw

First Edition

Printed in Taiwan, January 2014

CHAN AND ENLIGHTENMENT

by Chan Master Sheng Yen

ISBN: 978-957-598-637-7

North America distributor:

Chan Meditation Center

90-56 Corona Ave., Elmhurst, NY 11373

Phone: (718) 592-6593

Fax: (718) 592-0717

www.chancenter.org

Contents

Author's Preface

The thought of Chan is a clear current in humanity that is free, subtle, flexible, spacious, open, bright and clear. The life of Chan is a way of settling the mind, which is vigorous, at ease, simple, unadorned, and self-contained. The vision of Chan is to teach us that we must first learn to put down selfishness, self-deception, self-disparagement, self-conceit, and self-fettering. Only then can we have an open, liberated spirit to soar freely in the boundless sky. Chan teaches us that we must first practice to know ourselves, affirm ourselves, and further dissolve self-centeredness; only then will the state of enlightenment be revealed to us.

The purpose of Chan is to teach us to turn the hells of eight levels of heat of the practical world into a seven-jeweled lotus pool that is cool and refreshing; to transform our bodily, verbal, and mental activities that harm others and ourselves, into the compassion and wisdom that benefit others and ourselves.

This book is not Chan itself, but it attempts to convey to the reader some of the messages about Chan. Prior to this book, I had published two similar books on Chan: In December 1984, I collected twenty-five of my lectures about Chan practice and compiled them into a book entitled *The Life of Chan* (*Chn. Chan de shenghuo*). In December of 1986, I further brought together twenty-four lectures on Buddhist Dharma that I gave afterwards and compiled them into a book entitled *Holding a Flower and Smiling* (*Chn. Nianhua weixiao*).

In the blink of an eye, it is now the year of 1991. In the past four years, though I had as usual, given Dharma talks to the Meditation Group at Nung Chan Monastery, very few of them were transcribed into articles. The reason is that the *Humanity Magazine* was publishing in installments another of my books, *Questions about Buddhism* (Chn. *Xuefo qunyi*), for a year-and-half. So *Humanity Magazine* was not lacking in manuscripts for its issues, and, on the other hand, I did not have much time to revise the drafts transcribed from the tapes.

In 1982, Dharma Drum Publications, which I established in New York, published *Getting the Buddha Mind*. This was followed by *The Poetry of Enlightenment* and *Faith in Mind: A Guide to Chan Practice* in 1987, *Ox Herding at Morgan's Bay* in 1988, and *The Infinite Mirror* in 1990, and *The Sword of Wisdom* in 1992. At the same time, these books were also published by Dongchu Publications in Taiwan. In terms of the reprints and publication volume, these eight books in Chinese and English on Chan should be among the most well-received by general readers among my various works. Although Chan does not rely on words, the Chan teaching that I have strived to promote, through the media of words, in both the East and the West has produced some positive influence on the world.

Among the twenty-seven articles contained in *Chan and Enlightenment*, "Talking about Dreams while in Dreams" and "Discrimination and Non-discrimination" were lectures that I gave to the Meditation Group at Nung Chan Monastery. The other lectures that I gave at different places in Taiwan include ten articles: "Chan and Entanglement" at Tamkang University; "Right Path and Evil Path" and "True Enlightenment and Mistaken Enlightenment" at Zhongxing Hall in Taichung; "Emotion and Reason" and "Good and Evil" at the Sun Yat-sen Memorial Hall in Taipei; "Chan: Thus Come, Thus Gone" at the Zhongzheng Cultural Center in Kaohsiung; "A Pure Land on Earth" at Dr. Sun Yat-sen Memorial Hall in Yonghe; "Pure Mind, Pure Land" at Banqiao Gymnasium in Taipei County; "Chan: You, I, and They" and "Chan: Many, One, and Nothingness" at Kaohsiung Girls' Senior High School. The rest of the articles are lectures given in the United States and Hong Kong, such as "Chan and Enlightenment" at Harvard University in Boston; "Transcending Time, Space, and Life" at the University of Massachusetts at Lowell, Massachusetts; "Chan and Daily Life" at Washington University; "Chan: Human Consciousness" at the City University of New York; "Chan: Carrying Water and Chopping Firewood" at Zuang Yen Monastery in New York; and "Chan: Freedom and Liberation" and "Chan: Ordinary Body and Mind" at Sha Tin City Hall in Hong Kong.

The articles in this book include three lectures each given in 1986, 1987, and 1989 respectively, eight in 1988, and as many as sixteen in 1990. During these years I had given many public lectures, and the articles in this book are among those that I had revised and finalized in 1990.

As for the lectures, because they use a style of speech suited for the general public, they mostly received hearty responses when I delivered them, especially in Taiwan, with the lecture halls full, whether the halls were small or large, and the audience numbering from several hundred to as many as six or seven thousand. Because the lectures, whether at home or abroad, were targeted mainly at the intellectuals of middle and higher levels, I tried as much as possible to take a scientific and rational perspective to introduce the theories and methods of Chan practice that are practical, easily understood, wholesome, and with clear levels and distinct aspects. In a sense, this book allows readers spending a few hours to accompany me for a period of four years, listening to over twenty of my lectures on Chan practice, one after another. They can even obtain more information than if they personally attended the talks, because they have been abridged, revised, and enlarged as necessary, so that they became much more concise and richer in content than when they were first delivered.

Master Sheng Yen

Nung Chan Monastery, Beitou, Taipei

April 2, 1991.

Chan Enlightenment and Sitting Meditation

Zen Center in Saint Louis, Missouri, USA, April 16, 1990

To practice Chan, one need not necessarily do sitting meditation, but one should still use meditation as the foundation. Meditation is beneficial to our body and mind; it promotes physical health and mental stability; it helps us to reduce attachments and makes our mind calmer and clearer. Taken one step further, meditation generates wisdom and develops the spiritual domain. However, from the Chan view, unless one is guided by Buddhist teachings, any wisdom generated through meditation will still harbor vexations. A meditator who is still self-centered will struggle and experience mental afflictions when in conflict with people, objects, and surroundings. Sitting meditation has three aspects: harmonizing the body, harmonizing the breath, and harmonizing the mind.

Harmonizing the body means taking a correct and comfortable meditating posture, as well as dealing with bodily reactions during the sitting. Harmonizing the breath refers to the levels of breathing according to the depth of one's concentration: beginning with the most basic level, there is nasal breathing, abdominal breathing, "embryonic" (or womb) breathing, and "turtle" (inner) breathing. *Nasal breathing* is breathing where the air naturally comes in and goes out the nostrils. With *abdominal breathing* we still breathe through the nose, but one does not pay attention to the nostrils, nor senses the breath flowing through them; one is just aware of the rising and falling movement of the abdomen. With *embryonic breathing*, one does not breathe through the nostrils; rather, each and every pore of the body serves as a respiratory organ; at this time one is like a fetus while the universe is the womb. With *turtle breathing*, one doesn't need to inhale air from outside, and even the heart seems to stop beating. At this time, the body becomes independently like a universe in itself, and relies on the *qi (chi)*, the body's vital energy, for operation and circulation; being self-sustaining and self-sufficient, without requiring the supply of air or nutrition from outside the body.

And how does one take care of the thoughts in one's mind? Generally one uses methods of meditative calming and contemplation to collect the mind and focus the thoughts: counting the breath, reciting the Buddha's name, meditating on the impurity of the body, doing prostrations, sitting meditation, contemplation, and so on, help one achieve this purpose.

The main purpose of meditation is to bring a scattered mind to a concentrated state, and then to gradually turn the concentrated mind into unified mind. Generally, when one attains unified mind, one would think that one is already free of self-attachment and has reached the stage of no-self. In fact, one is just at the level of meditative concentration. As well, the meditative concentration may be shallow or deep, and that fact is reflected in the Buddhist classification of meditative states into eight kinds of meditative concentration attained in the four dhyana heavens and the four formless heavens, none of which is beyond the scope of a unified mind. That is to say, none of the eight kinds of meditative concentration is an attainment of no-mind, the wisdom of emptiness. According to the above, meditative concentration, in and of itself, does not necessarily equate to the meditative concentration of Chan.

What, then, is the meditative concentration of the Chan school? The *Platform Sutra* of the Sixth Patriarch Huineng says: "Externally, to transcend characteristics is meditation; internally, to be undisturbed is concentration." (McRae 2000) Also, "One does not see the right and wrong, the good and bad, the transgressions and faults of people. The mind of meditative concentration remains undisturbed when encountering the myriad external objects; within each moment of thought, one sees that one's intrinsic nature is pure."

This shows that the meditative concentration of Chan is founded in contemplating pure wisdom, not in the concentrative state of unified mind. If one still dwelt in unified mind, one has not fully departed from attachment. And what do we mean by attachment? When facing any person, thing, or situation, if you first emphasize that "you" have seen something and add a value judgment, then that is attachment.

So, what does Chan mean by non-attachment? When any thing, situation, or person appears in front of you, you do not add on any opinion but respond in an appropriate way to that person or situation, in accord with what the person or situation requires. When dealing with issues of property, or relations between parents and children, or between man and woman, it is easiest for us to feel self-centered attachment, and then with our own reputation and ideas. For spiritual practitioners, the deepest attachment is to their own achievements and experience; they can abandon anything except the value of their own viewpoints and experience, so they still have arrogance. Therefore, as long as one affirms the value of one's existence, one has not attained true liberation, and one has not really accomplished the wisdom without outflows.

In the Chan tradition, when one attains enlightenment, it is called "seeing the nature." After seeing the nature, one needs to maintain and enhance it. Thus, after attaining enlightenment, one embarks on the course of cultivation and works on nourishing it. In spite of the Chan School's emphasis that upon attaining enlightenment one's view is identical to the Buddha's, one is nevertheless not yet a buddha. This is similar in the Tibetan school, where one visualizes oneself as one's own *yidam*, or meditation deity; but even when one accomplishes this, the meditation deity remains the meditation deity, while one remains oneself. Nevertheless, now, one has more compassion than before engaging in the practice.

Therefore, in the Chan tradition, masters had to work hard before getting enlightened, and after attaining it they had to look for a more attained teacher. Only after enlightenment could one know who was a good teacher, and having found one, they had to redouble their efforts. Chan doesn't necessarily require one to sit in meditation, so Master Huineng's *Platform Sutra* says, "the seated meditation we teach does not attach to the mind or purity, nor does it mean sitting still." And it says, "the seated meditation some people teach requires one to observe the mind and contemplate purity without moving or getting up, putting their efforts into such practice. As deluded people have no understanding, they attach to sitting and practice wrongly." Huineng claimed: "Concentration is the essence of wisdom and wisdom is the function of concentration. At times of wisdom, concentration exists in that wisdom. At times of concentration, wisdom exists in that concentration." So, we have not seen any records about how Huineng engaged in sitting meditation. After Huineng's passing, his first generation disciple, Chan Master Huairang, on seeing his own disciple Mazu Daoyi meditating, asked him: "If sitting meditation can make one a buddha, wouldn't it be possible to make a mirror by polishing a brick?"

From many Chan records, however, we see that many lineage

masters of the Chan School also needed to practice sitting meditation. In the *Pure Rules* set up by Chan Master Baizhang, a disciple of Mazu, we find reference to "having sat in meditation for a long time." Nevertheless, the lineage masters didn't emphasize sitting; rather, they regarded each and every action in every moment of daily life as spiritual practice. The rules of daily life of Baizhang that we read do not say how long one should practice sitting meditation each day, but has a passage that says, "A day without work, a day without meals." This shows that his major practice was to work in the mountains or in the fields.

The same is true with Master Huineng. Before visiting Fifth Patriarch Hongren, Huineng was a woodcutter. After they met, Hongren did not tell Huineng to go sit, but sent him instead to mill rice in the kitchen. But we should understand that even when he was working, Huineng's mind was always stable and calm, without emotional fluctuations. Only such people will be able to attain true enlightenment.

However, it is also necessary to seek guidance through the concepts of Buddhism. Master Huineng gained true enlightenment when he heard a few words from the *Diamond Sutra,* which enabled him to realize the sameness and difference between [the concepts of] attachment and non-attachment, and between self and no-self. This shows that concepts are still very important. Although the Chan School claims to be "not dependent on words and language," what it means is that we should not be attached to words or language, though we still need to hear the teachings and get correct guidance from them. This is called "using the doctrine to awaken to the principle, [that is to say, from the teachings, one realizes Chan]."

If Huineng had not heard the words from the *Diamond Sutra:*

"Abiding nowhere, give rise to mind," he would not have gotten enlightened just then. And if he heard the phrase but only attached to it, he would not have gotten enlightened either. Therefore, Chan teachers liken the doctrines to a finger pointing to the moon; without the pointing finger, deluded people would not be able to see the moon. If deluded people just stare at the finger and refuse to look at the moon, the pointing finger is of no use. On the other hand, once people see the moon that the finger is pointing at, then the finger would also no longer be useful.

Since most people are unable to calm their minds, or even if they could, would have difficulties remaining calm and settled, they still must sit in meditation. We can also say that while Chan enlightenment does not necessarily require sitting meditation, the power of concentration from meditation is conducive to Chan enlightenment. Even so, to merely sit in meditation would not bring about Chan enlightenment.

I think the majority of you already have a fundamental knowledge about the Buddhadharma or Buddhism, and some are already engaging in Chan practice, while others are studying and practicing Tibetan Buddhism. I believe that you have many questions to ask. I'll answer what I can, and for what I don't understand, I'll say I don't know.

Q & A

Q: The Japanese Soto (Chn. *Caodong*) sect emphasizes practice and plays down the importance of seeking enlightenment, saying that sitting is itself enlightenment. What do you think about such a teaching?

A: I think that's a safer and more practical concept. If one simply seeks or stresses enlightenment, it may cause people to develop an opportunistic mentality of reversing cause and effect, and end up not wanting to practice, or thinking that they won't have to practice after attaining enlightenment. Moreover, emphasizing enlightenment may cause long-time practitioners to feel despair if they have not had a breakthrough to enlightenment, and even give up on practice. So I also advocate that it's better to emphasize just practicing, than to stress attaining enlightenment. Do you agree with my opinion?

Q: I certainly do. When I ask my master about the issue of enlightenment, he always advised me not to worry about it. Those who are attached to the experience of enlightenment take it to be a treasure and hold fast to it.

A: That's right. To pursue enlightenment and show it off is a kind of attachment in itself.

Q: I heard that a Korean monk placed in front of him a plaque with the word "Death" on it. Could you tell us whether one can only practice well when one has the determination to die?

A: We also teach people to make the determination to "go through the great death" when entering the Chan Hall. Death can be great death or small death. Small death is the death of the physical body, while one's karma—such as deluded thoughts and vexations, have not died yet. To undergo great death one should cast aside one's past, present, and future, regardless of whether they're good or bad experiences and concepts. Only this way can you really make an effort. I don't know what the Korean Son master's plaque with the word "Death" means. However, at a Chinese Chan Hall, the teacher would say, "Now we have to work really hard! You're only allowed to enter here alive and go out a dead person. As long as your thievish mind and deluded thoughts have not died, you should never leave the Chan Hall."

Q: Perhaps when this Korean Son master worked on a *huatou* or *gong'an*, he desperately wanted to break up the mass of doubt in this manner?

A: It's excellent to have this kind of determination, but it's dangerous to practice so fiercely. Only a few people with a very fit body and a very sound mental condition can adopt this approach.

Q: What kind of attitude should we take to handle emotions?

A: We should make use of emotions, but without being swayed by them, so as to not generate vexations.

Q: Can one teach people without resorting to emotions?

A: For sentient beings it's emotions; for bodhisattvas it's compassion. Take Avalokiteshvara Bodhisattva (Chn. Guanyin Pusa) for example. He takes on different appearances and uses a great variety of ways to help people. If he didn't help people with emotions, they would be in awe of him. Because bodhisattvas don't have attachment, they're also free of vexations. For people who don't follow Buddhism or engage in practice, the emotions will become their own vexations, and will also cause troubles for others.

Q: How can one apply emotions without giving rise to vexations?

A: There are two ways: one is to constantly use the concepts of the Dharma to correct and guide oneself, again and again. The other is to employ the methods of Chan to purify the emotions, little by little, into a compassionate heart.

Q: Emotion is something very natural. Once we try to restrain or deny it, it becomes unnatural.

A: When anything is subject to training or correction, it's definitely unnatural! It's natural for water to flow downward and it's unnatural if we pump it upward. However, we often have to pump water up into a dam or a reservoir. Only by giving it pressure can we utilize it.

Q: What is the position of compassion in the Chan teachings?

A: Compassion and wisdom are identical in meaning, but there are differences in how they are expressed. Those who truly have wisdom will truly have compassion. The manifestation of compassion lies in delivering sentient beings widely, yet there are neither the self nor sentient beings in one's mind—this is the selfless wisdom that realizes emptiness. Only with the wisdom that is free of the self and attachment will one display true compassion.

Chan and Enlightenment

Harvard University, November 12, 1988

Definitions of Chan

There are four ways we can define "Chan": as meditation, as the four *dhyanas*, as sitting practice, and as the Chinese school of Chan Buddhism.

Chan as Meditation

The Buddhist term in Sanskrit for meditation is dhyana, which was transliterated into "Chan" in Chinese. It contains various meanings, including concentration, quiet sitting, contemplative cultivation, and so on. Concentration consists of stilling the mind so that it rests on one object. Quiet sitting is equivalent to the English "meditation," whose contemporary meaning is "calming the mind." Contemplation refers not to thinking, but to continuously practicing on a method, and returning to it each time one departs from it, so as to make one's mind remain on the same method over a period of time. When explained with my concepts, dhyana means using the method to train a scattered mind into one able to concentrate, and then to reach the state where two successive thoughts are unified that is to say, there is but one thought. At this point one has entered meditative absorption. If one can take it one step further, breaking up the unified mind of meditative absorption and casting it away, then what appears is the state of "no-self" and "no-mind." This state is generally called "seeing the nature" (synonymous with "buddha-nature") or "enlightenment";

it is also the perfection of dhyana, the fifth of the *Six Paramitas* of Buddhism.

Chan as the Four Dhyanas

The Sanskrit term for the four dhyana heavens is *catvari dhyanani*. The first dhyana is the realm of joy after departing from the desire realm; the second dhyana, that of joy derived from meditative absorption; the third dhyana, that of wondrous bliss after transcending joy; and the fourth dhyana, that of equanimity and pure thoughts after transcending the bliss of the third dhyana. Fascicle 17 of the *Kindred Sayings* (Skt. *Samyukta Agama*) reads, "While in the state of the first dhyana, words become quiescent and extinct; in the state of the second dhyana, the reflection and investigation or the coarse and fine mental functions become quiescent and extinct; in the state of the third dhyana, the joyful mind becomes quiescent and extinct; and in the state of the fourth dhyana, the in and out breaths become quiescent and extinct. These are the foundational Dharma approaches for the *four immeasurable minds* and *eight liberations*, as well as for the four samadhis of the formless realm and the samadhi of complete cessation (Skt. *nirodhi-samapatti/nirodha-samapanna*), commonly practiced by Indian Buddhism and non-Buddhists. In addition, they are the most essential method of practice adopted by the arhats of the Hinayana and by Shakyamuni Buddha, the World-Honored One; up to the moment of attaining the Path and entering into *parinirvana*, they all relied on these four *dhyanas* for their achievement. There are very detailed narrations about this in Fascicle 4, 6, & 12 of the *Long Sayings* (Skt. *Dirgha Agama*), and Fascicle 1, 42, & 56 of the *Middle Length Sayings* (Skt. *Madhyama Agama*). However, non-Buddhists thought that entering the supreme mundane samadhi was already liberation. For example, before attaining enlightenment, the Buddha learned the four dhyanas under the rishi, Arara. The non-Buddhist rishis took them to be the supreme liberation, but the Buddha discovered that they are not yet liberation. (See Fascicle 3 of the *Sutra of the Past and Present Cause and Effect*).

Chan as Sitting Practice

As the term implies, sitting meditation is using the sitting posture to achieve the goal of meditation practice. Indian yogis discovered the method for meditative concentration. It is said that in ancient India a practitioner went into the mountains to seek the way to liberation, and discovered monkeys sitting cross-legged in a lotus posture and regulating their breathing, so he tried to imitate them, and ended up having a relaxed, refreshed body and mind. Therefore, he advocated that people practice sitting meditation. In fact, this may just be a legend. With their physiological construct, it may be possible for monkeys to sit crossed-legged or stretched out, but whether they can sit in the lotus position is a big question. Among the classical writings in India before the Buddha's time, the *Upanishads* for example, already talked about the methods for practicing meditation. "Upanishad" is a compound Sanskrit word meaning "sitting near," denoting sitting face-to-face with open-heartedness and utter devotion. This book advocated that one regulate the breathing, the body, and the mind as well as reciting the mantra OM to enter meditative absorption.

According to the collective experiences of generations of meditation practitioners, sitting meditation is called the sitting method with seven key points:

1. Sit with legs crossed, i.e., in the full lotus posture if comfortable, if not use half-lotus, simple crossed legs, or on a chair

2. Keep the back upright

3. Form the *dharmadhatu* mudra (oval) with the hands

4. Relax the shoulders

5. Place the tip of the tongue against the upper palate

6. Keep the mouth closed

7. Open the eyes slightly

(For details please refer to the chapter, "The Beginner's Methods for Chan Meditation" in *Chan Experiences & Chan Talks* (Chn. *Chande tiyan, chande kaishi*), by this author. The required conditions are to sit alone in a tranquil, secluded place, or a room that is quiet and free from disturbances. One also needs to have few desires, and be contented to achieve the level of meditative concentration described as "one-pointedness of the mind."

Chan as a School of Buddhism

With its origin in India, the Chan School in China developed and matured, and later spread to Korea, Japan, and Vietnam. Tradition has it that at the assembly on Vulture Peak, Shakyamuni, the World-Honored One, held a flower in his hand and Mahakashyapa, his foremost disciple, broke into a smile. Therefore, Mahakashyapa came to be regarded as the First Patriarch of the Chan School. Thereafter, the lineage was passed down generation after generation for 28 generations, and was transmitted to China at the time of Bodhidharma (6th century C.E.), who became the First Patriarch of Chan in China. Then after being transmitted for five more generations, the lineage passed on to Master Huineng (638-713), who became the Six Patriarch, and who established the unshakable foundation of the Chan School. Chan emphasizes not being based on words; it is a transmission outside the teaching, directly pointing to the human mind, allowing one to illuminate one's mind and see one's nature, to achieve sudden enlightenment, and become a buddha. Despite not being based on words, from Bodhidharma until the Sixth Patriarch Huineng, the Chan School has made many references to quite a few sutras. Since then, among all Buddhist schools in the history of China, the Chan School has left the largest quantity of written texts. The reason, it seems, is that to explain why Chan "is not based on words and is a transmission outside the teaching," it needs to use even more words. Among Buddhist schools in China, Chan has been the most popular; the most enduring, the most widespread. During the Tang (618-907) and Song (960-1279) dynasties, it branched out into five lineages and seven sects, but after the Song Dynasty, only two major schools remained over time, namely, the Linji (Jpn. *Rinzai*) and the Caodong (Jpn. *Soto*). In Japan, the Zen School came from the (late) Song Dynasty of China, and thus there are only these two sects. Due to the above factors, whenever the word "Zen" is mentioned in any part of the world, people will think of the Chan School.

The Definition of Enlightenment

In general, "enlightenment" signifies that what was originally unknown has become known all of a sudden. However, the enlightenment as referred to in Buddhism is different. What most people refer to as enlightenment can be roughly classified into five categories.

The Enlightenment of Art

The enlightenment of art can actually be called "inspiration." Whether they are writers, musicians, or painters, the majority of people's creative works do not depend on ordinary knowledge or learning, nor do they rely completely on the training of skills. In literature, some are said to write as if aided by a deity, finishing thousands of words at one stretch. For painters, by a stroke of genius, they can finish a painting in a dash, whether it is small or huge. For musicians who compose a piece of music, the scores often come flowing out incessantly like a continuous stream, without them resorting to thinking. Of course, there are cases where a beautiful writing only gets composed after one has racked one's brains, and a best example is how Jia Dao finished one of his poems only after repeatedly seeking a right verb. Nevertheless, a work without inspiration can only show one's skills, but cannot reveal the freedom of a powerful, unconstrained style. Therefore, artists are usually born great.

The Enlightenment of Science

For scientists to discover certain laws of physics, mathematics, chemistry, or biology, they should have the fundamental academic training, but discoveries mainly come from the power of insightful comprehension. Regardless of whether it is a significant creation, invention, or breakthrough of theory or technique, it is often a result of "finding something by chance after tracking miles in vain for it." Newton discovered the law of universal gravitation, Edison invented the electric lamp, and Einstein propounded the theory of relativity; none of these can be achieved by ordinary people.

The Enlightenment of Philosophy

For philosophers to obtain the experiences of life and universe, generally there are no more than three approaches as proposed by Confucians: to know by one's innate gift, to know when hard pressed by difficult situations, and to know by learning. To know by learning is of course important, but usually one cannot go beyond the scope of the experiences of one's predecessors. Only the great geniuses who are born to know and those who make discovery when pushed to the wall are able to open up a new frontier of knowledge, which is a state of enlightenment. The great philosophers of old left various philosophical theories and views as the history of our cultures and thought. For example, the doctrine of "achieving the innate knowledge of the good" that Wang Yangming propounded is something that he came up with when he was relegated to an outland region at Longchang in Guizhou Province.

The Enlightenment of Religion

The enlightenment of religion actually refers to incidents of revelations, oracles, manifestation of deities, etc. as a result of religious rituals or devotion, as well as the behavior of praying, prostration, reciting, etc. Some directly see a god's instruction as a vision, hear a god's words in their ears, receive a god's directions in a dream, or discover in a flash of inspiration that they are together with a god; they derive views that surpass those of ordinary people, suddenly enhance their own conviction, or give rise to a sense of mission to be compassionate to humanity. Or they really witness heavens, hells, or the worlds of immortals, or have other curious experiences. The person involved would usually take this to be enlightenment. In other words, unprecedented things suddenly happen, and impossible things become possible—the majority of religious faiths are generated in these situations.

From the standpoint of Chan, however, none of the above four categories is the true state of enlightenment. To achieve enlightenment, one must have dropped self-centeredness, rid oneself of selfishness and vexations, and eradicated discrimination and attachment. So, one should further transcend inspiration and divine responses to gain true enlightenment.

Chan Enlightenment

According to what is recorded in the sutras, the enlightenment of Chan signifies "awakening," which comes in three levels:

1. The self-enlightenment of the Theravada tradition: after eliminating self-centered vexations of greed, anger, ignorance, arrogance, doubt, etc., one will no longer receive bitter retribution in the cycle of birth and death because of various vexations. In order to achieve the level of arhatship where one breaks self-attachment and dwells in nirvana, one must cultivate the *Four Noble Truths*, the *Noble Eightfold Path*, the *Twelve Links of Dependent Origination*, and other Dharma approaches. In terms of the *"four fruits"* of Theravada practice, those who gain the "initial fruit" are considered as having attained initial enlightenment, while those who achieve the "fourth fruit" are completely enlightened.

2. Bodhisattvas in the Mahayana tradition are referred to as those who enlighten others. In Sanskrit, "bodhisattva" signifies an enlightened ("awakened") sentient being. Bodhisattvas not only cut off their own vexations, but in particular, also vow to widely deliver all sentient beings. The Bodhisattva Kshitigarbha (Earth Store) even said, "I will not realize bodhi until all beings in hell have been delivered." A bodhisattva wishes that all sentient beings will become buddhas, and whether they themselves will become buddhas is not an issue. In fact, if all beings become buddhas because of the bodhisattva, he or she is also bound to be a buddha. Usually, the bodhisattva path is divided

into fifty-two stages. If one can achieve the eleventh stage, one also counts as having attained enlightenment, and when one reaches buddhahood, he or she is said to have attained thorough, perfect enlightenment.

3. Buddhas are those who have enlightened themselves, enlightened others, and achieved complete enlightenment; whose vexations have been completely cut off, and who have nurtured the causes and conditions for the deliverance of all sentient beings. Buddhas benefit both themselves and others, and reach perfection in applying both the merit and wisdom, thus called the great, complete enlightenment.

4. Chan enlightenment has another higher meaning: one form of it does not require going through gradual stages; rather, under an enlightened teacher's guidance, enlightenment can be manifested by any incident. There are some who, while investigating Chan, [that is, while applying the method diligently], suddenly and spontaneously experience enlightenment. When such a state appears, one is open, magnanimous, broad-minded, whose mind is without obstructions, like a vast, blue sky without a single speck of dust in it. It is a mental state equal and identical to that of a buddha, with no difference whatsoever. However, upon attaining enlightenment a buddha is forever enlightened and the enlightenment will be complete; whereas, most Chan practitioners may have to go through one enlightenment after another [before becoming completely enlightened]. The duration of the enlightened state can be fleeting or lasting, a more powerful one lasting longer. However, since one has got enlightened, after all, one is very different from those who have never experienced it. Because they have seen the "original face," enlightened persons have steadfast faith and will keep practicing diligently. Therefore, a Chan

master once said, "I've achieved big enlightenment over thirty times, and innumerable small ones." This shows that one experience of Chan enlightenment does not amount to attaining liberation or becoming a buddha.

The above shows that, while Buddhist enlightenment can be sudden, gradual, deep, or shallow, the Chan tradition is identified with sudden enlightenment. While thorough enlightenment is possible through just one such sudden experience, most practitioners must experience it again and again, through one barrier after another.

The Evolution of Chan

The evolution of Chan may be seen through two historical passages in India: early and sectarian Buddhism, and later Mahayana Buddhism.

Early Buddhism and Sectarian Buddhism in India

This may also be explained from two aspects:

1. With regard to the concepts of Buddhism, one needs to take right view and knowledge as the basis, and take the precepts, concentration, and wisdom as the field of cultivation. By right view and knowledge we mean the firm belief that the Three Dharma Seals—"all activities are impermanent, all dharmas are without self, and nirvana is perfect quiescence"—are the unchangeable guiding principle. Then one also observes the five precepts and cultivates the ten virtues, so as to purify the bodily, verbal, and mental activities.

The five precepts are: not to kill, not to steal, not to engage in sexual misconduct, not to tell lies, and not to take intoxicants. The ten virtues consist of the first four of the five precepts, with the precept of not telling lies expanded into four virtues of speech: no lies, no frivolous speech, no divisive speech, and no abusive speech, plus the mental activities of no greed, no anger, and no delusions. The precept against intoxicants is special to Buddhism, which emphasizes cultivation of wisdom, whereas, intoxicants would befuddle and confuse one's mind.

To cultivate concentration is to cultivate the nine levels of concentration, namely, the four *dhyanas* of the form realm and the four samadhis of the formless realm, plus the arhats' samadhi of liberation, which is the samadhi of complete cessation—altogether nine. One enters and comes out of these states of concentration stage by stage, from shallow to deep and from deep to shallow, so they are called the nine levels of concentration.

There are two kinds of liberation for arhats. One is called the "liberation through concentration and wisdom," where one achieves liberation by means of the nine levels of concentration; liberation itself is wisdom. The other is called the "liberation through wisdom," where one directly realizes the state of liberation through contemplative wisdom; this is also the basic concept of Buddhism.

2. As for methods, one practices the Five Methods for Stilling the Mind, the four immeasurable minds, and the Four Foundations of Mindfulness. These are all methods for contemplative practice, and are also called the meditative contemplation or meditation in numerical categories. What we call the Five Methods for Stilling the Mind is to use the five kinds of contemplation to bring the scattered, disordered mind to stillness, so as to achieve the purpose of entering concentration: counting the breath, meditation on impurity of the body, meditation on causes and conditions, meditation on loving-kindness and compassion, and meditation on dharma categories (Skt. *dhatu*). In particular, the meditation on counting the breath and impurity are called the "two gates of ambrosia." Ambrosia is medicine

of immortality in the Indian legends. By means of these two gates, one will be able to enter the state of nirvana.

The four immeasurable minds are loving-kindness, compassion, joy, and equanimity. They are cultivated on the basis of the four *dhyanas* of the form realm, being the special characteristic of Buddhism. Why so? Generic worldly meditative concentration would indulge in the bliss of meditation, but the Buddhadharma requires that one use meditation to give rise to compassion, generate great joy, and renounce all attachments and states of meditative concentration, in order to benefit sentient beings, so that one can go beyond the three realms of desire, form, and formlessness.

The Four Foundations of Mindfulness refer to contemplating the body as impure, contemplating the perceptions as suffering, contemplating the mind as impermanent, and contemplating dharmas (phenomena) as selfless. This practice is also a special characteristic of Buddhism. Ordinary people take the impure body as pure, and as a result become attached to it; undergoing the phenomena that change and go by incessantly, they do not feel that it is a suffering; their thoughts constantly vary from moment to moment, but they take them to be permanent. None of the phenomena they experience are real, but they take their body and mind as the self. By contemplating the Four Foundations of Mindfulness they will be weary of the body and mind, and won't cling to any phenomena in the world, and thus achieve the purpose of transcending the world.

Mahayana Buddhism

Mahayana Buddhism in India can be discussed in four aspects:

1. The meditative concentration of Mahayana Buddhism takes samadhi as its goal. Among the scriptures of early Mahayana, there

are altogether twenty-four sutras that contain "samadhi" in their titles, such as the *Shurangama Samadhi Sutra* and the *Pratyutpanna Samadhi Sutra* (see the *Origin and Development of Early Mahayana Buddhism* by Master Yinshun). What does samadhi mean? In earlier times it referred to concentration, while in later times it referred to the power of liberation generated by concentration and wisdom, and can be said to be another name for liberation. For example, Fascicle 20 of the *Treatise on the Great Perfection of Wisdom Treatise* (*Skt. Mahaprajnaparamita Shastra*) says, "The three samadhis all rely on One Reality to reach nirvana without outflows," and "the Three Dharma Seals are the One Reality." Already stated in the *Agama Sutras* are the three samadhis of emptiness (without self), without marks (without characteristics), and wishlessness (without desire), in other words, the three liberations. The three liberations all rely on the "One Reality"; that is, they are realizations of the Three Dharma Seals. The "Citta-samyutta" (Skt. citta-samprayukta) in the *Samyutta Nikaya* of the Pali Canon takes four kinds of samadhi as the liberation of the mind (pp. 450-452, Vol. 15, the *Theravada Canon*).

What we call liberation is no other than wisdom. The wisdom without outflows can result in the liberation from vexations, so the accomplished masters in ancient India all placed importance on the practice of meditation methods that takes samadhi as the goal.

2. The four kinds of samadhi in the meditative concentration of Mahayana: According to Fascicle 2 of the *Great Calming and Contemplation* (Chn. *Mohe zhiguan*) of Master Zhiyi (538-597) of the Tiantai School, the methods of meditative contemplation applied in Mahayana Buddhism of India are categorized into four kinds of samadhi as follows:

(1) The samadhi of constant sitting derives from the

Mahaprajnaparamita Sutra as Spoken by Manjushri. It is also called "the samadhi of a single practice," and refers to sitting still constantly, which is what we generally call sitting meditation.

(2) The samadhi of constant walking: This derives from the *Pratyutpanna Samadhi Sutra*, and thus is also called "the pratyutpanna samadhi." One practices this in the manner of walking meditation, without resting, sleeping, or sitting down, for a period of ninety days.

(3) The samadhi of half walking and half sitting: This derives from the text in the *Mahavaipulya Dharani Sutra* and the *Lotus Sutra*, and thus is called the "lotus samadhi." Besides sitting meditation, the methods of practice such as worshipping the Buddha, reciting the sutras, and repentance are added. As a rule, most of the Chan practice in a Chan hall adopts this manner of practice consisting of both walking and sitting meditation.

(4) The samadhi of neither walking nor sitting: This is also called the "samadhi at free will (Chn. *Suiziyi sanmei*)," or the "samadhi of awareness (Chn. *Jueyi sanmei*)," that is, it does not rigidly stipulate that one adopt the posture of walking, standing, walking, or lying down. As long as one does not slacken the mind and practices diligently according to one's own intention, one may achieve the purpose of attaining samadhi just the same.

3. The meditative concentration of the Mahayana is no other than daily life. According to the *Akshayamati Sutra*, which was translated into Chinese by Dharmaraksha (265-318), it reads, "To make this meditative concentration abide in an equal mind is called 'a bodhisattva cultivating meditative concentration'... The state where one's mental activities are equal, one's mental characteristics are equal, one is ultimately equal, and how one gives rise to any activity is equal is called concentration. To abide in giving, observing the precepts, in

patience, diligence, meditative concentration, wisdom and the equality of all dharmas is called concentration… As one's own mind is equal, the minds of others are also equal—this is called concentration." This is to take the state where the mind abides in equality—the equality of sentient beings and that of dharmas—as the meditative concentration of a bodhisattva. This text means that a bodhisattva who practices meditative concentration does not necessarily have to do it in the manner of sitting meditation. It is the same in meaning with the saying of "A straightforward mind is the place of practice" in the *Vimalakirti Sutra*, and that of "An ordinary mind is the Path" of Eminent Master Mazu Daoyi.

4. The meditative concentration of Mahayana is no other than the four postures of walking, standing, sitting, and lying down. For instance, Fascicle 1 of the *Bhadrakalpa Sutra* says, "The practice comes in three manners: the first one is walking, the second one, standing, and the third one, sitting. All conditions of disharmony are harmonized and thereby transformed." (The lower part of P. 1, Vol. 14, *Taisho Tripitaka*)

Also, Fascicle 1of the *Sutra of Akshobhya Buddha's Land* says, "As a seeker of the supreme Path," if "I have become a *shramana* from one life to another but do not often sit under a tree, or do not often diligently do three things, namely, walking, sitting, and standing… I would have deceived countless buddhas, the World Honored Ones." (The middle part of P. 752, Vol. 11, *Taisho Tripitaka*)

In addition, the "verse of the analogy of a dragon" in the middle of Fascicle 2 of the early *Dragon-Elephant Sutra, Middle Length Sayings Agama*, praises the Buddha as a great dragon, saying, "A dragon is in samadhi when walking and standing, as well as when seated and lying down. A dragon is in samadhi at all times." (The lower part of P. 608,

Vol. 1, *Taisho Tripitaka*)

The chapter on "Disciples" of Fascicle 1 of the *Vimalakirti Sutra* also says, "To display various comportments without coming out from the samadhi of cessation is to sit in meditation." (The lower part of P. 539, Vol. 14, *Taisho Tripitaka*)

We can see from the four sutras mentioned above that the meditative concentration of the Mahayana has a great diversity. It emphasizes daily life, in that one may practice meditative concentration at any time. In other words, it stresses the concentrated state of the mind, without being particular about taking the sitting posture with the body. This is exactly the basis for the later theory of the Chinese Chan tradition.

The Chan School of China

The Chan School in China can be seen as Chan prior to the coming of the Sixth Patriarch Huineng, when he became the Sixth Patriarch, and after his passing.

Prior to the Six Patriarch, Master Huineng

Prior to Sixth Patriarch Master Huineng, the Chan School took shape in two directions, one of them being passed down from Bodhidharma, and the other being transmitted by the lineage masters of other schools. When the lineage of Bodhidharma was passed down to the Fourth Patriarch, Master Daoxin (580-651), it branched into two lines of Niutou Farong (594-657) and Dongshan Hongren (601-674). Generally, Hongren is taken to be the Fifth Patriarch of the Chan School because he was the teacher of Huineng. In fact, Farong was also the disciple of the Fourth Patriarch, and his line was carried on for seven generations, and gradually disappeared after Niaoke

Daolin (741-824). As for the Chan masters outside the lineage of Bodhidharma, they include Zhu Daoshen (355-434), Sengchou (480-560), Facong (468-559), and other masters of the early phase, who all exerted an influence on the subsequent thoughts of Chan School. Moreover, Nanyue Huisi (515-577), Tiantai Zhiyi (538-597), and other masters of the Tiantai tradition as well as Qingliang Chenguan (738-839) and Guifeng Zongmi (780-841) of Huayan School were also renowned meditation masters.

The approach during the period from Bodhidharma to the Sixth Patriarch, Master Huineng, is not necessarily all just that of sudden enlightenment. For example, *The Two Entrances and Four Practices* of Bodhidharma advocated entry through principle and entry through practice (see "A Brief Explication of Mahayana's Four Practices for Entering the Path" in the *Essentials for Cultivation and Realization in the Chan Tradition* (Chn. *Chanmen xiuzheng zhiyao*), compiled by this author.) Entrance through principle is to enter the essence of the teaching (to perfectly understand the teaching) through the method of direct contemplation, and to awaken to one's buddha-nature through sudden enlightenment. Entrance through practice includes four kinds of contemplative practices, namely, accepting karmic retribution, adapting to conditions, non-seeking, and acting in accordance with the Dharma. The entrance through practice is a gradual Dharma approach with stages of progress.

The Gate of Essential Expediencies for Entering the Path and Calming the Mind by the Fourth Patriarch, Master Daoxin, also says, "Directly contemplate the body and mind as well as the four elements and *five skandhas* in a quiet place." It further says, "By constantly contemplating the grasping, awareness, delusive consciousness, thinking, and wandering thoughts till the scattered mind no longer arises, one attains coarse calm abiding (or stillness). If one's mind has become completely still and free of grasping thoughts, one will become calm and concentrated bit by bit, and one's various vexations will also subside bit by bit." (See "The Expediencies for Entering the Path" in the *Essentials for Cultivation and Realization in the Chan Tradition*.)

"On the Essentials for Cultivating the Mind" (alias "On the Supreme Vehicle"), the work of the Fifth Patriarch, Master Hongren, maintains that it is first and foremost to guard the mind, saying, "Guarding the mind is the root foundation for nirvana, the essential gate for entering the Path, the core of the twelve divisions of all sutras, and the progenitor of all buddhas in the past, present, and future." It further says, "If only one guards the mind with absorption and without giving rise to wandering thoughts, the Dharma of nirvana will naturally manifest." ("An Excerpt from the Essentials for Cultivating the Mind" in the *Essentials for Cultivation and Realization in the Chan Tradition*). In this approach, there is a mind for one to guard, so it is not a sudden teaching. In particular, he also said, "Based on the *Sutra of Contemplating on the Amitayus Buddha*, if a beginner practices sitting meditation, he or she should sit up straight, focus on the right thought, close the eyes and the mouth, and look straight forward, visualizing a sun—far or near as he or she pleases—and guard the true mind, without abiding from one instant of thought to another. (The same as "On the Essentials for Cultivating the Mind," mentioned above). This also has a method, and what is more, it is based on the visualization of the sun from the Pure Land sutras.

From the three afore-mentioned citations, we can see that the Chan School before the Sixth Patriarch is still a continuation of the meditative contemplation in India. It is only until the time of

Huineng that there appeared the mode of Chan, which is said to directly point to an individual's mind and not fall under gradual stages.

The Chan of Master Huineng

Master Huineng attained enlightenment when he heard the phrase "without abiding, give rise to the mind" from the *Diamond Sutra*, so he placed special emphasis on that sutra. When he ascended to his seat to expound the Dharma, he said to the audience, "Purify your mind everyone, and meditate on *mahaprajnaparamita.*" "*Mahaprajnaparamita*" signifies "crossing over with great wisdom." In other words, one crosses over with the great wisdom from this shore of samsara and vexations to the other shore of liberation. However, the patriarchs before him asked people to recite "*mahaprajnaparamita*" orally, while he advocated reciting it with the mind.

Huineng did not maintain that one should empty the mind and sit meditating quietly, or that one should seek the Buddha outside the mind. If one cannot attain enlightenment by oneself, one needs to seek guidance from a virtuous teacher. In addition, he maintained that concentration and wisdom are inseparable saying, "Concentration is the essence of wisdom, and wisdom is the function of concentration. When wisdom is present, concentration is contained in wisdom. When concentration is present, wisdom is contained in concentration." This is the simultaneity of concentration and wisdom, and is different from the traditional concept of first cultivating concentration and then generating wisdom. He said, "Don't say that concentration comes first, and then one generates wisdom, or that wisdom comes first and then one generates concentration. What can concentration and wisdom be likened to? They are like the lamp and its light. With the lamp, it is bright; without the lamp, it is dark. The lamp is the substance of the light, and the light, the function of the lamp."

He had the following concept about seated meditation: "What is 'seated meditation'? In this teaching, there is no impediment and no hindrance. Externally, for the mind to refrain from activating thoughts with regard to all the good and bad phenomena is called 'seated.' Internally, to see the motionlessness of the self-nature is called 'meditation'." Therefore, he said: "Some people teach meditation in terms of viewing the mind, contemplating tranquility, motionlessness, and non-activation, putting their efforts on the basis of these. These deluded people do not understand, so they attach to such a practice and develop distorted views. There are many people like this, and they in turn teach others. You should know that it is a great mistake."

These teachings all derive from the concept of "taking the four postures of walking, standing, sitting, and lying down to be samadhis" as quoted earlier from the Mahayana sutras. Therefore, Master Huineng cited in particular "a straightforward mind is the place of practice" and "a straightforward mind is a pure land," the two statements from the *Vimalakirti Sutra*, and extended the idea and said, "Simply apply a straightforward mind, and don't be attached to any dharmas." (The above-mentioned citations can all be found in the *Platform Sutra of the Sixth Patriarch*. Please refer to the "Excerpts from the *Platform Sutra of the Sixth Patriarch*" in the *Essentials for Cultivation and Realization in the Chan Tradition.*)

Chan after the Sixth Patriarch
Nukariya Kaiten, a former president of Komazawa University in Japan, has classified the periods of Chinese Chan into several phases:

from Bodhidharma to Huineng he called "the time of pure Chan"; from Huineng to the late Tang and the Five Dynasties (907-ca. 960), "the time of extemporaneous approaches"; and from then to the Song Dynasty, "the very ripe time." Thereafter Chan gradually declined, and it was in modern times that Eminent Master Xuyun and Chan Master Laiguo revived the Chinese Chan School.

The extemporaneous approaches refer to applying the means of shouting, beating, and other extemporaneous methods to help Chan practitioners eliminate self-attachment. During the "very ripe time" that began from the Northern Song Dynasty, the methods of *gong'an, huatou*, and Silent Illumination came into being. *Gong'ans* are historical anecdotes (literally, "public cases") about the individual enlightenment experiences of certain ancient Chan masters. Before then, nobody collected, sorted, and compiled these accounts. During the Northern Song Dynasty Fenyang Shanzhao (947-1024) first compiled *One Hundred Instances of Earlier Masters* (Chn. *Xianxian yibaize*); Xuedou Chongxian (980-1052) compiled *In Praise of One Hundred Ancient Instances* (Chn. *Song'gu baize*); and Wuzu Fayan (1024-1104) initiated the *gong'an* of "*wu*," (literally, "no," "not", or "without") exhorting people to investigate Master Zhaozhou's answer, "*Wu*," when asked by a disciple if a dog had buddha-nature. Later, Master Dahui Zonggao (1089-1163) devoted great effort to advocating Zhaozhou's *wu*, whereas his contemporary, Hongzhi Zhengjue (1091-1157) was the first to advocate Silent Illumination. To know more about *gong'an* and silent illumination, please refer to the chapter of "The Chan of Chinese Chan School" in the work *Chan Experience & Chan Talk*, by this author.

What Is Enlightenment?

Only the person who drinks the water will know how cold or warm the water is; just so, only one who has attained enlightenment will know what it is like. Also, the manner of enlightenment and the degree of enlightenment will vary among people and with the time. The karmic roots (spiritual capacity) of people can be sharp or dull, and the effort put into practice can be shallow or deep. Thus, for different people and under different circumstances, the enlightened state that results will be different. Nevertheless, there is a principle by which one may judge whether one has really got enlightened. If your mind corresponds to mental states such as self-centered greed, anger, ignorance, arrogance, doubt, and so on, then no matter how great the mysterious experience, or how you claim to have an earth-shattering change, it is nothing but a "perceptual experience" rather than enlightenment. At the moment enlightenment occurs, if you feel overjoyed, it may be enlightenment, and afterwards you may feel nothing in particular. You are no different from ordinary people; what is different is that you are free of the self-centered frame of mind of greed, anger, ignorance, arrogance, doubt, and the like. If you still have vexations after "enlightenment," yours may be a small enlightenment or you have not actually attained it. After attaining true enlightenment, for a long period of time at least, your mind will be like a vast, entirely cloudless blue sky without even the sun and moon, but it will not hinder the workings of any worldly phenomena, and you will interact with people as normally as ordinary people, or even with more humility.

Now I will point out some false kinds of enlightenment, which we can also call "look-alike" states of enlightenment, but which are fundamentally illusory.

Lightness and ease is not enlightenment. By means of sitting meditation, prayer, recitation, and so on, one may feel refreshed, comfortable, soft/pliable, and relaxed physically, as well as mentally open and cheerful, but this does not necessarily amount to enlightenment.

Mental acuity is not enlightenment. With the methods of practice one may derive a strong ability of association and reasoning, ability to read very fast, a great eloquence, or a sharp wit for literary writing, but this does not amount to enlightenment.

Supernatural power is not enlightenment. Supernatural powers are of two kinds: those derived from cultivation, and those derived from karmic result. The deities and ghosts all have the miraculous power derived from karmic result. Ordinary people may derive from cultivation the miraculous powers such as the power of divine vision, that of divine hearing, that of knowing others' thoughts, that of knowing past lives, and that of appearing anywhere at will. Non-Buddhist practitioners, as well as deities and ghosts, may know the past and future, appear and disappear unpredictably like a shadow, transform something from nothing, transform something into nothing, and know the thoughts of other people. However, having supernatural powers is not tantamount to attaining enlightenment, and even has nothing to do with an enlightened state. The general situation, however, is that once someone has some minor supernatural powers, he or she would usually be worshipped as a sage. As a matter of fact, a sage will not often resort to supernatural powers, using them as a tool for teaching and transforming people. Those who often display supernatural powers will mostly boast about having attained a deep state of enlightenment, which is not trustworthy.

Author's Note: This text derives from a lecture given at the Harvard-Yanjing Library at Harvard University on November 12, 1988. Due to insufficient time, I did not present all of the information I had prepared. After I returned to New York City, Ms. Ye Cuiping assisted me by transcribing the recorded lecture. I then added some content according to the outline drawn up earlier, and finished this article. That is why it may in part be somewhat inconsistent with the lecture I delivered back then.

Chan and Entanglement

Right Wisdom Buddhist Society, Tamkang University, Taiwan, September 30, 1988.

Who Is "You," "He," and "I"?

Greetings to all the teachers and students attending this lecture! Our topic today is "Chan and Entanglement." I will first talk about what is meant by "entanglement," and go on to talk about Chan. The reason for these two topics is because Chan came into existence in order to solve the problem of entanglement.

I will begin by introducing four phrases: "All sensations are characterized by suffering; all activities are impermanent; all dharmas are without self; and nirvana is quiescence." In this context, the word "suffering" in "all sensations are characterized by suffering" is synonymous with "entanglement." Because one is entangled, there is suffering. Who is entangled? It is the "I" that is entangled. Where there is the "self," one will not be free and at ease. Most people do not understand the impermanence of all phenomena, and not able to experience the "selflessness" of phenomena, they are entangled and unable to be free.

Let's cite two *gong'ans* (Jpn. *koans*) of the Chan School. [*Gong'ans* are historical anecdotes of encounters between Chan masters and disciples.] The first one is about the Fourth Patriarch, Master Daoxin (580-651). When he was 14, Daoxin visited for the first time, the Third Patriarch, Sengcang (d.606), saying, "Venerable Master, please be kind and teach me how to attain liberation." The Third Patriarch asked, "Who is binding (preventing) you?" Daoxin replied, "Nobody binds me." Then the Third Patriarch said, "Why then do you seek liberation?" Upon hearing this, Daoxin became enlightened. (Fascicle 3 of the *Record of the Transmission of the Lamp Composed in the Jingde Era* (Chn. *Jingde chuandeng lu*)

In the second *gong'an*, a monk visited Master Shitou Xiqian (700-796), a second-generation Dharma heir of the Sixth Patriarch. The monk asked the master, "What is liberation?" Xiqian said, "Who is binding you?" But then, the monk asked another question: "What is the pure land?" Again, instead of answering the question, Xiqian asked another, "Who is contaminating you?" The monk further asked, "What is nirvana?" Xiqian still asked in return, "Who gave you birth and death?" (Fascicle 14 of the *Record of the Transmission of the Lamp Composed in the Jingde Era*)

In responding to the disciples, the two Chan masters used the means of answering with another question instead of explaining. It would seem that they had not answered the questions, but in fact, their responses were actually the best, as well as the most pertinent and useful. In asking, "Who is binding you?" "Who contaminates you?" "Who gave birth and death to you?"—the "who" and "you" obviously refer to the "self" from the phrase, "all dharmas are without self." Not aware that there is no "self," most people suffer as a result. They don't know why they suffer, simply thinking that there are numerous "he's," "she's" and "you's" that cause "me" to suffer. As a result, people of superior capacity would hope to achieve liberation with the methods of practice, those of lesser capacity would seek the blessing of deities to turn their ill fortune into good, and those of least capacity would blame heaven and others, not knowing where to put themselves in the world.

Dual Emphasis on Concepts and Practice

Just now, on our way from the Nung Chan Monastery in Beitou to your university, one of your students was discussing with one of my monastic disciples how to really apply Buddhadharma in actual life. After all, if the Buddhist teachings are of no use in actual life, they are just a kind of knowledge or shallow belief. The student said, "The most troublesome matter is emotions. Buddhist believers can usually speak convincingly, but once they are involved in emotional issues, they get all tangled up!" Please think about this: who has entangled whom? There should not be anyone who can entangle you unless you entangle yourself for failing to "let go."

To solve this problem of entanglement, we deal with it from two aspects: first is to guide and straighten ourselves out with conceptual understanding; second, to engage in spiritual cultivation by practicing the methods. Conceptual understanding is like the software in a computer, and practicing a method is like the hardware. If you only have the concepts but not the methods, it won't work; if you only have the methods but not the concepts, you will get nowhere, either. Therefore, Buddhism maintains equal emphasis on understanding and practice. Next we will first talk about the concepts, and then the methods.

Four Kinds of Entanglement

Entanglement concerns the issue of suffering which is also known as "vexation." There are many different kinds of vexations, which we can classify into four categories: psychological, physiological, ethical, and those of the material world.

Psychological conflicts: the issues of arising, abiding, changing, and perishing as spoken by the Buddha, which means that one's earlier and later ideas contradict with each other, and that one's different ways of thinking conflict with one another. Let me ask the male students here; if you fall in love with two female students at the same time, what would you do? Besides the emotional issues between men and women, even when buying a T-shirt, a book, a pair of shoes, or a pair of eyeglasses, we will experience the struggle within. I knew a young man who got some money and planned to buy a camera. He browsed in many shops on many streets, and came back empty-handed. He went out to look for a camera a second time, and once again didn't buy any. So, whenever he needed a camera, he borrowed one from friends. People asked him, "You've got the money, so why don't you buy one for yourself?" He said, "I've looked around but could not find any ideal one. I'll reserve the right to buy the latest model, so I'll wait for some time." As a matter of fact, he was just unable to make up his mind, undergoing a struggle within himself.

Last month, six of my disciples at Nung Chan Monastery made up their minds to take the monastic vows, and had their head shaved in the tonsure ceremony. It seemed so easy: the heads of the six persons were all shaved clean in a short while. However, is it really such a simple matter? In fact, before they decided to take the monastic vows they had already struggled for a long time, and after they began to reside in the monastery they were still undergoing the trials. There were even those who had much anxiety when their heads were being shaved, thinking, "I'm making the first step onto such a path. Have I taken the right path after all?" I would like to ask the students here who are married: when you got married, did you just step forward and get married so easily? Or did you consider the marriage again and again, struggling within, again and again, and only then did you determine to marry your spouse?

Physiological troubles: the issues of birth, aging, illness, and death as expounded by the Buddha. Our body comes into being from birth, and every second after birth, it undergoes the transition between birth and death. Most of you know something about metabolism, which is the normal phenomenon involved in the process of birth, aging, decay, and death. People call the time when bodily life comes to an end, "death," and they call the change from birth to death of the body's local cells, "metabolism." As a matter of fact, the death of a cell also counts as death. There have never been people who eat the five kinds of grains without eventually falling sick. Whether it is a minor disease or a grave one, falling ill is always a trouble, and always makes one suffer.

Ethical relationships: the vicissitudes of our human world are generally called "the joy of meeting and the sorrow of parting." Please do not limit ethical relationships of humanity to the scope of five ethics between a superior and a subordinate, parents and children, wife and husband, elder and younger siblings, and friends. Broadly speaking, the interdependence and interaction among people are all ethical relationships. Divorce, sibling rivalry, father-son discord, contention between boss and employee, disorder between levels in a company, and the like, are all ethical tragedies. Then also, the variance of ideas between two generations will also bring us troubles. Nowadays we call it a "generation gap," but it is not a problem that just appeared today. In addition, conflicts among nations and races, different interpretations of religious beliefs, opposition of political thoughts, conflicts of interests in business, and so on, are all hotbeds of vexations. In sum, a pleasant time is very scarce in this world. Not only the savage, bloody fighting with each other makes one's life difficult and causes one to suffer, but minor frictions also make one uncomfortable.

Impermanence in the material world: becoming, abiding, destruction, and emptiness as expounded by the Buddha, referring to the natural phenomena of the celestial and heavenly bodies. However, because they involve processes on the order of eons, it is hard to be aware of these changes. The natural phenomena that closely concern us include the climatic issues of wind, rain, water, fire, and drought, as well as damage from insect pests, which bring troubles to humanity. In particular, we are vexed at all times by the needs of modern life— clothing, food, housing, and transportation, as well as air pollution, environmental hygiene, the exploitation and destruction of natural resources day by day.

Now let us turn back and ask: why do we have all these problems? As a matter of fact, it is because there is the belief in the "self." All our mental activities are the operation of this self. For example, each and every one of us has opinions, thoughts, ideas, joy, anger, sorrow, happiness, etc., and they are all but the expression of this subjective self. As with psychology, so it is with the body: if someone points to your body and asks, "Whose body is it?" you will definitely say that it is "mine."

The active and passive aspects of ethics are all affected by our self—yours, mine, his, and hers. The material world is the environment in which I find myself: when we look roughly at the environment, it is not an "I" but an "it" that stands opposite to me, so it can benefit as well as harm me; it can make me suffer as well as make me happy. In terms of Buddhadharma, our body/mind is the direct reward (or retribution), while the environment where the body/mind is located is the circumstantial reward (or retribution); they are all the results derived from the karma that the self has created. The body is my small "clothes," and the environment is my large body. For the sake of the self, we created a variety of good and evil karma with bodily, verbal, and mental actions; and again, we receive the karmic results of the body/mind, and that of the environment through the "self" of another future life. This is indeed reaping what we sow.

Impermanence and No-Self

If we want to solve the problem of the "self," we must first understand conceptually what is called "no-self." When observing in accordance with the Buddhadharma, we find that the self does not exist. "All activities are impermanent," one of the four phrases I mentioned just now, means that none of the phenomena—or activities—is forever unchanging, and thus is called impermanent. *Psychologically* there are arising, abiding, changing, and perishing; *physiologically* there is metabolism—birth, aging, illness, and death; *ethically* there are the vicissitudes of sorrow, joy, parting, and meeting; *with the material worlds* there are becoming, abiding, destruction, and emptiness. Since theses four categories of phenomena are changing constantly, the self that is represented by them is of course not truly existent, either.

Therefore, when one understands the meaning of "all activities are impermanent," one will also grasp the meaning of "all dharmas are selfless." Because of impermanence, the dharmas are without self. If one knows impermanence, one is aware of selflessness; if one realizes selflessness, one attains liberation. On the contrary, if one is still an ordinary person with heavy hindrances, then because one cannot endure the impermanence of all activities, one will suffer. These are two opposite poles. The fact of arising, abiding, changing, and perishing is suffering; so are life's vicissitudes of sorrow, joy, meeting and parting, birth, aging, illness, death, and the fact of becoming, abiding, destruction, and emptiness. There is a saying that "a person gets old, and a pearl grows yellow." This is because of impermanence: a person who lives for a long time will get old, a pearl set aside for a long time will grow yellow. All things in the world will change, and will depreciate. The longer one practices the better, and the longer a friendship the better, but our bodies are bound to depreciate from day to day. The bricks and tiles of the Qin or Han dynasties are valuable because rare antiques are taken to be precious. The older an accomplished monastic, the more he or she will be respected, partly because there are very few accomplished monastics. It is not because the thing has existed for a long time or because the person has gotten old. As a matter of fact, most elderly people feel great suffering from aging, and others do not necessarily believe the older, the better.

Quiescence and an Unmoving Mind

Why do people regard impermanence as suffering? If one is unable to accept the fact of impermanence in spite of one's knowledge about it, one will find it suffering. For instance, the passing of loved ones and the breakup between lovers are mostly suffering. If such a thing happens to someone and you tell them, "All things are impermanent, so take it easy and don't be upset," they will almost certainly say, "Things are indeed impermanent, but I'm still unable to bear it!" Now this is suffering.

Therefore, if one only knows conceptually the principle of impermanence and no-self, one will still be unable to really depart from suffering. Only when one truly realizes through direct experience that "nirvana is quiescence," can one then depart from suffering. "Quiescence" means "unmoving," which signifies that there is no "self" to move. If there is no action of the self and no existence of the self, and if one does not seek the value of self, nor seek to assert oneself, then it is no-self. The quiescence of nirvana is not a state of deadly stillness lacking any sign of life as described by most people. Rather, though I am unmoving, I do not hinder any thing from moving; though I am devoid of a self, I do not hinder anything from existing.

Because of the power of their karma, ordinary sentient beings undergo the suffering of samsara and vexations, whereas, through the power of vows, bodhisattvas deliver sentient beings in the ocean of suffering. But for them, there is neither quiescence nor nirvana. When, then, can one reach quiescence and nirvana? They can be reached when one attains the arhatship in the Hinayana tradition, or the eighth ground (Skt. *bhumi*) of a bodhisattva for Mahayana tradition. The eighth ground is called the "ground of immovability" (Skt. *acalabhumi*) or the "effortless stage." What is immovable? There is no self moving, so it is called "quiescence." Being effortless means that one does not intend to do anything; that is, one does not engage in samsaric activities that are driven by karma; not thinking there are sentient beings in samsara to be delivered, one does not need to vow to deliver sentient beings. Those who reach this level are able to deliver sentient beings in the status of a buddha; at this time, they exist as far as sentient beings are concerned, but are nonexistent as far as they themselves are concerned.

Removing Evil and Doing Good

It is said that it will take three great *asamkhyeya kalpas* (incalculable eons) for one to attain buddhahood, and it will take two great *asamkhyeya kalpas* to achieve the eighth ground. The common methods of practice should proceed along the three disciplines:

precepts, concentration, and wisdom. The precepts amount to avoiding all evils and doing all good. That is to say, a bad thing may be insignificant, but one should not do it, while a good thing may be trivial, but one should do it.

Meditative concentration (samadhi) normally includes nine graduated stages, of which the first eight stages are commonly shared with non-Buddhist traditions and are called eight kinds of meditative concentration attained in the four dhyana heavens and the four formless heavens. The eight stages of meditative concentration include the four dhyanas of the form realm, and the four formless concentrations of the formless realm. They are still samadhi levels within the three realms (desire, form, and formless), and their realizations are still not yet liberation. When one reaches the samadhi of extinction of sensation and thought, the ninth stage realized by an arhat, the wisdom of liberation without outflows has been accomplished, and one has transcended the samsara of the three realms.

Wisdom can be realized with outflows and without outflows. In wisdom with outflows, there are still traces of the self. For example, one recognizes and believes that impermanence is a reality, and can accept it conceptually, but once one is confronted with the issues of success or failure, gain or loss, or parting in life or death, one is still unable to accept such a fact with an ordinary mind. One must achieve wisdom without outflows that accords with liberation in order for wisdom to truly function. Only when one reaches the first fruit of the arhat (Hinayana) path, or the first ground of the bodhisattva (Mahayana) path, can one manifest a portion of wisdom without outflows. It is only at the level of the fourth fruit of the arhat and above the eighth ground of bodhisattva that the sheer wisdom without outflows will appear. Therefore, it is called the approach of gradual practice.

Calming the Mind, Not Thinking about Good and Evil

Sudden enlightenment means that one does not need to go through the gradual stages of three great *asamkhyeya kalpas*, but one achieves wisdom without outflows while still an ordinary being. This is the method of Chan. Let me cite two examples:

Not finding a mind to be calmed: After Bodhidharma sat facing the wall for nine years, Huike (487-593)—who became the Second Patriarch—went to the master to ask for help to calm his mind. Huike thought his own mind was very disturbed and he sought a method for calming it, and then practiced hard. Instead of helping, Bodhidharma ignored Huike and kept him standing outside the cave. Huike had no choice but to keep waiting with great persistence. Eventually his mind was no longer scattered, and the deluded thoughts came to a stop. At that moment, Bodhidharma came out to take a look at him. Huike thought that he had a chance, so he knelt down again to request a method for pacifying his mind. Thereupon Bodhidharma told him, "Since you ask me to help pacify your mind, just bring it to me, and I'll calm it for you!" At that moment, Huike searched for his mind, but could not find it. He could only say, "I can't find my mind! I don't know where my mind is." Bodhidharma then said, "I've already pacified your mind."

This story appears to be very simple: the disciple asked for help to calm his mind, and the teacher responded by asking him to show his mind. The disciple searched for his mind but could not find it; thereupon the teacher said that he already calmed the disciple's mind. If we repeat this process in this manner today, can we bring about the same result? Certainly not. Why not? Because Huike's practice had already reached the level where his mind did not attach to phenomena, and if Bodhidharma did not point it out bluntly, Huike would continue to look for the mind to calm it. When Bodhidharma asked him to find his mind, Huike discovered that there is no mind to be found. This is to search for the self and to discover that there is no self to be found. What we are used to regarding as the self is just the illusion formed by stringing together the mind's distracted, wandering thoughts. Check it yourself by looking for your mind; if you look closely, you will discover that the mind, as we are used to calling it, is nothing but the relation of one thought to the next, and when this relation continues without cessation, it is what we conceive to be the self, and our attachment to it. Since such thoughts are constantly changing, there is no fixed and unchangeable self. If we can understand this situation, we will grasp the meaning of Huike's not being able to find his mind. For us, this is still a conceptual understanding, whereas, at that time, Huike was already in a state where he could actually experience no-mind.

Not thinking of good or evil: After the Sixth Patriarch Huineng obtained the ceremonial robe and bowl from Fifth Patriarch Hongren, and crossed the river to Dayu Mountain [in order to escape jealous monks], the monk Huiming chased after him, wishing to seize the robe and bowl, which symbolized the transmission of the Chan lineage. When Huiming caught up with Huineng, the latter relinquished the robe and bowl by putting them on a rock, but Huiming was unable to pick them up, so he said, "Actually, I have followed you to seek the Dharma." Huineng then told him, "Since you've come for the Dharma, I will tell you: thinking neither good nor evil, put down all the questions in your mind, then tell me what your original face is." This "original face" refers to the fundamental self that leaves behind the four categories of phenomena: 1) birth, aging, sickness, and death; 2) arising, abiding, changing, perishing; 3) the vicissitudes of sorrow, joy, parting, and meeting; and 4) becoming, abiding, destruction, and emptiness. What is the fundamental "self" after all? In reality, apart from these four categories of phenomena, it is impossible to find the "self." So, Huiming did as the Sixth Patriarch said, and discovered his "original face." This is because the enlightened state will manifest upon the removal of the attachment to the self.

Not Abiding in Anything

The stories of Huike and Huiming illustrate the sudden approach of Chan. Someone may ask, "Does the sudden enlightenment approach mean that one doesn't need to practice?" Also, someone once asked me, "Huineng never practiced before, but he got enlightened upon hearing the *Diamond Sutra*. Is such an instance very common?" As a matter of fact, Huineng was a woodcutter before he heard the *Diamond Sutra*. At that phase in his life, he did not engage in sitting meditation, worshipping, or reciting the sutras, the Buddha's name, or mantras, but he did cut the firewood one chop after another, picked up the logs, bound them piece by piece, and, shouldering the firewood, walked step by step to sell them at market. He was able to keep body and mind unified while doing all these things, and normally his mind already could settle as still water. That is why he attained enlightenment the moment he heard the phrase, "Without abiding in anything, give rise to mind," from the *Diamond Sutra*.

In the phrase "without abiding in anything," the word "abiding" is a manifestation of the "self," and signifies attachment. So "not abiding in anything" amounts to selflessness. To "give rise to mind" means that though one does not attach to any subjective or objective phenomena, one does not deny the constant arising and perishing of those phenomena. Instead of shutting down the faculties of seeing, hearing, perceiving, or knowing, we do not give rise to vexations such as anger or craving when coming into contact with anything. Therefore, this mind is not the deluded mind of ignorance, but the mind of wisdom that is free of outflows.

Burning Down a Practice Hut

In the *Record of the Transmission of the Lamp Composed in the Jingde Era*, there is a *gong'an* called "The old woman who burned down the practice hut." According to the record, a mother and her daughter made offerings to a Chan monk who practiced very hard for a long time in a hut that they provided for him. One day, the mother sent her daughter to bring a meal to the monk, and told her, "When you bring the meal there, give the practitioner a big hug, embracing him tightly." The daughter did what the mother instructed, but the monk had no response. The second day, the mother brought the meal by herself and asked, "Master, my daughter hugged you yesterday. How did you feel?" The Chan practitioner replied, "A withered tree leaning against a cold cliff." The monk took the young girl to be a dry tree, and took himself to be a cold cliff. Thereupon, the old lady told the monk, "I never realized that I have been making offerings to the wrong person. Get out of here!" Then she drove him away with a broom, and set fire to the hut, burning it down.

Why did the old woman throw out the monk whose mind did not move when embraced by the young girl? It was because he had not attained the mind of wisdom. He was good at meditative concentration, but was not liberated yet. If he were truly a thoroughly enlightened Chan master, he would have perceived the girl as a girl;

how could she be taken as a withered tree? And the Chan practitioner himself was a human being; how could he turn into a cold cliff?

Some people say that a practitioner goes through three phases in Chan practice: at the beginning, seeing a mountain as a mountain and a river as a river; next, while practicing diligently, not seeing a mountain as a mountain and not seeing a river as a river; and finally after attaining enlightenment, once more seeing a mountain as a mountain and a river as a river. When the monk in the hut perceived being hugged by the girl as like a withered tree leaning against a cold cliff, his mind was neither that of an ordinary person nor of a thoroughly enlightened person, but of being in the midst of practicing diligently. The old woman chasing away the monk and burning down the hut seems to be a brusque action, but it is actually the best method in the Chan tradition to force a person to push oneself ahead, and is an approach for sudden enlightenment.

Ordinary Practice

To achieve the purpose of sudden enlightenment, you must first be mindful at all times of every action you make and every thought you give rise to in your everyday life. Not only should you be clearly aware of the details of your life, but you should also make unremitting efforts with a steady, balanced, and relaxed mindset. How can you achieve such a level? Whatever you do and whomever you interact with, you must first put down the self-centered perspective involved with anger, craving, gain, and loss, and then engage in various activities in a practical and down-to-earth way, handling each matter according to the needs of the occasion. For instance, whether you cook, sweep, sleep, read, or work, put whole-hearted effort into it; if you harbor no selfish thought and concentrate only on the work at hand, then that is practicing Chan in daily life. Consistently keeping up such a practice, you are already a happy person, even without attaining sudden enlightenment.

However, it is not as easy as one may wish to reach such a level of cultivation. When encountering simple matters and regular people, most people would probably be able to deal with them with an ordinary mind. But when they are confronted with emotional issues such as those between family members or lovers, or significant gain or loss concerning property, reputation, position, etc., they would find it difficult to handle it with an ordinary mind. An ordinary mind means the mindset of reacting to what we habitually see, hear, undergo, or do in daily life. We treat all unusual phenomena with a habitual mindset. Facing any terribly serious matter, we can accept it and deal with it by regarding it as a usual, everyday matter.

Introducing Three Methods

The ordinary mind of a Chan practitioner is the mind of wisdom, so wonderful, but quite rare. Therefore, we need a method to purify the unstable emotional states and restore the mind's balance. A most practical and simple method is to join the palms, and look at the tips of the two middle fingers. Hold this posture in an attentive manner and after thirty seconds or one minute, your emotions will naturally become settled.

Another method is to pay attention to your breathing and be mindful of the breath going in and out the nostrils. This can also put your emotions to rest. One more method is to recite the name of a buddha, such as "Namo Amitabha Buddha," or a bodhisattva, such as "Namo Guanyin Pusa (Avalokiteshvara Bodhisattva)." Reciting the names of Amitabha and Guanyin will bring us peace and blessings in the present life, as well as enable us to be reborn in the Western Pure Land.

These are all the methods for cultivating ordinary mind. The reason these methods can calm our emotions lies in the effect of shifting one's attention elsewhere. We replace the thoughts that cause our emotions to fluctuate with the attentive thoughts of joining the palms, observing the breathing, or reciting the name of a buddha. If we often act this way, we will be able to always maintain a stable and harmonious mental state. It is like installing a lightning rod beforehand in order to protect the building if it is struck by lightning.

If you often use the above-mentioned methods to pacify fluctuating emotions, then when you become proficient with the practice one day, and suddenly turn to ask yourself, "What is my original face?" or "Who is joining the palms?" or "Who is reciting the Buddha's name?" Any of these questions may enable you to suddenly realize that all the buddhas of the past, present, and future are "breathing through the same nostrils as you." My dear friends, do you want to attain sudden enlightenment? You do! If so, please begin by always maintaining an ordinary mind.

Q & A

Q: Master, could you tell us what kind of state you've already achieved now?

A: Let me tell you in the clearest language: I've achieved the state that I achieve now.

Q: We are living in a realistic world and are constantly bombarded by all sorts of sounds from the world. How should we restrain ourselves so we won't be subject to their influence?

A: As I just said, we must first take the theories or concepts as our guidance, and then actually apply the methods of spiritual practice. We must act by coordinating the theory with the method. Only a theory-based method can be a correct method for putting things into practice, and only by applying the method to fulfill the goal that the theory points to will it be a useful theory or concept. Talking about the theory can also give us some guidance, but merely talking about theories or concepts may not be able to resolve our fundamental issues. Therefore, we must apply the method to put them into practice.

Q: Just as the Master said, this world of ours is so chaotic, and all things in the world are so impermanent. Besides the psychological and physiological problems of individuals, there are also interpersonal and environmental problems. So, Master, could you tell us whether our world can still be saved?

A: If I thought that the world cannot be saved, I wouldn't be here to give this talk. It is because it *is* possible for all sentient beings and all people to be saved that I've come to lecture on the Buddhadharma. Don't be so negative or pessimistic. The way of the world is just like this, and chaos and impermanence are normal phenomena. As to how to lessen our troubles, conflicts, and suffering to a certain extent amidst these normal phenomena, it is necessary for us to use the methods and concepts of Chan to educate and train people and settle these problems.

Q: Why is sitting meditation beneficial to our mind? Could it be said that the outer behavior may exert an influence on our inner activities?

A: It is definitely beneficial. The internal and the external may indeed act on each other. Sitting meditation appears to be an external behavior, but if we were unwilling to sit in meditation, we probably would not have created the external behavior of sitting meditation, and would not be able to sit well. If we are willing to do sitting meditation, we will keep sitting. As a result, it will enable our mind to calm down little by little. In addition, sitting meditation will help us regulate our endocrine system, and improve our digestive system and circulative system, so that our mindset will also be influenced and adjusted.

True Enlightenment and Mistaken Enlightenment

Zhongxing Hall, Taichung, Taiwan, August 18, 1988.

Tonight I will be talking about enlightenment in five aspects: what is enlightenment, the categories of enlightenment, the levels of enlightenment, the phenomena of enlightenment, and last, the methods for attaining enlightenment.

What Is Enlightenment?

What is generally referred to as "enlightenment" signifies understanding, being inspired, awakening, and corresponding. "Understanding" means that what was not known previously is now known. You probably had the experience of being teased as a child, when someone covered your eyes from behind and said, "Guess who?" You tried hard but simply could not guess who. Finally they let go and you turned around to look: "So, it's you!" That is enlightenment in the sense that what was previously unknown is now known.

What about being "inspired?" There is something you don't understand no matter how hard someone tries to explain it. They give you some hints and suggestions, maybe using analogies or other methods, so you can see it from another angle. When you finally understand, that is being inspired.

What about "awakening?" Originally you may be clueless and muddle-headed, but once reminded by someone you will suddenly see the light, saying, "So that's how it is. I did not know it before, but

I know it now."

The Chinese word for "corresponding" means to be "in front of" someone. You may have had the experience of sitting face-to-face with someone, yet you don't know who that person is. Four months ago a public official from Taipei wanted to take refuge in the Three Jewels. Since a close friend of his wife is a lay disciple of mine, he decided to take refuge with me and came to Beitou. After the ceremony I invited him to the parlor. He saw the words "Master Sheng Yen" on the scroll hung on the wall, and exclaimed in surprise, "Ah, you are Master Sheng Yen!"

The enlightenment that Buddhism speaks of can be illustrated by the Mahayana sutras. For example, the *Shurangama Sutra* says that deluded people are walking on the road of delusion, whereas enlightened people attain enlightenment from being in the midst of delusion; they need someone to point out to them how to convert themselves from delusion and attain enlightenment. The chapter on "Skillful Means" in the *Lotus Sutra* says that there are definitely causes for the buddhas, the World-Honored Ones, to appear in the world. What are the causes? They are to disclose the Buddha's insightful views to sentient beings, allow them to attain the ultimate purity, enable them to know what the Buddha's insightful views are, and, eventually, cause them to enter the Buddha's insightful views.

Therefore, the Tiantai School says that the Buddha's appearing in the world can be put in four words: "disclosing, showing, awakening, and entering." This means the Buddha came to disclose his insightful views to sentient beings, to show them his insightful views, to make them awaken to his insightful views, and then to enter into his insightful views. In Chinese we refer to the Dharma talks given by Dharma masters as *kaishi*, which means disclosing and showing, precisely as discussed above. You can say that I am here tonight to disclose and show the Buddha's insightful views to you, and enable you to awaken to and enter the Buddha's insightful views. Based on the *Lotus Sutra's* definition, all Buddhist teachings are meant to enable sentient beings to awaken to and enter the Buddha's insightful views. Now, what are the Buddha's insightful views? They are views of the formlessness of self, of others, of sentient beings, and of lifespan (the cycle of birth-and-death). No-form is the true form (reality), which means no-self, as well as no-attachment.

As far as the patriarchs of Chan are concerned, it is just as what Chan Master Foyan said, "Deluded people are deluded amidst enlightenment, while enlightened people are enlightened amidst delusion. The enlightened know the direction, while the deluded take the south for the north." Delusion and enlightenment are actually the same thing. Nevertheless, deluded people are always unable to let go and cast aside, and reluctant to give away, whereas enlightened people feel that all things are innately natural. Greed is a bad thing, and greediness is a kind of vexation, especially the craving for wealth. One may also crave other things such as sleep, profit, reputation, sex, and status, but as long as one craves anything it is a bad thing and there is no exception. Someone asked me, "If trying to get money is greedy, then does that mean that I should not do business? Doesn't Buddhism also encourage people to give and perform meritorious deeds by donating money? Isn't that also greed?" I replied, "If the money donated to the temple goes into my pocket and I employ it for my personal use, then it is greed."

If I employ the money to sustain the activities of the monastery, and these activities are for spreading the Dharma and benefiting sentient beings, then it should not be called greed. Another person asked, "After my company has earned a profit we use it to show gratitude and contribute to society. When we run our business, it is also for the benefit of the general public. So is it also called greed?" I answered, "Of course not." Therefore, whenever one pursues something with a self-centered purpose it is called greed, while anything that one carries out not for one's own sake or for the self is not called greed. The enlightenment that the Chan patriarchs talked about refers to attaining the realization that we do not need to cling to the possession a self center, so that we can let go of everything. Only people who are able to let go can take up great responsibilities. In other words, the more one is able to let go, the broader one's mind will be, and the profounder one's state of enlightenment.

The Categories of Enlightenment

Enlightenment can be worldly enlightenment or Buddhist enlightenment. Worldly enlightenment can further be classified into the inspiration which dawns upon one, and the divine revelation of god(s). Inspiration refers to the inspiring thoughts by which poets, painters, and novelists create their works. Once I met a painter in America who was also a photographer. He was looking at a dried leaf that had fallen to the ground, and it showed traces of having being eaten by insects. Then he took pictures of that leaf. I asked him what was so attractive about a dried leaf. He said, "Through it I see the principles of the whole universe; I see God talking to me, and I see the Buddha speaking of the Dharma within it. Within it, there is the beauty of completeness and there is also the beauty of incompleteness and flaws. I see the history of development of the whole natural world. I could simply write a thick book about what I've discovered today." Did you ever have this kind of experience?

Then at another time I saw a poet observing ants going up and down a tree, back and forth. When I asked him which ant he was following, he said the commander-in-chief. I was amazed at the time, but it was just his observation and artistic association, and the reality was not necessarily like that. Look at the pictures painted by Hong Tong in Taiwan in which flowers grow on people's heads, and people grow on top of flowers. Just as there are birds in the trees, trees can also grow from the heads of birds. This is his inspiration. I also met a little boy who was hiding under a table. I asked him what he was doing there. He told me that there were many people under the table. I took a look and saw no one else there at all. He pointed at the legs of the table and chairs, as well as the stripes of the table, showing me who this was and who that was, and he said, "My father is just like this."

The divine revelations of god(s) can be said to be a phenomenon of folk beliefs or popular religions. Have you ever seen a person who was possessed by a ghost or spirit? Many people have. For example, there was the incident of Liu Hemu in Taiwan, and there is also a certain "living Buddha," originally from Taichung, who presently lives in Seattle (USA). Both used manifestations of sounds, lights, reflections, and the like, to make you think they are enlightened. They also claimed to be thoroughly enlightened. There are many non-Buddhists nowadays who express themselves this way to show that they are "enlightened." Some of them may also resort to emotional appeals or act in a very romantic or artistic way, but that is not true enlightenment. One who relies on the power of ghosts and spirits to claim they are enlightened are just being delirious or deceptive, not really enlightened. However, by saying that, we do not mean that they have no useful purpose, and we are not saying that art and academic researches are no good, or that folk beliefs do not have their uses.

Buddhist enlightenment can be three kinds: through faith, through understanding, and through realization.

Enlightenment through Faith

One believes in the buddhas, the bodhisattvas, and the Three Jewels with great piety; and through this piety one obtains spiritual responses from buddhas and bodhisattvas, and is protected by heavenly spirits, so that one's faith becomes very steadfast. When I was a young novice, who had just left home, I was unable to recite the Buddhist liturgy from memory. So, my then-master instructed me to prostrate to the bodhisattva Guanyin 500 times every morning before others woke up. He said that if I did that I would become clever and would soon be able to recite the liturgy. After three months, I suddenly became able to very quickly memorize the liturgy. Did I become enlightened doing this? Certainly not. But it can also be regarded as a kind of "enlightenment." In that situation, the empowerment that Guanyin Bodhisattva bestowed on me helped me remove my karmic obstructions so that I was no longer dull. This may sound uncanny, and it is like the Yiguan Dao sect where you receive the five words, "The Supreme One Maitreya Buddha," and a dot is placed between your eyebrows and suddenly, you become really clever! But you cannot say that they are heretical; there seems to be reason in what they do.

Nevertheless, Buddhism differs from the prophecies and revelations of folk beliefs or popular religions in that it accepts Buddhadharma as its guideline and criteria. Although we may experience spiritual responses or empowerments, we will not proclaim ourselves as buddhas or great bodhisattvas, or claim that we have attained great or thorough enlightenment. However, some non-Buddhists, as well as so-called Buddhists who do not understand Buddhadharma, may make such claims.

Enlightenment through Understanding

Having read sutras or Buddhist books or listened to Dharma talks, one develops faith in the Buddhadharma and comes to understand it. One thinks that the Buddhadharma is inconceivable and is the best teaching in the world, and hence one develops some realization. The sutras say that conceptual enlightenment is like counting treasures that belong to others, like clerks in a bank counting other people's money. Therefore, from the perspective of one who has achieved true Buddhist enlightenment, Dharma masters who lecture on the sutras but who are not yet enlightened are just "counting treasures." They have the enlightenment of understanding but not the enlightenment of realization. When I asked my disciples to expound the Dharma they would say modestly, "Oh Master, we have not attained enlightenment! It would just be like counting treasure if you want us to expound on the Dharma!" I said: "Don't the banks need clerks too? So you might just as well count treasures tentatively." Some would also ask me whether I am enlightened. I usually say, "I don't know." They would then ask, since I don't know if I am enlightened, how can I expound the Dharma? I answer, "It is enough for me to enable others to become enlightened; it doesn't matter whether I myself am enlightened." That is to say, it does not matter whether I have treasures or not, but it would be enough if I help you to count treasures. Therefore, enlightenment of understanding is enlightenment too, and one should use it to help others to further engage their practice.

Enlightenment through Realization

One has personally experienced the fundamental principles of Buddhadharma and practiced them accordingly, cultivating precepts, concentration, and wisdom; one has eliminated greed, anger, and ignorance one by one, and has finally reached thorough enlightenment. Enlightenment of realization can be the enlightenment of the Hinayana (Lesser Vehicle) or of the Mahayana (Greater Vehicle). The enlightenment of Hinayana is the realization that the self does not exist; that life is impermanent, and bodies are also impermanent; one comes to realize that there is no [enduring and separate] self, and thus will not have any attachments—no greed, anger, or ignorance. With Hinayana enlightenment, one only realizes life is impermanent, but one does not yet realize that dharmas (phenomena) themselves also do not exist.

Therefore, with the enlightenment of Hinayana one looks upon birth and death as something extremely terrible, so one seeks to depart from samsara and enter into nirvana. With Mahayana enlightenment, one has the profounder realization that the scenes of samsara are also empty, and therefore one neither attaches to, nor avoids the problems of samsara. Rather, one comes and goes freely amidst samsara with a compassionate heart. Departing from samsara does not mean escaping from the human world nor running away from the three realms, but to be free from bondage to samsara and its troubles. There is no country that is without prisons; those who break the laws are imprisoned and lose their freedom; so, they long to be freed from prison and when released, long never to go back again. This situation is similar to what ordinary people need to engage in spiritual practice, and to depart from the prisons of three realms. Once our practice reaches the level where we depart from the three realms, we don't want to go back. This is the enlightenment of Hinayana. However, the bodhisattvas of Mahayana are not afraid of entering the prisons of the three realms. The bodhisattvas certainly would not break laws and be imprisoned; rather, they would enter the prisons to teach the Dharma so they are free to come and go.

Levels of Enlightenment

Chan Master Guifeng Zongmi (780-841) in the Tang Dynasty said that there are five kinds of meditation practice. This first is that of certain non-Buddhists who attach to either eternity or nihilism, and aspire to the superior state while detesting the inferior state. Holders of the view of eternity believe that they originated from the root source of the god(s) and will return to the god(s). They also think that they will become supreme deities in the future (often seen in non-Buddhist religions such as polytheism and monotheism, whether or not they believe in permanent souls or an eternal God). Nihilism is the view of there being no supramundane cause or effect; usually those who have no religious faith or oppose it will hold nihilistic views. You may ask doubtfully: would those without religious faith still practice meditation? Yes, they would. Nowadays there are many people who practice qigong (methods for directing the *qi* or life energy), taijiquan (a kind of Chinese martial arts), and seated meditation. However, they do not necessarily have anything to do with religion; they only wish to have a healthy body and a tranquil mind. This is close to the nihilistic view of certain non-Buddhist faiths. The patriarchs in ancient times said that it would be better to hold a view of eternity as huge as Mount Sumeru than to hold a nihilistic view as tiny as a mustard seed. Buddhism regards both eternalism and nihilism as non-Buddhist, but generally speaking, eternalism with religious faith would value morality more than materialistic nihilism.

The second kind of meditation is that of ordinary people; although they have the right faith in cause and effect, they still have attachments. They are attached to the joy and calmness of meditative concentration, thinking that meditative concentration in the desire realm is already liberation. In fact, one will not be able to go beyond the three realms if one gets attached to meditative concentration and clings to it covetously. The third kind of meditation is that of the Hinayana followers who have awakened to the emptiness of the self and attained liberation without being attached to meditative concentration. To transcend the three realms, one needs to let go of coveting meditative concentration. The fourth kind of meditation is that of Mahayana followers who awaken to the emptiness of the self as well as dharmas. The fifth kind of meditation is that of those who suddenly awaken to their intrinsic nature, discovering that their mind is one and the same as that of the buddhas, this being the unsurpassed vehicle.

A Chan master once said that he had experienced major enlightenment thirty-six times and minor enlightenment numerous times. This shows that Chan enlightenment does not solve all problems at once. There is a Chan saying: "Great doubt, great enlightenment; small doubt, small enlightenment; no doubt, no enlightenment." The doubt that is aroused in practice inspires one to "investigate Chan." There is a *gong'an* from the records of Chan, in which a disciple of Master Zhaozhou (778-897) asked him: "All sentient beings have buddha-nature. Does a dog have buddha-nature?" The Master answered "Wu" (meaning "no," or "without") in order to break the disciple's attachment. Clearly, the disciple knew that all sentient beings have buddha-nature, but purposefully asked whether a dog had it. After Zhaozhou answered "Wu," the disciple was in trouble, for in the Chan tradition the disciple heeds the master. So, now this disciple had to rack his brain to find out why the master denied that a dog has buddha-nature.

Long afterward, in the Song Dynasty (960-1279), Chan Master Dahui Zonggao (1089–1163) asked his disciples to investigate "Why does a dog not have buddha-nature?" As a result, thirty-six people became enlightened during one night. Dear audience, please give this method a try and see how many of you would become enlightened.

Question: Why does a dog not have the buddha-nature?"

Master Sheng Yen: Can you become enlightened just by asking this question? Someone can go crazy if they keep on asking this! (*Laughter*) As those with great doubt will achieve great enlightenment and those with small doubt will achieve small enlightenment, there are levels of enlightenment. When ordinary people see their nature, they "realize the principle." Many people make the mistake of thinking that Chan enlightenment resolves all things. As a matter of fact, it is not necessarily so.

Let me explain Chan enlightenment with three points: first, you see for yourself that your intrinsic nature is that of a buddha. This is called "seeing the nature"; it is a breakthrough in one's investigation of Chan. As an example, when investigating Master Zhaozhou's saying that a dog does not have buddha-nature, one suddenly realizes why he said this! However, seeing one's intrinsic buddha-nature does not yet amount to being a buddha—having seeing the mountain, you still have to climb it. Second, having attained enlightenment, you must embark on cultivation—this is setting out to climb the mountain. Having seen the nature, one departs from the erroneous views of eternalism and nihilism; one will surely not regress from right faith in

Buddhadharma; one will put effort into spiritual practice. Meanwhile, vexations definitely still exist, so one must continue to practice. The third level is the enlightenment of the sage in which one experiences that reality, the true nature of phenomena, is formless. Chan traditionally speaks of three barriers on the path of enlightenment. The first is the *initial barrier* in which one "shatters the ball of doubt" and sees one's buddha-nature. The second barrier is the *manifold barrier* in which one attains major and minor enlightenment one after another as we mentioned earlier. The third barrier is the *imprisoning barrier*; only when one has broken through this barrier does one truly transcend the three realms, and attains the forbearance based on the insight of non-arising of phenomena (Chn. *wusheng faren*). At this time one is at ease, free to come and go in samsara.

The Phenomena of Enlightenment

The phenomena that accompany enlightenment can be divided into common and uncommon. Common phenomena can be achieved as long as one engages in spiritual practice, and are further divided into sensation and cleverness. "Sensation" means that one *feels* that one benefits from the experience. Take for example, the feeling of lightness and ease. A fellow monk I met at the full ordination ceremony was reciting and prostrating to Guanyin Bodhisattva one day, when he suddenly felt totally relaxed and at ease throughout his body. He was also walking while doing prostrations, so he began to walk faster and faster. After more than twenty kilometers, he finally began to feel tired, and then realized that he was not doing prostrations anymore, but was just walking. This is the so-called state of lightness and ease. Moreover, when he became tired he found that the world was different from what it used to be; there was a sense of stability in calmness and relaxation, and everything was clean and pure in his eyes. Therefore, he thought he had attained enlightenment, and if no one pointed out his mistake he would have continued to think that he had.

Next, there is the state of "cleverness." A Buddhist monk sat in meditation and a few days later, he had a strong urge to write poetry; all beautifully composed, he was able to generate over four hundred poems and verses in just one night. The monk thought that he had got enlightened; otherwise how could he have composed more than four hundred poems in just one night? However, this was not the true enlightenment! Then there is another phenomenon called "keen sensitivity." One time during sitting meditation, he seemed to hear two oxen fighting. When he opened his eyes he did not see any ox; instead he found two ants grappling together on the floor.

I once met a person from Myanmar, who received a PhD in chemistry in the U.S. He came to learn sitting meditation with me but stopped coming after two weeks. Three months later he showed up again. I asked him why he had not come for such a long time. He said, "I didn't have to come because I could see you when I meditated at home. Whatever I asked you, you would answer me accordingly, so I could learn meditation with you without having to come to your place!" I thought it was strange and wondered whether he had come to me or I had gone to him. (*Laughter*) If other people encountered this situation they might be pleased with themselves, thinking that they have become buddhas. However, I just told him, "You've strayed into a demonic state. You'll have troubles." As a matter of fact, none of these examples of common phenomena is enlightenment. If one takes them as enlightenment, one is surely making nothing but mistakes!

The second category of common phenomena can be compared to the states described in a Chan saying: "At first, seeing mountains as mountains, and rivers as rivers; then seeing mountains not as mountains, and rivers not as rivers; finally, again seeing mountains as mountains, and rivers as rivers." And these are not true enlightenment either. When one has not yet engaged in spiritual practice, we say that they see mountains as mountains and rivers as rivers. When one practices so hard they become oblivious to the environment, we say that they no longer see mountains as mountains, and rivers as rivers. The third state, where once again mountains are mountains and rivers as rivers, may be because one stops practicing and once again becomes aware of the environment. But it may also be because one has attained enlightenment, but now is able to see mountains and rivers without attachment.

As for unusual enlightenment phenomena, before attaining enlightenment, one feels grief-stricken—as if bereaved of both parents—and after attaining enlightenment, one is even more grief-stricken. Before enlightenment, the practitioner is in deep grief for not having realized the all-important truth. He or she believes that they need to make special efforts in practice. After enlightenment they see themselves having great responsibility to strive vigorously to deliver all sentient beings. Or, before becoming enlightened, all that one could do is to practice; afterwards there is nothing for one to do, and nothing that one cannot do. For example, Venerable Master Guangqin (1892-1986), who just passed away three years ago, said, "There is neither coming nor going, and nothing has happened at all." That is to say, after attaining enlightenment, one realizes nothing has ever happened—after enlightenment, one is very modest and open-minded, acts like an ordinary person, but their compassion and wisdom are entirely different from those of ordinary people. He or she has nothing to do, but they can also do anything as long as it involves delivering sentient beings.

Methods for Attaining Enlightenment

Regarding the methods for attaining enlightenment, there are three kinds. The first is the gradual approach, and it is the method of practicing slowly; the second is the sudden approach, and it is the method of attaining enlightenment all of a sudden. Within the gradual approach are three stages: first, we go from a scattered mind to a focused mind; then we go from a focused mind to a concentrated (single-pointed) mind; finally, we go from a concentrated mind to a mind of wisdom and hence, enlightenment. One does not necessarily have to resort to sitting meditation or investigating Chan. So long as one single-mindedly recites the Buddha's name or does prostrations, one may also go through these three stages and reach enlightenment.

In the second method—the sudden approach—it is not necessary to use any specific method, but one simply keeps sitting or keeps investigating a *huatou*. Now, the third method is to recite the Buddha's name. In fact, reciting the Buddha's name is the best method for many people as everyone can recite the Buddha's name. By reciting "Namo Amitabha Buddha" one may go from reciting the Buddha's name with a scattered mind to reciting it with an undivided (one-pointed) mind and will eventually attain the samadhi of mindfulness of the Buddha, and then one will surely attain enlightenment. If we cannot achieve enlightenment by reciting the Buddha's name, we may request Amitabha Buddha to receive us by vowing to take rebirth in the Western Pure Land of Utmost Bliss. Therefore, reciting the Buddha's name is the easiest and most reliable way to attain enlightenment. It would be the best if we can attain enlightenment this way; if not, then Amitabha Buddha will take us to his Pure Land when this life of ours comes to an end, and so we can diligently practice once again and achieve enlightenment after taking rebirth there.

Finally, I remind you that one has to rely on one's own practice in order to attain enlightenment. Do not expect to achieve it by taking shortcuts or easy ways; do not ask someone else to help you attain enlightenment with a mantra or empowerment; that is impossible. If something of the kind happens it would still be worldly enlightenment, not true enlightenment. We need to embrace this kind of right view and understanding; otherwise we would be misled and be mistaken rather than becoming truly enlightened.

Emotion and Reason:
Dealing with Complex Relations

Sun Yat-sen Memorial Hall, Taipei, July 11, 1990.

We often hear people say something like, "He is a nice person and has a kind heart, but he doesn't get along well with others." Let me ask you, would you say this was a nice person? In terms of himself, he is a good person; in terms of society, he is just "half" a good person. In particular, if a Buddhist does not get along well with others, he or she cannot exercise a purifying influence on society. So, I would like to talk about emotion and reason today, to explore how we should establish interpersonal relationships, so that there will be more harmony.

Definition of Emotion and Reason

What, then, are emotion and reason? Subjective attitude is emotion, while objective attitude is reason. Selfish viewpoint is emotion, while impartial viewpoint is reason. To pursue something for oneself and for the present is emotion, while to pursue something for the public and for the endless future is reason. To do something with an intention is emotion, while to do something without any intention or purpose is reason.

Emotion keeps the activities and survival of society running, just like lubricant in a machine, making life more meaningful. Nevertheless, from the Buddhist point of view, we must dissolve emotion layer by layer, and enter the state of reason. What we mean by a subjective attitude is caring only about one's own ideas and opinions, disregarding the thoughts of others. Not considering others, not putting oneself in their position, is "emotion." On the other hand, thinking first of others in all situations, seeking to lessen one's own self-centered mentality and behavior, is "reason." When considering our own benefits, we should also try to help others obtain benefits and assistance. It's as if we were all in the same boat; we repair the craft and improve its performance so that all may reach safe landing earlier. As we are also on board, we will arrive at the other shore safely as well. The broader our scope of mind becomes, the more people we can help, the greater our progress and achievement will be. Therefore, though we are not working for ourselves, we obtain the greatest benefit ourselves. This attitude is called "without intention," yet it gets the most things done.

Types of Emotion and Reasoning

We can speak of five kinds of emotion: love between man and woman; affection between family members; friendship; kindness and gratitude between givers and receivers; and companionship between practitioners on the Path. The first four kinds of emotion are worldly, while the fifth is the emotion related to the Dharma. The existence of emotions is why Buddhism calls living beings "sentient beings," or beings with feelings.

Is there friendship, kindness, gratitude between a man and a woman? The answer is yes, and this shows that it is not necessarily just romantic love between man and woman. For spouses who are Buddhist followers, there is also friendship on the path of practice. Moreover, the Chinese traditionally think there is only family love, kindness, gratitude between parents and children. However, in

Western society, people regard their parents as friends; at the same time there is certainly love between parents and children, as well as children's respect and love for their parents. Of course, besides friendship, there may also be kindness, gratitude, and friendship on the path of practice. Between givers and receivers, some people give simply for the sake of giving, without thinking that they are performing an act of kindness. We may say that these people are doing selfless giving.

When I pursued advanced studies in Japan, very few people helped me or made offerings of support. But an anonymous donor regularly sent me money from Switzerland. I asked him, "What do you want me to do for you? How can I repay your kindness?" He replied, "I don't want anything from you, or expect you to do anything for me. Hopefully you'll also help others when you have the ability to do so." This is friendship on the path of practice. Therefore, helping anyone with Buddhist teachings, money, or physical strength to enable him or her to obtain the benefit of the Dharma is friendship on the path of practice.

Let's talk about the different types of reasoning. From common knowledge or the Buddhist perspective, reason can be classified into six types: physics, the laws of matter; physiology, the bodily structures and processes; psychology, the workings of the mind; ethics, morality in interpersonal relations; truth, as in philosophy and religion; and, finally, true suchness or true nature, which is called "one's original nature" in Buddhism.

Reasoning from Physics

Last night we had a typhoon, and fortunately, it didn't strike our city. Yet it was still quite windy this morning. Someone said, "Shifu, it's the first day that you'll be giving a lecture, and we're having this typhoon. What a nuisance!" I replied, "There must be a reason or cause when a typhoon occurs. Since the typhoon has its reason and cause, we shouldn't be complaining."

Two years ago, a lay Buddhist drove me to visit a place. On our way there, the rain was pouring and this lay Buddhist said, "Hopefully the rain will stop when we get to our destination, so Shifu won't get wet from the rain." I said, "You're really selfish! For the sake of one single person, you want the rain to stop." But strangely enough, when we were about to arrive, the rain stopped all of a sudden. He said joyfully, "This is your meritorious blessing, Shifu. It's not raining now." I said, "Amituofo! It's not my meritorious blessing when the rain stops as we wish. If there's a drought here and people need rain badly, but the rain stops when I come, wouldn't it be causing harm to many people? So, the rain stopped because it *should* stop, not because I've come here." By using this example, I want to show that there are always causes for every phenomenon in the world. If a Buddhist says that it stops raining as soon as an eminent practitioner arrives somewhere, and it begins to rain soon after he leaves, then this is non-Buddhist thinking, and not Buddhist teaching. The Buddhadharma explains everything in terms of the workings of causes, conditions, and karmic result.

Reasoning from Physiology

Our body is like a machine, so please do not overuse it, and do not leave it unused too much. If you use a machine nonstop everyday, it would break down very soon. So it needs to be given rest, be lubricated and maintained from time to time, so that it can be used for long. My body has never been fit and I have always been ill, but

I am always in action everyday. Many people urge me to take a rest, but I say that this machine of mine cannot be given a break, or it will rust right away. However, sometimes when I am very busy and people want to talk to me, I still see them and use the time to rest. For example, someone asked me how to deal with his headaches. I said, "Don't worry! Besides seeing a doctor, just recite the name of Guanyin Bodhisattva." He talked for a long time, but I only said one sentence. He gladly accepted my words, and his problem was solved.

Reasoning from Psychology

Usually, our thoughts are uncontrollable, which is why we have the Chinese idioms, "a mind like a monkey's" or "a mind like a wild horse." However, if we can find the patterns in our mental processes, and understand what causes the arising and perishing of our thoughts, we will not be afflicted or troubled by uncontrollable thoughts. Nowadays there are professional psychotherapists who can help people analyze the causes of the thoughts arising in their minds, and find out ways to deal with their emotional problems, enabling them to achieve temporary relief. Nevertheless, these methods are just stopgaps, relieving the symptoms but not the disease, and the patient's mind will still fall back into chaos.

The Buddhist teachings, however, can thoroughly solve emotional problems by dealing with them at their roots. First, Buddhism teaches us how to be aware of how mental afflictions originate; it is, in a sense, somewhat like psychoanalysis. Then, no matter what problems we have, we just "kill the devil upon meeting a devil, and kill the buddha upon meeting the buddha." Of course we should cast away bad thoughts, but we should cast away the good ones as well, and completely put down all thoughts at any time. If one reaches this level, there will be no trace of mind to be found. So, would there still be any mental troubles? Of course not! That is what we mean by "attaining enlightenment," "eliminating vexations," and "realizing bodhi." Therefore, while a psychotherapist can help many people, the Buddhadharma can offer help to psychotherapists.

Among my students and disciples, there are more than ten psychotherapists, including Asians and Westerners, the latter being greater in number. I asked them, "Aren't you physicians yourselves?" They replied, "Shifu, you're the physician of physicians." I said, "I'm not that capable. I fall ill myself and seek to be cured. But I just work to help the new patients as an old patient. Only the Buddha, the one with great compassion, is the physician of all physicians." The Buddha is also known by another honorific: "King of Medicine." The true physician is no other than the Buddha.

Reasoning from Ethics

Chinese people emphasize ethics, especially the five ethics, which refers to the responsibilities and obligations resulting from relationships among people. That is to say, everyone should act in accordance with the roles they play, and the status they are in. If we do not fulfill our duties or obligations, then we have failed to be upright people. For example, if a husband and wife perform their respective duties and obligations, they will definitely enjoy a harmonious marriage; if not, they will quarrel and fight, demanding that the other fulfill *their* duties, rather than fulfilling *one's own* duties.

Reasoning from Theories of Truth

This refers to metaphysical ideas, theories, or concepts. One starts from practical society, and infers that there should be an ideal, unchanging truth. Phenomena are changing but the truth is unchanging. So, philosophers and religious teachers believe that there is a primordial and ultimate truth. If people can believe that there is a truth, they will feel comfort and a sense of belonging. So, people cultivated in philosophy will not be irritable or impatient, but will definitely have a sounder character. It is because they believe that, in spite of the unfairness of the practical world, the truth is definitely impartial.

Reasoning from True Nature

In Buddhism, one's true nature is also called true suchness, nirvana, buddha-nature, dharma-body (Skt. *Dharmakaya*), and so on. Many people mistake "death" for nirvana; in fact, nirvana means that the mind is like still water, and it is free and at ease, not troubled by any favorable or unfavorable situations, or right or wrong, good or evil, etc.

When I arrived in the United States in 1975, an American asked me to teach him the method for attaining liberation. He said, "I have no liberty now. I want to get divorced, but I can't because my wife puts forward requirements and wants money from me. Master, I heard there are methods for liberation, aren't there?" I replied, "It won't work. After I help you out and you get divorced from this wife, you'll marry another woman. You'll keep replacing one wife with another, and you'll never be liberated." He said, "I won't get married any more. I have enough of it from women; how could I get married again?" I told him, "Being afraid of women, you also won't be liberated. You won't feel at ease. If you aren't afraid when you meet her, if you aren't afraid when she sticks to you like a limpet, then it's liberation. Besides, not feeling distressed when one goes without woman or wife is also liberation." In other words, when confronted with a problem, if we can readily, joyfully, and calmly face it, accept it, and deal with it, we are liberated right at that moment.

Making Good Use of Emotion and Reason

From the Buddhist perspective, compassion and wisdom are actually the purification of the emotions and reason as found in worldly situations. By purification we mean that we try to keep others and ourselves from being caught up in troubles and vexations. How do we simplify complex relationships? The answer lies in four simple words: use reason and emotion. It signifies handling our interpersonal relationships with compassion and wisdom. When we have a bit more loving care for others, we can create a bit more warmth and affinity. Some people are rude and unreasonable, and it's impossible to reason with them. But if we use emotions like family affection, love, or friendship, then problems can be solved. Chinese people use emotion more, giving others a sense of warmth and amiability. However, if we simply apply emotion and ignore reason, we would most likely confound right with wrong, or confuse good and evil. Therefore, when it comes to ethics among family members, friends, and relatives, we may apply emotion. As for social relation, we should handle them with reason; in other words, we may apply emotion to deal with personal matters, but we must apply reason to deal with public affairs. Applying emotion will bring harmony to our environment, while applying reason will ensure fairness in the environment. We should not adhere to just one of the two nor lack the other.

A disciple of mine is very rational, and in doing everything he wants it to be reasonable. As a result, he is filled with perplexity. He said, "What a mess! There are so many unfair and unreasonable things in our world!" I told him, "You're not being compassionate! When interacting with people, we shouldn't simply apply reason. People shouldn't be treated like material objects. You should put compassion into your interactions with people. Only then will you have peace of mind, and at the same time make the people related to you joyful."

Compassion is similar in meaning to sympathy, except that it is more purified and genuine. Using emotion is tinged with personal feeling, but using compassion is not. When some people create unreasonable incidents or behave illegitimately around us, in terms of reasonableness, they may have to be sent to prison. From the perspective of compassion, however, their offences may have arisen from their family background, social environment, or physical and psychological factors. So, from a different angle, we forgive them with empathy, and try to help them in various ways. This is called compassion.

We should feel compassion for others because of their troubles, but this does not mean that we just always approve what they do, saying, "Fine, just fine." As for our own problems, we should release, guide, and reform them with wisdom; this is what is meant by spiritual practice. We are often confronted with problems that trouble us; these problems are mostly of our own making, but they may also be caused by the environment. Under these circumstances, it is no use resenting ourselves or blaming others; it is best to resolve them with the Buddhist concepts of karmic causality. Otherwise, we would feel bitter or resentful.

According to the Buddhist concept of karma, all our troubles and difficulties are the present results that come from past causes. With such a concept in mind, we would feel less afflicted, or we don't even need to feel afflicted at all. Nevertheless, karmic causality does not mean we should not change our environment or solve our problems. Rather, we should create positive causes and conditions to facilitate the change of environment and the solution of problems. Only then is it the attitude of wisdom.

The Buddhadharma places great emphasis on compassion and wisdom. To promote Buddhist teachings is to carry on the campaign of compassion and wisdom. If everyone can cultivate a mind of compassion and wisdom, our society will certainly be purified, and our lives will definitely be happy. Therefore, we need more people to join us to spread the Dharma, and to urge people to embrace and practice the Dharma.

Hopefully you are all practitioners with compassion and wisdom, as well as promoters of the Dharma. Blessings to you all!

Good and Evil:
Establishing Correct Values and Concepts

Sun Yat-sen Memorial Hall, Taipei, July 10, 1990

I do not consider the contemporary era to be the worst of times, in which people confuse and confound good and evil. In reality, good and evil have always stood side by side, in all times and all environments. Good represents positive values and symbolizes brightness, while evil represents negative values and symbolizes darkness. The two alternate and grow and decline in turn with the changes of time and environment. Therefore, in each era, it is necessary to elucidate the value and criteria of good and evil in order to offer help to everyone in society.

The Judgment of Good and Evil

We may judge good and evil from three aspects: behavior, results, and motives.

Judgment Based on Behavior

Most people habitually judge good and evil from the behavior of others. In fact, people with bad behaviors are not necessarily bad, while people with good behaviors are not necessarily good. Recently I led a seven-day Chan retreat in the United States, and something happened to a participant on his way to our monastery. And for the first three days, this incident kept him from settling himself into the retreat. At last he spoke his mind to me: while he was driving on the highway, a deer of about two hundred pounds dashed out from the forest, and failing to brake the car in time, he ran over the deer. He was very upset, thinking, "I've come here to practice. How could I have killed a life?" So he was deeply troubled. I told him, "You didn't do anything bad, but what you did isn't necessarily good. You didn't commit an act of killing; it's your car that killed a deer."

If a Buddhist thinks that this incident is an act of taking life or doing evil, then this concept is wrong. From the Buddhist perspective, to judge whether a person is good or bad, two conditions must be met; namely, "what the mouth speaks must correspond with the intention," and "the effect derived from the bodily action must correspond with the intention." If the mouth speaks something or the body makes an action without corresponding with the intention, then it does not count as committing an evil or breaking a precept.

Judgment Based on Results

Judgment based on results means finding good or evil based on the results of a behavior. Some people originally harbor the intention of doing good deeds or speaking good words, but they end up with bad results. On the contrary, some people have bad intentions but unexpectedly, their actions turn out to be beneficial to others. These situations can be found frequently in daily life. This shows that to judge whether something is good or bad based on the results is incorrect.

Judgment Based on Motives

By motives we mean one's own intention. This is very important from the Buddhist standpoint. Buddhadharma stresses causes and conditions, which refer to the contributing factors that underlie all events and all phenomena. There are always some primary factors for whatever every one of us does or says. If someone harbors an ill intention but brings about a good result due to changes in external factors, then according to Buddhism, such a person is not credited as having done something good. Though he has not done anything bad, his motives are improper. Therefore, the goodness or badness of motives is the essential basis for judging good or evil.

The Definition of Good and Evil

Good and evil are value judgments; "good" refers to positive values, while "evil" refers to negative values. The criteria for the value judgment of good and evil usually vary with the times, the environment, and the existing culture, but their influence over individuals, society, and history has never been negated. If an individual's behavior can progress along with the development of morality, knowledge, and techniques, then its value is good, or positive; otherwise, it is evil.

We will next look at this in terms of society, which includes individuals, families, and interpersonal interaction and influence. The issues within one's mind are private and individual matters, but if one's thoughts are manifested in speech or action, that will influence the family and all the related people in the living environment.

Today, lots of young people are doing drugs, and some began since elementary school years. What is the cause? It has a lot to do with their families, fellow students, and friends they come in touch with. If such drug users exert a negative influence on other people, then what they do results in evil [even if the young drug users may not have evil intent in mind].

It is said that quite a few people in Taiwan like to eat snakes and the more poisonous the better, claiming that this can ward off cold, counteract poison, and invigorate the body. In addition, others delight in sumptuous feasts with all kinds of gourmet cuisine. They don't do this for nourishment, but for satisfying their self-importance and vanity. This practice is quite prevalent in Taiwan.

The famous singer Ho Dejian, who just returned from Mainland China, said, "Mainland China is so poor, yet Taiwan is much too wasteful." I also met some American friends who had been to Taiwan who said to me, "The living conditions in Taiwan are better than that in America." Hearing this, I felt worried about Taiwan. Some Taiwanese people may spend over ten thousand (Taiwanese) dollars for one meal, but they are loath to donate even one or two thousand dollars to charities. Is this kind of custom and value good or evil?

We can also judge good and evil based on historical value. The reader understands that we should not contend for the momentary fame and gain of the present or for the practical matters of the moment, but should strive for the history that will always be remembered. Putting aside for the moment whether we leave behind a good reputation, we must think first what influence our actions will have on the future of our offspring, our races, and even all humanity. In the *Book of Documents* (Chn. *Shujing*) it is said, "A family that accumulates virtues will definitely have felicities reserved for their descendants, while a family that accumulates non-virtues will definitely have disasters reserved for their offspring." This is a judgment of long-lasting value about one's own whole family.

As for historical figures, perhaps in their time many people worshipped them blindly, but viewed from the historical perspective, they may be regarded as bad people. Therefore, as the thoughts vary in different times, the judgment on historical figures will also vary.

Nevertheless, from the Buddhist perspective, it is impossible for the Buddhadharma to have different standards of value because of the differences in time.

Criteria of Good and Evil

The criteria of good and evil can be summed up in the four points as follows.

An Individual's Interests as the Criteria

This is to take a selfish standpoint as the criteria for judging good and evil. It is not correct because many wicked people claim that they are good people. There are two kinds of good people. One kind is "one who sees everyone as a good person"; the other, "one who looks upon everyone as either good or evil."

In this world, how can there be individuals who regard all as good people? This is the attitude of buddhas and bodhisattvas. If you help them in a favorable way, they say, "How nice of you! Thank you!" If you covertly cause them troubles, they also say, "How nice of you! Thank you!" Why is it so? When you help them in a positive way, it is a "favorable condition as contributory factors." When you make their life difficult in a negative way, it is an "adverse condition as contributory factors." Regardless of whether you treat him in a positive or negative way, he always feels that you are a good person.

As ordinary people, we may also make judgments in this manner. When we know clearly that someone will cause us harm, and that we have no way to avoid it, then we can only accept it. Such acceptance is a test, and going through this kind of test or trial will make us more mature, so we should be thankful to them. As Buddhists, we should learn to take this kind of attitude, discerning good and evil distinctively, yet without taking the wicked person to be beyond any remedy, or to be an enemy we shall hate forever.

Social Customs and Habits as the Criteria

If the cultures and civilizations in the world could interact with one another, the criteria of social customs and habits would be the same. However, owing to the differences of races and beliefs, there are differences in the value judgment of different areas and times. Consequently, in Shakyamuni Buddha's time, he thought that in any time, place or country a Buddhist stays, he or she should not go against the local social customs and habits at the time. Otherwise, he or she would have done an evil. That is because when you object the things those people require for their living, you would not be able to survive, not to mention spreading the Dharma. The idea of "following the time and the place" means that each one upholds a different standard by adapting to the environment and time they live in. This is the thought of the World-Honored One. Summarizing the above discussion, we know that there are no fixed criteria of good and evil for social customs and ways.

Philosophical Thought or Critical Thinking as the Criteria.

A portion of people may always believe any given philosophical thought, but it can never be universally accepted in any way. Therefore, it is not right to take the philosophical thoughts or critical thinking as the criteria.

The Religious Belief as the Criterion

From the perspective of the *Koran* and the *Old Testament*, those who worship idols are doomed to hell. Once, on the flight from Taiwan to

America, I met a Protestant priest from Korea on the airplane, who sat next to me. He took a look at me and began to chat with me in English. Hearing what I said, he shook his head and said, "What a shame!" I asked him, "What do you mean?" He said, "How could an outstanding person like you believe in Buddhism?" I asked, "Then what's the best religion?" He said, "The only best religion, of course, is Christianity." I said, "You're right." He said, "If so, why do you believe in Buddhism, and not Christianity?" I told him, "As far as you're concerned, Christianity is the best. But as far as I'm concerned, Buddhism is the best. Do you agree?"

In fact, regardless of traditional religions or new religions, they do not approve the faiths of one another, and all regard the other faiths as problematic. However, open-mined people will not publicly criticize because it is barely tolerable in our times. Nevertheless, when making judgment in private, they still think that theirs are the best, while all other faiths have problems. This shows that the thoughts of religious faith cannot be taken as the criteria for value judgment.

Then, apart from religion, are there other methods for curbing people's minds? There are, but they are not very reliable. Therefore, with no other alternatives, we still need religion; it is always better to have religion than be without it. Therefore, from the Buddhist standpoint, we think that all religions should exist, and that different people, people of different levels and different interests, may choose to believe in different religions.

Buddhist Concepts of Good and Evil

This may be elucidated in four points as follows.

Existence of Both Good and Evil

That both good and evil exist is the worldly standard that arises out of the common social judgment and criteria of the human realm. This is making judgments based on the influence of ordinary people over the individual self, family, and society. If the influence is positive, it is said to be good; if the influence is negative, it is said to be bad. This includes ethics, morality, customs, habits, and legal standards. So, as a Buddhist, one should affirm the standard of good and evil of the current society in the first place.

Generating Good and Eliminating Evil

This is the function of Buddhism for transforming people; it takes current society as the basis, and then elevates society to a purified level. That is to say, since there are good and evil in society, we wish people to do as much good as possible by applying the Buddhist approach of observing the precepts, cultivating concentration, and fostering wisdom. They begin by improving their physical and verbal behavior, and then adjust their fundamental ideas and concepts at the psychological level, to achieve the goal of generating good and eliminating evil.

Having Good but Not Evil

This is the state of bodhisattvas, far beyond the reach of ordinary people. If ordinary people see everything and everyone as good, they are confusing good and evil and being a hypocrite; this will bring no good to individuals and society. However, despite there being quite a few people who have wicked minds and evil conduct, as Buddhists we believe that "everyone will be able to perfect themselves and become buddhas and bodhisattvas." It is just that, presently, most people's causes and conditions have not yet matured. If we can create the right causes and conditions for them, encourage them to move in the direction of virtues, they will also be able to attain buddhahood in the future. So, they too are future buddhas and bodhisattvas, and we should not be too concerned about whether they are presently "good" or "bad."

All sentient beings have buddha-nature, so bodhisattvas will not give up on any single living being, and will treat all sentient beings equally. There is not any single sentient being with unaltered wickedness, so we should not give up on anyone.

Neither Good nor Evil

Being without good or evil is the buddha state; this is a higher state than "having good but no evil," since good and evil do not exist for beings in the buddha state. The Eminent Chan Master Yongjia (665-713) said, "In dreams, perceiving clearly the six paths of existence in the Saha World; upon awakening, realizing the great universe as completely empty." "In dreams" refers to the situation where one is still in the midst of vexations before wisdom arises. [The "six paths" are the six kinds of rebirth in the three realms.] "Upon awakening" refers to attaining enlightenment and achieving buddhahood.

Before one attains enlightenment, one perceives that good, evil, and all the variety of different phenomena are existent. After attaining enlightenment, or buddhahood, one perceives each and every thing as completely equal, so there is no longer any single thing in his or her mind to cause worry or obstruction.

Levels of Good and Evil in Buddhism

The levels of good and evil include the five categories as follows.

Human Beings

At the human level, believing in the Three Jewels, practicing giving, and observing the five precepts are good. Vilifying the Three Jewels, not practicing giving, and not observing the five precepts are evil. But why do we not say that believing in religion is good, and not believing in religion is evil? This is because the standards for defining religion are subjective and cannot serve as criteria. However, the Three Jewels—the Buddha, the Dharma, and the Sangha—are not a kind of religion. The Buddha is the person who spoke the Dharma, the Dharma is the methods or principles one employs to prevent evil and do good, and the Sangha are those who practice the Buddhadharma, teaching and spreading the Buddhadharma, and taking charge of its activities.

Buddhadharma does not necessarily direct us to believe in or obey a specific object, but directs us to act and practice in accordance with the teaching. For example, we practice charity or giving (Skt. *dana*) to bring benefit to other people. Using our wisdom, or knowledge, financial resources, physical strength, or language to encourage or help those in difficulty, to offer benefit, assistance, or relief. All such matters are giving. Observing the precepts means always doing whatever good one *should* do, and never doing whatever one *should not* do. Vilifying the Three Jewels means dissuading people from believing in the Three Jewels and speaking ill of the Buddha, the Dharma, and the Sangha.

Heavenly Beings

Heavenly beings are at one level above that of human beings. In addition to cultivating the morality of ordinary human beings, one must also cultivate the ten virtues and practice meditation; only then can one be reborn in the heavens of the desire realm and the dhyana heavens. Those reborn in the heavens of the desire realm are still in the heavens of material world, while those born in the dhyana heavens are in the heavens of the spiritual world (the form and formless realms).

From the Buddhist perspective, if people behave according to the moral standard of ordinary human beings, they will be reborn in the human realm. If they attain higher moral standards than most people, they will have earned the merit to be reborn in the heavens of desire realm; there they enjoy sensuous pleasures which are more exquisite, more pleasant, and of longer duration as compared to those in the human realm. If they cultivate meditative concentration, they will go beyond the material world, and enter the purely spiritual world, the dhyana heavens.

Supramundane Beings
Those who regard the world as too chaotic, too full of suffering, and wish to never return again, belong at the supramundane level.

Bodhisattvas
The level of bodhisattvas is actually a level of engaging oneself in the world. Bodhisattvas just want to give of themselves; they just help all sentient beings without expecting anything in return. They have no intention of returning to the human realm, or of taking rebirth in the heavens to enjoy the blessings and fortunes, neither do they aspire to forever dwell in the world of pure spirit, and never return to this world.

Buddhas

Buddhas abide in the world, being ever-present and omnipresent, and they deliver all sentient beings, without any thought of having delivered any sentient beings. As far as buddhas are concerned, there is no such question as good or evil.

Good and Evil Attributes of Mind in Buddhism

There are two kinds of mind in Buddhism: one that harbors notions of good and evil, and one that is pure. The former is the ordinary people's mind and the latter is the mind of buddhas. Having the notion of "good" and "evil" is the function of human consciousness. It is how we judge all things, objects, and phenomena we perceive or encounter; and it originates out of self-centeredness. This can be explained in two aspects: First, because we make judgments about good and evil, we remain in samsara, leading to birth after birth, and death after death. Second, whether we accept and acknowledge it or not, the karmic force of good and evil will make judgments and decisions on its own. Buddhism sums up these points and calls them "karmic force," which is another name for the "mind."

Next we will talk about "attributes" of the mind which include both good and evil. According to Buddhism, our mental activities fall into three categories of attributes: good, evil, and neutral (not-cognizant). In other words, the responses and effects of thoughts arising in our mind may be "good" or "evil." As for the attribute of neutrality (not-cognizant), these are mental activities which are not distinguishable as good or evil.

In terms of Buddhism, good, evil, and neutral (not-cognizant) are phenomena experienced only by sentient beings. To the buddhas, all sentient beings have buddha-nature, and all are pure and all are good; the distinctions between the three attributes of good, evil, and neutral (non-cognizant) do not exist

Buddhist Relativism of Good and Evil

From the Buddhist scriptures, we can find several hundreds of explications about the relativity of good and evil. I will list only five points as explanation:

Judging Good and Evil in Terms of Cause and Effect

Good causes will produce good consequences, while bad causes, bad consequences. This is like the saying "those who sow peas will reap peas, and those who sow beans will reap beans." However, the causal relationship is not that simple. Two persons both committed homicide, but as a result one of them may have to pay back two lives, while the other does not necessarily have to repay the one life, and possibly wind up only receiving two slaps on the face.

Nevertheless, the principle that "good will bring about good karma, and evil, evil karma" surely does not change. When the karmic results of one's actions cannot be seen in this life, it will definitely manifest in future lives. Also, why do two persons who both committed homicide not necessarily receive the same karmic result? This has a lot to do with good causes, good conditions, bad causes, and bad conditions.

Good Causes and Conditions vs. Bad Causes and Conditions

A good cause may meet with good conditions, and may also meet with bad ones. The relationships of causes and conditions are extremely complicated. That is why we say "causes and conditions are inconceivable." Moreover, cause and effect are also inconceivable, but there is a never-changing principle: "we must increase positive causes and conditions, and try our best to avoid creating negative causes and conditions." We do this by staying close to virtuous friends more often.

Staying Close to Virtuous Friends, Staying Away From Wicked Ones
It is said, "He who stays near vermilion gets stained red, and he who stays near black ink turns black." The same is true with the principle of staying close to virtuous friends. Therefore, we should associate more with virtuous friends, and keep away from wicked ones. But how do we discern virtuous friends from wicked ones?

Virtuous Path and Wicked Path
The good teachers and beneficial friends who encourage us to strive to improve ourselves, and who help us to have a healthy body and mind, a harmonious family, and a steady society are "virtuous friends," and the methods and approaches they use are the "virtuous path." On the contrary, those who teach us to kill, commit arson, steal, engage in sexual misconduct, and tell lies are "wicked friends," and the path they follow is the "wicked path."

Some people would rather be ruthless in order to succeed in obtaining something than having the bad luck of failing to do so. So they unscrupulously resort to every trick and scheme to obtain illegal gains. These are, of course, also wicked ways. Also, some people think, "When I do something bad, it is my bad luck if I get caught and go to prison for several years. And it's my good luck if I don't get caught. You try to be a good person, but what good does that get you?"

Good States of Existence and Miserable States of Existence
Without doubt, those who follow the virtuous path will be born in

good states of existence, while those who follow the wicked path will be born in miserable states of existence. In the human realm, there are also good and miserable states of existence. For example, to be born where one has no clothes, no food to eat, and frequently encounters disasters and diseases amounts to a miserable state of existence. Moreover, the Buddhist scriptures say that those born in the three realms of hell, hungry ghosts, and animals are also called miserable states of existence. In contrast, those born in the heavens or in a peaceful society of human realm are good states of existence.

I recall that when I first arrived in Taiwan, the material conditions in society were quite poor, and many people had no shoes. However, back then everyone worked diligently, and lived a frugal life. I thought to myself, "Taiwanese people are blessed. Our fellow citizens living in Taiwan have virtuous roots." After forty years, however, our living standard gets higher and higher, but the social climate becomes worse and worse. If we continue this way, knowing only craving for enjoyment and being selfish, not to mention how our next life will be, the karmic blessings of our next life will be used up now and disasters will befall us earlier than expected.

Today people who believe in Buddhism are increasing in number. This phenomenon has a tremendous influence on society. I believe that our society is still hopeful, and this hope rests on you and me.

Talking about Dreams While in Dreams

Nung Chan Monastery, Taiwan, August 17, 1986

Today I will talk about dreams—dreams of sentient beings, and dreams of the buddhas. As a matter of fact, the buddhas themselves have no dreams; rather, they come into the dreams of sentient beings in order to respond to their needs. Before achieving buddhahood, sentient beings remain in the dream state without being aware of it. Therefore, to the buddhas, the dreams of sentient beings are like flowers in the sky and the reflected moon in the water, neither of which are real. Sentient beings dream without knowing they are dreaming, taking their dreams to be real and existent.

The Dreams of Sentient Beings

Before they learn about Buddhism, the dreams of sentient beings are all illusory; after they learn Buddhism, their dreams are half-awake and half-illusory. What ordinary people dream mostly falls within the following scope:

1. The dream is clear and distinct, and remains clear after one awakens; it lingers in the mind without being forgotten for a long time.

2. The dream is seemingly clear and yet vague; it seems clear while one dreams but is elusive after one wakes up.

3. The dream is vague and messy; it requires strenuous effort, and when the dreamer wakes up he feels physically and mentally fatigued, knowing he had a dream but unable to recall it.

4. The dream is a premonition of something that will happen

in the future. Those who dream premonitions are more or less oversensitive; there is nothing wrong with being oversensitive, but it is easy for such people to receive responses from some paranormal powers. If they overemphasize the presages of dreams, they will have troubles in their life. Since not many dreams are premonitions, there is no need to fuss over them and seek an interpretation. Just be prudent with everything, often harbor virtuous thoughts, and diligently recite the holy name of Amitabha Buddha or Guanyin Bodhisattva, and that will be fine.

In terms of the Consciousness-Only doctrine of the Yogachara School, dreaming is one of the activities of the "independently arising thought consciousness" (mano), which, together with the five sense consciousnesses, makes it the sixth consciousness, and its function is thinking. According to Yogachara, consciousness has eight aspects. Those related to the senses of the eyes, ears, nose, tongue, and body; with their respective functions, are the five base consciousnesses. The function that corresponds to the brain's central nerves [and which forms thoughts] is the sixth consciousness. The function of storing the karmic seeds and reactivating them in a new birth is the eighth, or "store consciousness" (Skt. *alaya*). That which takes the store consciousness to be the "permanent" self is the seventh consciousness.

If the sixth consciousness generates functions concomitantly with the first five consciousnesses, it is called the "thinking consciousness that arises (in tandem) with the five (sense) consciousnesses." If the sixth consciousness does not correspond with the first five consciousnesses but acts independently, it is called the "independently arising thinking consciousness." The thinking consciousness that arises while one dreams is called "independently arising in a dream," and the thinking consciousness that arises while one is in samadhi, "independently arising in samadhi." Therefore, if a dream results from pressure on parts of the body, or from certain muscles being stimulated, then it is not the independently arising thinking consciousness; rather, it is the function of the thinking consciousness that arises with the five sense consciousnesses.

Categories of Dreams

Most people's dreams roughly fall into four groups:

1. When one has enough sleep but is not yet fully awake, it is easy to dream, and because the body is fully rested, the dream is clearer and more distinct.

2. When one has just begun to sleep but not yet soundly, and the body has not fully rested yet, a dream may be chaotic, or half-muddled and half-clear.

3. When one is woken up but dawdles in bed, turning around and covering up to sleep again, it is also easy to have a dream.

4. When a spirit or a paranormal force appears in one's dream to foretell something, what one sees and hears comes from communicating with the paranormal force from outside. As mentioned above, not everyone has premonitions; when this occurs, it is usually very clear. However, according to general experience, most dreams that occur in the first half of the night will not come true; after one has had a full, sound sleep, the rate of dreams coming true is higher. The followers of Buddhism, especially Chan practitioners, will treat dreams as delusions or illusions; even if they actually have an apparent premonition, they will not be troubled by it.

One who dreams a premonition learns in advance of what has not yet happened but has been foretold. For instance, rats know beforehand that there will be a fire, and ants know beforehand that it will rain. Legend has it that in Taiwan, a certain kind of broad-leaved grass can foretell a typhoon, that some dogs can forecast a disastrous incident, and the like. This is all because before an incident takes place, the karmic forces have already been activated, the causes and conditions are already existent, and the cause and effect have already ripened; so it is impossible to avoid it. In terms of the phenomena, they are all things that have not occurred yet; in terms of their potentiality, that has already been completed. For those with the predictive power, or those whose consciousness is more sensitive, or those who have special karmic relations with a given incident, they would see in their dreams the circumstances of the incident that is about to take place.

By means of meditation, one may also derive the power of knowing, feeling, or seeing something in advance. When in the course of meditation your mind becomes so clear and lucid, with only few wandering thoughts, you may foresee a sound or a sight before it comes about. This is not a miraculous power, but a high sensitivity. When Venerable Jicheng of Malaysia attended a seven-day Chan retreat at the Chung-hwa Institute of Buddhist Culture in Beitou, he already heard the sound of the hand-chime before the time-keeper struck it to mark the end of one sitting session, as if time had flowed backward, with the sequence of events reversed; he was very amazed about it. If we can explain presages in this manner, there is no need to explain them with mystifying stories or tales about ghosts and deities; otherwise, we would be fostering superstition. Indeed, ghosts and spirits do exist, and those with more sensitive nerves would certainly have a sharp receptivity, so it is easy for them to receive the powers sent forth from ghosts and deities. However, the presages and premonitions are not always furnished by ghosts and spirits; as long as one has a stronger mental power, one could generate this kind of power, too. Therefore, in the dreams of ordinary people, both distinct and premonitory dreams are mostly phenomena manifested by their own physical and mental reactions.

The dreams of most people as mentioned above are the long night dark dreams made within the dream of samsara. Those who have not transcended the three realms have the "dream of sectional birth and death," while those who have transcended the three realms but have not achieved the buddhahood have the "dream of transformational birth and death." For example, the *Song of Enlightenment* by Eminent Master Yongjia says, "In dreams there are clearly six paths for sentient beings; upon awakening one sees that the great *chiliocosm* is completely empty." This dream mainly refers to the dream of vexations in the sectional birth and death. In other words, sentient beings amidst the vexations of samsara are dreaming at all times and all places. Since time without beginning, if they do not go beyond samsara, they will have to transmigrate among the six destinies of existence, as if remaining in a long, dark night that drags on and on, in which they dream one horrible dream after another.

Beautiful Dreams Are Always Short

Of course, amidst the three realms, one would also have happy dreams occasionally, such as taking birth in the heavens or abiding in meditative concentration. However, "a pleasant night in spring is always too short"; happy dreams are transient and one wakes up in no time. After one's blessings are exhausted or the power of meditative concentration has subsided, one will reenter into the interminable nightmare of samsara that drags on and on. For instance, Zhuangzhou's dream of himself being a butterfly, and the dream of enjoying a wealthy, glorious life in the imperial city of Handan, wherein a dreamer experiences 50 years of courtly life in one short dream, are all happy dreams and fantasies. In the records of Chinese Buddhism, we also read about the dreams that revered masters experienced during spiritual practice, such as Venerable Master Xuyun's dream of "ascending to the Tusita Heaven," Hanshan Deqing's dream of "visiting the bathing pool of Majushri," Yuan Zhongdao's dream of "receiving the invitation from Yuan Zhonglang, my younger brother, to go to the Western Pure Land," and so on.

These dreams are all very vivid and clear. Are they real or unreal? We may say they are unreal because all dreams are unreal; we may say also they are real because they represent the practitioners' mental states; however, once we know they are dreams, they have of course already departed from the dream state.

Recently, a lay follower of mine brought a laywoman to visit me. He told me, "Some time ago, this lady fell sick and was hospitalized. Because the disease was rare, the doctors were at a loss how to treat her, and just tried to keep her alive by giving her injections and infusing fluid nutrition through her nostrils, so much so that they could not find on her body any veins to make injections, and the muscular tissues shriveled like an ant's nest; finally she went into a coma, and was declared by the doctors to be in a vegetative state. So, she lay on the sickbed like this. And after six months, a miracle happened; she came around little by little from the coma, eventually moving her body and speaking softly. However, she had come back from another world, and was not the person born to her parents anymore."

This is the story this lady told me: "As I personally perceived it, those six months were just a short while. I strolled buoyantly and arrived at a carefree and uninhabited world, where there was no dust, no mess, and no noise, and all the grass, flowers, and trees as well as the ground were all made of gold, silver, pearls, and other jewels, which could not be compared to or described with any treasures in the human world; I just felt that they were so solid, pure, and subtle. Then a thought occurred to me: why is there no mud at this place? I would like to pluck a flower and take it back. Then I had a second thought: since everything is so perfect, it is superfluous to pluck the flowers. So I withdrew my hand. In that uninhabited world, I felt an indescribable happiness in my mind. Soon after, I left that world of flowers and trees, and came to a hill. On top of the hill, I came across a couple, a man and a woman. The woman walked in front, and was apparently pregnant. Somehow she suddenly stumbled and fell, so I rushed forward to help her up. In the meantime the man had caught up on us, so I left the pregnant woman to the care of the man. In the next moment, I floated down the hill idly and woke up. After regaining consciousness, my family told me what has happened. Only then did I know I had remained unconscious for six months; nevertheless, it was just a short while in my conscious mind. The dream was so brief; why was it already six months when I came round? I remained puzzled despite much thought. And so, Master, I purposely came to ask you to tell me in which realm was my dream after all."

I said, "I'm unable to interpret dreams; however, according what I read in the sutras, your situation was similar to that of the birth from a womb in the border region described in the *Infinite Life Sutra* (Skt. *Amitayu Sutra* or *Sukhavativyuha Sutra*), taking the lotus womb of spontaneous birth as the palace, the small one of which is one hundred yojanas (about 7 or 9 miles) in diameter, and the large one, five hundred yojanas in diameter. In this big palace, for five hundred years in the time of the Western Pure Land, one does not see the Buddha, hear the Dharma, or see any bodhisattvas or *shravaka* sages. The reason for this is that although one makes a vow to be born in Amitabha's Pure Land, one still harbors a doubt in one's mind. As a result, one is born in this lonely palace."

Why was this lady able to go there and return again? Mostly likely, she had too much hindrance from her attachment to affections. Although she cultivated meritorious deeds by engaging in giving and charity, she does not understand Buddhadharma, and was unable to cut off her attachments. Therefore, being unwilling to part with her husband and children, she had come back to the human world. Then she said that, after the recovery, she did give birth to a quite healthy boy for her husband.

The Interminable Dream of Sentient Beings

From this instance, we see that with a very brief time fleeting by in a dream, six months had elapsed in the human realm. This shows that pleasant dreams are always transient. However, there is also a situation where a short time in the human realm turns into a long period of time, such as the dream of enjoying a wealthy and glorious life in Handan. The reason is this: usually the standard of time is calculated on the basis of sunrise and sunset as well as the body's biological working; under the dual restriction of the tangible body and environment, we establish a common standard. Once we depart from the tangible physical body and the world it relies on, time will have no fixed standard, but can be long or short depending on the perception of one's own thoughts. When there are many active thoughts, one feels that time is long, and when there are very few active thoughts, one feels that time is short.

Therefore, we beginners on the Buddhist path have been immersed in a long, interminable dream for eons—since time without beginning—and enduring it with a lot of suffering. As the sagely, liberated buddhas and bodhisattvas look at it, they do not perceive time at all. This is because the *tathagata* always remains in concentration, without a moment outside of concentration; since there are no delusive actions in concentration, there is naturally no perceivable time. Sentient beings perceive time as long or short exactly because they are having dreams within the dream of samsara.

Yesterday, a disciple of mine came with a sorrowful look to give me advice, saying, "Master! You should take good care of yourself, because last night I dreamed that you died. Thinking that the Master was not old enough and should not leave us so early, I was so upset that I cried out loud, 'How could the Master have died?' Then I woke up weeping."

I said, "How ignorant you are! The Master in your dream died, but the Master outside of your dream isn't dead. I have nothing to do with your dream at all."

Another disciple asked, "There are many people who have dreamed that the Master taught them and helped them in their dream. Did it have nothing to do with you, Master?"

I replied, "It's true that they did dream such a dream, and it's truly me while they're dreaming, yet it's their own business, something within their own mind. Even those who have never seen me may dream of me. I do not need to enter into their dreams, but I could still be a part of their dreams."

Likewise, the buddhas, bodhisattvas, and those who have attained liberation know that sentient beings suffer when living in the dream of samsara. Sentient beings also perceive the buddhas and bodhisattvas entering the ocean of samsara to fulfill universal deliverance. Yet there is no need for the buddhas and bodhisattvas to become trapped in sentient beings' ocean of samsara and suffer together with them, so they have already departed from suffering. As far as the buddhas and bodhisattvas are concerned, though sentient beings exist in the ocean of the pure nature of the buddhas and bodhisattvas, their existence amounts to non-existence. As far as sentient beings are concerned, though the buddhas and bodhisattvas do not really appear in the interminable dream of sentient beings, sentient beings perceive buddhas as real.

Who Awakens First from the Interminable Dream?

When sentient beings—especially Chan practitioners—practice Buddhadharma after hearing it, it is easy for them to be aware that they are dreaming amidst samsara. Once they know they are in an endless dream of samsara, they are already on the threshold of leaving behind such a dream. Why? Because when they gain the power of Chan concentration, it is easy for them to reflect that in the past, their minds have been deluded, scattered, muddled, and vague, like dreaming an illusory dream. Therefore, as long as they derive some benefits from practicing Buddhadharma, they will see the life of practice more clearly, and enable themselves to practice diligently. If this is coupled with the guidance of the Buddhist principles of no-self, impermanence, and emptiness of self-nature, etc., they will be able to waken themselves from their illusory dream.

If one knows for sure that one is dreaming an endless dream of samsara, one should try to find a way to get out of it. And one should not only get out of the dreams of suffering but also of happiness, because it is easiest for happy times to flee by, whereas difficult and painful time will last endlessly.

I read about a government official at the minister rank, whose three generations of ancestors were all in high government positions. Someone said, "This minister differs from the mass of people. He was born with a silver spoon in his mouth, having strong backing and superior background; therefore, he has a smooth sailing career and a meteoric rise, getting promoted to higher and higher posts quickly." Most people think that blue-blooded young people from wealthy, noble families lead a luxurious, easy life since their childhood, doing whatever they want, having a fortunate life that many people dream of. However, this minister himself perceives it differently. In an interview, he said that he was not born to be a minister. Although he had ample food and clothing and did not suffer from hunger and cold, born of a prominent family, he had to bear the pressure from the family and society, and the sense of duty to exert all effort. He worked hard for his education; learning—from primary school to earning a doctorate from abroad—was by no means easy. After returning to Taiwan, he went through various trials, and had to remain vigilant and careful at all times and places. These stressful, demanding situations are not something that outsiders can understand.

This shows that the dream of wealth and glory is not necessarily a pleasant one. Even if it is, when one awakes from the dream, there will be nothing left. Nevertheless, we still should not be careless or absent-minded before we awaken. If we wish to not dream bad dreams, of course we should endeavor to engage in virtuous deeds, such as giving. If we wish to have the happy dreams of a prosperous life and ascend to heaven, we must first cultivate the five precepts and ten virtues, and even the mundane meditative concentration. If we wish to wake up from the dream of samsara in the three realms, we must further develop selfless wisdom. Therefore, before waking up from the dream, we should first perform the "Buddhist work in the dream" well. If we can in everyday life avoid doing bad deeds, speaking bad words, or harboring unwholesome thoughts, we can be sure that we will not have bad dreams at night or have bad luck in the daytime, and that the day for us to awaken from the dream of samsara will not be in the endless future.

Dharma Joy and Chan Delight

Chan Meditation Center, New York, June 1, 1990.

When this seven-day Chan retreat ends after breakfast tomorrow morning, I hope that you all have experienced the "joy of the Dharma in every moment, and abiding in the bliss of Chan in all places." As we all have vexations, we often feel uneasy; since on this retreat we have heard the Buddhadharma, we should use it to dissolve the vexations.

The Methods of Practice

Chan practice requires both the guidance of concepts and the cultivation of body and mind. The guidance of concepts consists of dissolving the vexations in our mind through hearing Buddhadharma; from this we derive the joy of the Dharma. We use the concepts to help ourselves eliminate delusions and attachments, and to eradicate self-centeredness. Whenever confronted with difficulties or distress, we apply the concepts of Buddhadharma to relieve the pressure, the burden, the uneasiness in our minds.

To cultivate our body and mind we use the methods of Chan—sitting meditation, prostrating to the Buddha, chanting, and so on. These methods enable us to replace wandering thoughts with right thought; they further unify wandering thoughts with right thought until gradually and finally, we reach the stage of no-thought. Through this process, we will attain the delight of Chan.

Unifying Body and Mind

After we replace our wandering thoughts with the right thought, our self-centeredness goes from a scattered state to one of concentration. When we are concentrated, we gain control of ourselves. When concentrated mind becomes unified mind, we find that our own existence is not important any more—the self no longer stands in opposition to the environment and other people, the body no longer stands in opposition to the mind. Since there is no opposition, the body has no burden; moreover, there is no seeking or rejecting—thus, the mind remains in a state of peace and happiness.

According to sutras, in a time and a place without the Buddhadharma, one can still derive immeasurable joy just by hearing a spirit, deity, or supernatural transformation of someone who speaks a line or two about the Dharma. In our world there are many who have not heard the Buddhadharma; but you here not only heard the Dharma, you listened to it for a whole week. Although you have not yet attained liberation, you can, at any time, apply Buddhadharma to help resolve your various mental and conceptual challenges. Since you practice at all times under the guidance of the Buddhadharma, not for a single moment should you feel despair, distress, sorrow, hatred, or jealousy.

Knowing about Dharma Joy

Now, what Buddhadharma have you heard after all? Having listened to the Dharma for seven days you might ask, "How can we make ourselves happy? Which lines of words will make us joyful?" If so, it is because you heard so much Buddhadharma during seven days that you became somewhat confused about what it is. This is like breathing air every day without being keenly aware that it is air that gives us life and vitality.

During seven days, did you hear about cause and effect, causes and conditions, faith, repentance, and shame? Did you hear about making offerings, making vows, transferring merit, relaxing the body, and opening the mind? You heard these words: "Don't close the door of mind or keep it tightly blocked. Open up the mind to let all thoughts come and go freely, yet without mentally grasping or rejecting anything." And so on. Do these words count as Buddhadharma? In fact, these are all the outline of Buddhadharma, and can be said to be the essentials of Buddhadharma too.

By believing in the Three Jewels, you will not be disoriented, not knowing which direction to go; by believing in the law of cause and effect, you will not blame fate or others, nor be carried away by your success. By believing in causes and conditions, you will not regard a distressful matter as something permanent, and a fortunate thing as something substantial. By applying the sense of shame, you will not be prideful or conceited, nor will you be jealous.

We vow to make offerings; making offerings means dedicating our body and mind to the Three Jewels to receive and cultivate Buddhadharma and to contribute to sentient beings. After we have dedicated ourselves, our own problems are not as important as before, because sentient beings are more important than ourselves. When you can regard sentient beings as more important than yourself, you will not be troubled by yourself any more, so you will of course be joyful!

Buddhism teaches us to have few desires, to be content, and to feel shame. Only by having few desires and being content can we have a calm and stable mind for studying and practicing Buddhadharma. Only by having few desires and being content will we truly generate a mind of shame. Only after we feel shame will we be able to repent the evils and karmic hindrances we have created in the past. Only after repentance will we obtain peace and happiness. This is the Buddhadharma and this will bring us Dharma joy.

What I elaborated above shows that there are really many things that can make us elated in the Dharma joy. The sutras say, "It is rare to hear the Buddhadharma, yet we have heard it." You have been able to listen to a lot of Buddhist teachings during the past seven days. Even though you have not personally realized the essence or empty nature of all dharmas (phenomena), you should feel all the more joyful for being able to hear the right Dharma (teaching) of the Buddha.

Experiencing Chan Delight

During these seven days we have worked intensively to train our body and mind. When we first entered the Chan Hall, we had lots of hindrances because our body had not yet adapted to the life of Chan practice; we felt stressed, painful, and uncomfortable. However, after practicing sitting meditation, the muscles and nerves became relaxed; the body's energy flowed smoothly, enabling it to feel calm and relaxed, as if relieved of a heavy burden. This kind of relaxed, calm, and serene sensation brings us the delight of Chan.

We used Chan methods to focus our attention, make our scattered, chaotic mind gradually become concentrated, and then become unified or close to it. At this time emotional fluctuations and the sense of not being able to control ourselves naturally diminished; we were living a life full of self-confidence, vigor, with a bright and calm mind. We always knew what situations we were in, and always knew that all we needed to do was try our best, and there was no concern about gain or loss, or comparing ourselves with others, or feeling worried, sorrowful, or afflicted. Isn't this the delight of Chan?

During seven days, I constantly taught you to relax the body and mind, and you were able to do so little by little. Since you know that you can turn the tension of your body and mind into relaxation, this means that you already began to have a taste of Chan delight.

Knowing How to Relax

When doing seated meditation, we can practice relaxing our body and mind. We can also practice this at any time. If we can practice the method of relaxation for a period of time, we will be able to relax our body and mind at any time. To relax the body and mind is to rest. When the brain cannot but rest, we allow it to rest. When the body, muscles, and nerves are tense, we make them rest. If we can let the brain and body take a full rest, without using the brain to think, without seeing with the eyes, or hearing with the ears, or touching with the body, how comfortable it will be! To keep our body and mind settled, relaxed, and at ease in daily life is also an experience of Chan delight. Therefore, in the surroundings where we live our life, we can abide in the delight of Chan at all places.

This morning I talked about Chan delight and Dharma joy. They are interrelated and mutually coherent, and you have now possessed at least one kind of them. So, after you go away from the seven-day retreat, my best wishes for you is that you feel the joy of the Dharma in every moment, and abide in the delight of Chan in all places.

Pure Mind, Pure Land

Banqiao Gymnasium, Tapei, July 19, 1990

At the present time, our world cannot yet be called a pure land on earth. The environment in which we live is actually a reflection of our mental state. Different individuals with divergent states of mind will experience the world differently. When we feel happy we perceive the world as a happier place. If we are psychologically unhealthy, afflicted, or depressed, the world we perceive, as well as our immediate environment, will also fall short of our expectations. Before we achieve buddhahood or attain liberation, the environment influences our mind. Put another way, our mind changes with the environment. Of course, our mind can also change our environment, in which case the environment changes with our mind.

In ancient times, the mother of Confucian sage Mencius changed their family residence three times to find a good environment for her children to develop a sound character and mental disposition. From a Buddhist perspective, there are too many temptations and obstructions in this world to facilitate smooth practice. Shakyamuni Buddha therefore introduced Amitabha Buddha, who, through power of his great compassionate vows, guides all those who aspire to be reborn in the Western Pure Land. Upon arriving in that realm, those who are reborn there find themselves in a good environment where success in spiritual practice is easy.

For those in the earthly realm, since our immediate environment affects us greatly, it's imperative that we improve our environment, or go to a purer environment and let it influence us, thus elevating our character and purifying our minds. Alternatively, the environment changes with the mind. This world is not a pure land, nor is it like the Pure Land of Amitabha Buddha. But before we arrive in the Western Pure Land, through our own efforts devoted to spiritual practice, the world we perceive will be purer.

What is "mind"? The mind has two aspects: the material and the spiritual. The material mind refers to the heart and the brain. People say, "I do mind, and I'm really upset" or "This kind of thing gives me a headache." Being upset means feeling tense or anxious, the heart overburdened. A headache means feeling vexed and irritable.

The spiritual mind includes emotions, reason, thoughts, and concepts. Although these things are all associated with the brain, the brain and the spirit are not the same thing. The brain is what the spirit depends on, and the spirit is a function produced by the brain. Buddhist teachings tell us that the mind comes into being only when consciousness is added to the mental faculties in our brain cells. After someone dies, although their brain still exists, emotions and thoughts do not. A computer or audio tape can record information, but they cannot think. Only a brain with life and spirit can function as a mind.

Afflicted Mind and Pure Mind

In Buddhism "mind" refers to the afflicted mind as well as to the pure mind. States associated with you, I, they, greed, anger, ignorance, impermanence, suffering, and the like are expressions of afflicted mind. What we call "you," "I," and "they" denote the function of discrimination, and the reactions generated upon coming into contact with people, affairs, and things.

Someone asked me, "The Buddhist scriptures say that to have

no attachment is to have no discrimination and no vexations. Is it possible for us to be free from discrimination?"

I replied, "That's impossible. In the moment that you asked and I answered, was there no discrimination between you and me?"

This person responded, "All religions are the same. They just use different names. Some call it Buddha; others call it Jesus, God, or some other deity."

I said, "They're different. There are differences within the similarities, and similarities within the differences."

Let's take a typical woman as an example: To her father, she is a daughter; to her husband, a wife; to her children, a mother; and to her teacher, she is a student. Although she is the same person, when viewed from different perspectives and different levels, she's not the same person. So if a difference in religious or social status results in the perception of a different environment or object, how could there be no discrimination?

All events, phenomena, and individuals have different circumstances, perspectives, and environments; however, we should not regard them as either being in conflict or not in conflict, with our own subjective feelings. The more we perceive things this way, the more harmonious the world will appear.

"You have a problem. They have a problem. I have no problem." I have used these phrases to delve into the problems that arise between "you, them, and me." The mentality and magnanimity of bodhisattvas is revealed when they do not give rise to vexations, even though differences between "you, them, and me" are present. Even though we are not yet bodhisattvas, we can learn from, and emulate them. If other people have a problem, we help them. If you have a problem, we help you. And if you yourself have no problems, then whatever you do is for others. With this kind of attitude—caring more about other people—we reduce the chance of conflict or disharmony, and we decrease the likelihood that vexations will arise.

Greed, anger, and ignorance are concrete manifestations of "you, they, and I." What we call "you, they, and I" is actually self-attachment. Only when an "I" is present does the knowledge of "you" and "they" appear, as well as ideas such as "I want" and "I don't want."

There are those who exhort other people to not be greedy or angry. But if we ask the exhorters themselves to be totally without greed or anger, we see that's impossible. It is the sage who is completely free from greed and anger. And while it is right to measure ourselves by the sage's standards, we should not demand that others, as well as we ourselves all be sages.

Even if people do not crave wealth, they often crave fame. Even if they do not crave either fame or wealth, they still crave the five desires. Our bodily existence depends on the five desires. Since we are born in the realm of desire, before we have truly entered samadhi or attained liberation, we still crave sights, sounds, smells, tastes, and contact. People in general crave the five desires. Even ascetics who do not covet the five desires still have cravings—what they crave is sagehood, or some level of sagehood. Only by attaining liberation can one be truly free from cravings.

When we want to be free of people, things, or environments that we dislike or that cannot fulfill our desires, then feelings of anger, hate, or resentment may arise. This is very much related to our bodies and conceptual outlook. Our bodies and our daily lives are of course intimately interrelated. When something benefits our lives, we crave it, and if we cannot get it, we are likely to become angry. We also get angry when, against our wishes, we are compelled to part with something that benefits our bodies. Any conflict with our own personal fame or gain, or divergence from our way of thinking, can make us unhappy; this can also give rise to anger, hate, or resentment.

Wisdom Like a Mirror, Vexations Like Dust
A pure mind is also the buddha-mind of wisdom. The afflicted mind makes us suffer, and to be reborn again and again, among the six destinies of the three realms. The fewer our afflictions, the higher the level at which we will be reborn, and the more our wisdom will grow. Wisdom is like a mirror and vexations are like dust. The mirror covered with dust is ignorance; wipe away the dust and wisdom is revealed. Here is what happened when a young layman named Huineng visited the monastery of the Fifth Patriarch, Master Hongren. When the Fifth Patriarch was drawing closer to *parinirvana*, he wanted to transmit the robe and bowl symbolizing the Chan lineage to a successor. So he instructed each of his disciples to compose a verse in order to see which one was most worthy to receive the robe and bowl. The leading disciple, senior monk Shenxiu, wrote the following verse on a wall:

> *The body is the bodhi tree*
> *The mind is like a clear mirror stand.*
> *Be always diligent in polishing it*
> *Do not let it attract any dust.*

This verse speaks to removing vexations from the mind to reveal wisdom. After he read the verse, the Fifth Patriarch instructed his disciples to burn incense, learn the verse by heart, and recite it diligently, so as to earn great merit. Huineng, who at this time was just a layman who worked in the kitchen, also composed a verse:

Bodhi is fundamentally without any tree;
The clear mirror is also not a stand.
Fundamentally there is not a single thing—
Where can any dust be attracted?

Huineng perceived that bodhi is fundamentally not like a tree, and the mind is not like a mirror. And since there is [in the mind] no tree and no mirror, there is also no dust, and no need to clean away any defiling dust. This showed that Huineng perceived things at a higher level. The Dharma body, however, should be cultivated through the physical body; we use the physical body of flesh and blood to cultivate the Buddhist path. Only then is it possible to become enlightened, attain liberation, and achieve buddhahood. The body is thus very important; it is an instrument of spiritual practice, as well as a breeding ground for vexations.

Our mind, when not greedy, is angry; it is ignorant, and cannot perceive wisdom. So, only by reducing greed and anger can we discover wisdom. When we are reciting the Buddha's name or a sutra, if impure thoughts or deluded ideas arise, this is normal. It is precisely because our minds are not pure that we need to practice. Beginning practitioners should acknowledge that they suffer from vexations, which is why they need to seek wisdom. When afflictions have been severed completely, wisdom manifests. When wisdom is perfected, it is identical to the mind of a buddha, which is originally the same as the minds of sentient beings. The difference is that the minds of sentient beings are afflicted, while the mind of a buddha is not. This is illuminating mind, the illumination of a buddha's pure mind of wisdom, so one sees the unmoving and empty nature of the buddhas.

The pure mind is the wisdom that illuminates oneself and others. Buddha-nature is the "original face" which is no less present in ordinary people, and no more present in the sages. After attaining enlightenment, a Chan Master was asked, "What happened?" He replied, "After I got out of bed in the morning, I turned around and bumped my head on the wall. Only then did I discover that my nostrils point downward." This tells us that buddha-nature is everywhere and inherent in everyone. As long as our minds are afflicted, we are deluded and cannot see our buddha-nature. When wisdom is manifest, one has already attained enlightenment, and whatever one perceives manifests the buddha-nature, the non-discriminative mind, or non-differentiated nature.

No Craving and Attachment Is Pure Mind

The saying "a pure mind is a pure land" is derived from the "Buddha Land" chapter of the *Vimalakirti Sutra*, which says "as the mind is purified, the buddha-land is established." This tells us that after the mind is purified, the environment will also be purified. Here, environment refers to the realm of the five desires: whatever the eyes see, the ears hear, the nose smells, the tongue tastes, and the body touches, also called the "five sense objects." Beautiful colors and forms are pleasing to see, beautiful sounds are pleasing to hear, and delicious food and drink are a pleasure to taste. When encountering all of these things, if the mind is clear, unmoving, and not craving or afflicted, it is the pure and unmoving mind. Whether the mind is imperturbable or untainted does not depend on contact with the environment, but on whether or not we can let things go and cast them aside. If we build up our practice slowly, unaffected by things that happened in the past or that may happen in the future, our minds will gradually approach a state of purity.

The koans of the Japanese Zen tradition include this interesting anecdote: There were two monks devoted in their practice, a senior disciple and a junior disciple. One day while traveling by foot the two monks came to a river. As they were about to cross the river, they encountered a young woman who was anxious to make the crossing. But due to recent heavy rains, the water level was high, and there was no boat available. So the senior monk offered to carry the woman across the river, after which the woman and the two monks went their separate ways. As they continued down the road, however, the junior monk kept complaining to his senior, saying, "How is it that a monastic touches a woman? By carrying a woman across the river today, you broke a major precept." The senior monk ignored him, and carried on as usual. That night the senior monk slept soundly till daybreak, whereas his junior tossed and turned restlessly, brooding over the senior monk's behavior that day, thinking that he breached a precept yet was unrepentant. Upon rising, the senior monk saw that his junior had not slept all night, and asked him why. After hearing his response, the senior monk said, "After carrying the woman across the river, I put her down. Why are you still holding on to her so tightly, and won't put her down?"

This story explains how not to be contaminated by the environment. Although there is contact with the environment, the mind does not waver, or give rise to anger or craving, as a result of that contact. At the time of contact, simply perceive the object of contact as it is. Then, whatever contact you have had with the environment, let the past be past—don't dwell on it. This, then, is a pure mind. It is not easy to maintain a pure mind, but we can try, based on the concepts discussed above. Then even if we cannot always maintain a calm mind in every situation, we can at least use those concepts to reduce our afflictions.

Keeping the mind pure is not a great problem. If we cannot keep it pure forever, a single hour, or even one minute of purity is still a good thing. As long as we practice purity, we can enjoy one minute's worth of the happiness that comes with purity and ease. Those who misunderstand Buddhist teachings or do not practice will most likely become alienated and disgusted with the real world, and seek escape. So here is another story for everyone to consider.

During the Tang dynasty, a mother and her daughter gave offerings to a practitioner for many years. One day the mother wanted to test whether the practitioner had succeeded in his practice. The mother told her daughter, "When you take food to the practitioner today, hold him in a tight embrace." The daughter did as she was told. The next day, the mother asked the practitioner, "How was my daughter?" The practitioner replied, "Like a wilted tree leaning against a cold cliff."

Many people think their minds can remain unmoved by a pretty face, and that they are already quite accomplished in their spiritual practice. This mother, however, thought that the practitioner had not yet achieved the proper level of cultivation, so she rousted him out with a broom, and set fire to the thatched hut that she provided for him, burning it down.

This story tells us that a practitioner like the one in the story had already attained a certain level in his spiritual practice, but had not yet attained enlightenment. Though his mind remained calm, he contravened the codes of common sense and practical living. His practice was moribund. So remaining untainted by the environment means that we need to be aware of the environment, without being moved by it. After the mind is purified, the environment can be purified.

A Subtle Influence that Transforms from the Inside Out

How can we purify the environment and make a pure land? We should start from within, correcting our concepts and establishing our faith. At the same time, we need to purify our bodies and minds through cultivation methods such as the precepts, concentration, and wisdom. In the cultivation process, we become aware that we are impure in both body and mind. Becoming aware that our bodies and minds are impure is a sign that we are gradually moving towards purity. Through our own individual purity, showing loving concern and offering guidance, and giving of our time and patience, we influence the people we interact with in our own families and in our daily lives. We ourselves have to gradually examine our own behavior, concepts, and thoughts, and at the same time reach out to other people to have a subtle, transforming influence on them, so that we can help purify the land.

The purpose in our establishing Dharma Drum Mountain is "to uplift the character of humanity and build a pure land on earth." That means that the starting point for improvement lies within the mind of each individual. Whenever vexations arise, or we are unkind to others, we should immediately be aware of precisely what kind of mind, or what kind of thought, we are generating in that moment. Unlike the sages, of course we cannot be completely free from unwholesome thoughts or actions. But we must gradually come to know what we are doing, and engage in self-reflection every day. Perhaps we have said or done something wrong, and feel shame or repentance. If we are frank and sincere, our humanistic qualities will be heightened, our character will rise above the crowd, and we will be respected. As Buddhists, if everyone can move in this direction, our environment will become more and more pure. "Building a pure land on earth" is neither a slogan nor is it an empty ideal. It is a cause that everyone, every individual, that cares about contemporary society should support with their unstinting efforts, and the only means by which we can hasten the realization of a pure land on earth.

A Pure Land on Earth

Dr. Sun Yat-Sen Memorial Hall, Yonghe, Taiwan, September 20, 1990

The Human Realm

The Chinese *renjian*, translated as "humans," usually denotes interpersonal relationships. However, in the Buddhist context it means "human beings" or "humankind." The Japanese *ningen* means the same thing. Humankind is just one category of sentient beings. In the Buddhadharma sentient beings are classified in three ways:

1. as the five samsaric destinies: namely, the five categories of sentient beings,

2. as the six samsaric paths: namely, the six categories of sentient beings,

3. as the ten dharma-realms: namely, the ten categories of sentient beings.

Both the five samsaric destinies and the six samsaric paths refer to ordinary people, while the ten dharma realms include ordinary people and sages(enlightened beings).

Human beings are one of the five samsaric destinies. With the five samsaric destinies, we must look at the differing results from the standpoint of causes. Here, "destiny" means "going toward" some fate. Depending on what varieties of karma we have created in previous lifetimes, we will go to the destiny where we should be reborn. Usually the five destinies are the realms of hell, hungry ghosts, animals, humans, and heavens. From being reborn in one of these five places we know what kinds of karma we created in the past. For example, having created the karma of the hell realm, we go to hell; having created the karma of humans, we go to the human realm.

Human beings are one of the six samsaric paths, or "roads." From the standpoint of destiny, depending on what road we walk, we are called by the name of that path. For example, having created the causes of human beings, one goes on the path of humans; that is, one walks on the road of human beings. It is called the "six samsaric paths" because it has one more path than the five samsaric destinies—that of the ashura. The ashura is not one of the five samsaric destinies because ashuras can be found in the human realm as well as in the heavenly path, and they can be in the animal path as well as in that of hungry ghosts. Any humans, ghosts, or deities that are very ferocious, and any animals that are ferocious as well as clever, can be called ashuras.

According to the sutras, ashuras often cause trouble in the human realm, and fight with heavenly beings (devas) in the heavens just as Sun Wukong, the legendary Monkey King, created a disturbance in the heavenly palace. Each time the ashuras fight with heavenly beings, they are defeated, and then escape to the human realm. When they fail to find a hideout in the human realm, they will hide in water, or in plants, or in the opening of lotus roots, being able to become large or small.

Coming to the ten dharma realms, human beings are one of them. The ten dharma realms include the six types of ordinary beings plus the four kinds of sages. In other words: the six samsaric paths make up the first six dharma realms, to which are added the four types of sages: shravakas, pratyekabuddhas of Hinayana as well as bodhisattvas and buddhas of Mahayana. Therefore, all sentient beings—from the lowest to the highest levels—are within the ten dharma realms.

Meanings of the Human Realm

Based on the sutras, the "human realm" has several meanings.

1. In the chapter, "Trayastrimsa Heaven" of the *World Account Sutra*, fascicle 20 of *the Longer Agama Sutra (Skt. Dirghagama)*, the Buddha says, "When I was in the human realm in the past, my body did virtuous deeds, my mouth spoke virtuous words, and my mind thought of virtuous thoughts." When the Buddha practiced in the human realm, all his bodily, verbal, and mental actions were virtuous; namely, they are the ten virtuous deeds. Cultivating the ten virtuous deeds contributes to the karmic reward of humans and heavenly beings.

2. In the *Sutra of the Virtue of Listening*, fascicle 36 of the *Middle-length Agama Sutra* (Skt. *Madhyamagama*), it says, "Having come and gone between the heavens and human realm for seven times, one reaches the border of suffering." This means that in order to attain the fourth fruition of the arhat, the sages who have entered the path must come to the human realm for seven times. When they eventually attain full arhatship, they are liberated from the ocean of suffering in samsara and need not return to the human realm.

Aspects of the Human Realm

We can look at the human realm (Skt. *manushya*) from several aspects:

1. Fascicle 6 of the *Lokasthanabhidharma Treatise (Treatise of Cosmology)* explains that the human realm has eight characteristics: clever, superior, with subtle mind, with right awareness, with higher intelligence, able to discern true or false, being the right vessel for the noble path, and born from intelligent karma. This sounds complicated but they are actually simple: sentient beings that

can distinguish, analyze, memorize, and think are called "human beings." Most important is that among the six realms of sentient beings, only human beings can cultivate Buddhadharma and be a vessel for the Path. In other words, the human body is a fit tool for cultivating Buddhadharma, while for other sentient beings that do not have this tool, it is not easy. Exactly because sentient beings can achieve different bodies, those who are human in this lifetime will not necessarily be human in future lifetimes. Therefore, when one is rewarded with the human body, it is the best for spiritual practice.

2. Fascicle 18 of the *Mahaparinirvana Sutra* says, "The appellation 'human beings' means those who are capable of feeling grateful and indebted; moreover, being human signifies being gentle and soft in bodily and verbal actions; moreover, human beings are said to have arrogance; moreover, human beings are those who are able to remove their arrogance." As a matter of fact, human beings are equipped with many other characteristics, such as jealousy, in addition to arrogance. Perhaps other animals also have jealousy, but the jealousy of human beings is stronger. Other animals may also have suspicion, but only human beings have arrogance. Why do they have arrogance? As human beings are able to think, have a self-center, and make judgments, it is easier to for them generate arrogance.

3. From the above we know that *manushya* can also be translated as "thinking" and "thinker." There are four constituent conditions for animals to have: cells, nerves, memory, and thinking. The lower an animal species is, the fewer conditions it requires; only the humankind is equipped with all the four conditions. Other higher animal species, such as dogs and monkeys, merely have some memory at most, and only humans can think above the animal level.

Where Is the Human Realm?

We know clearly that human beings live in this world, but is it the only world with human beings? According to the sutras, this world is located on a tangible mountain, which, however, is invisible to us. It is called Mt. Sumeru. The top of Mt. Sumeru is inhabited by heavenly beings and the lowest level by hell dwellers. At each of the four sides of Sumeru is a large continent, all inhabitable by human beings. We are living in the continent at the south side. The lifespan and karmic reward of humankind, as well as the natural environment, are all different in these places. We do not know where exactly the east, west, and north sides of Mt. Sumeru are. However, the sutras say that those living on the north side have the longest lifespan, and may live to be one thousand years old.

Apart from the Earth that we know, are there also human beings in other places? The Buddhist sayings, "It is rare to obtain a human form" and "Once one's human form is lost, one cannot regain it in ten thousand kalpas" seem to indicate that it is very hard to become a human being, and that the chance of losing the human form are many, while the chance of gaining it are few. At the same time, however, there are more and more people on earth. Is this inconsistent with the Buddhist doctrines?

In fact, the sutras mention that the Saha World takes Mt. Sumeru as its center, and the world with Sumeru as its center is a small world. A thousand small worlds are called a small chiliocosm (a thousand-world universe); a thousand small chiliocosms are called a medium chiliocosm (a million-world universe); and a thousand medium chiliocosms are called a large chiliocosm (a billion-world universe or trichiliocosm). In this Saha World of ours, how many places like Earth are there? Although we cannot see it with our eyes, the whole

Saha World is the domain in which a buddha gives his teachings, and Shakyamuni Buddha is called the supreme teacher of the Saha World. Please do not misunderstand, thinking that Shakyamuni Buddha is just the supreme teacher on our earth. In fact, he is the supreme teacher of a whole trichiliochosm. Moreover, before this world system (trichiliochosm) appeared, there already existed many world systems. When this world system of ours falls into ruin, many other world systems will arise.

Where Did Humans Come From?

Where did humankind come from at the very beginning? Christianity says that human beings were created by God—that the Earth was created first, and then human beings were created afterwards. No matter whether such a statement is correct, let us see what the sutras say about this.

According to fascicle 14 the *Sutra of the Motion of Brahma*, as well as the chapter on the "Original Conditions of the World" of the *World Account Sutra* in fascicle 22 of the *Long Agama* (Skt. *Dirghagama*), we find the introduction about the origin of human beings, which says: the world goes through four stages from existence to destruction, namely, formation, existence, destruction, and voidness. The total span of these four stages is called a large kalpa (eon). When the world has completed these four stages, some sentient beings among the heavenly beings of the Heaven of Radiant Sound at the second dhyana heaven, after depleting all their karmic rewards and ending their lifespan, will gradually descend to the Brahma Heaven, and further go down to the material world of the earth.

The heavens include those of the desire realm, the form realm, and the formless realm. All the heavenly beings in the desire realm have tangible forms, whereas those of the form realm are only mental and spiritual phenomena, without the existence of material phenomena. Originally sentient beings in the Heaven of Radiant Sound of the second dhyana heavens had no physical phenomena, no physical bodies, but they had spiritual and mental phenomena. However, after gradually descending to the earth, they could still fly freely at first, without the sensation of a physical body. Little by little, they took on the energy of the earth and ate the things on the earth, so that, with their bodies becoming coarse, they could not fly and gradually began to age and die. These are our ancestors.

So, where did the people of the Heaven of Radiant Sound come from? They have cultivated meditative concentration in different worlds, and having succeeded with cultivation, they were born into the dhyana heavens. Therefore, sentient beings existed since time without beginning, while human beings on the earth had an initial starting point.

How to Be Born as Human Beings

In addition to the sentient beings of the Heaven of Radiant Sound who arrived here to become the ancestors of humankind, where did the later human beings come from?

1. The *Mixed Agama* (Skt. *Samyuktagama Sutra*) says: "Those who create the ten evil karmas (deeds) will be born in the hells; if they are born as human beings, they will suffer from various hardships. Those who create the ten virtuous karmas (deeds) will be born in the heavens; if they are born as human beings, they will be free from various hardships." What is said here refers to the retribution or reward of karmic causality. The ten evils refer to the ten evil deeds, including killing, stealing, sexual misconduct, false speech, divisive

speech, harsh speech, frivolous speech, greed, anger, and ignorance; namely, three for bodily conduct, four for the verbal conduct, and three for the mental conduct. If one creates all of the ten evil causes, one will fall to the hells; if one only creates a portion of them, one may be born in the human realm, and yet suffer from various hindrances and hardships. On the contrary, the ten virtues refer to no killing, no stealing, no sexual misconduct, no false speech, no divisive speech, no harsh speech, no frivolous speech, no greed, no anger, and no ignorance. As human beings, it is not easy to do all the ten virtuous deeds. If one can do all of these deeds, one can be reborn in the heavens; if one does just a portion of them, one will be born in the human realm and be free from various hardships.

2. The *Sutra of the Buddha Speaking to Suka the Elder about Different Karmic Retributions* (Chn. *Fowei shoujiazhangzhe shou yebaochabie jing*) says, "When one performs the ten virtuous deeds incompletely, lacking in some of them, one will attain the results of the human destiny due to ten such deeds."

3. Fascicle 1 of the *Treatise for Discerning the Correct* (Chn. *Bianzheng lun*) quotes from the *Sutra of a Demon Transforming Himself into a Monk* (Chn. *Mohua biqiu jing*), saying, "The five precepts are the roots for human beings, and the ten virtues, the seeds for heavens." That is, people who uphold the five precepts can all be born as humans in the human realm, and people who cultivate the ten virtues can take rebirth in the heavens. The five precepts refer to no killing, no stealing, no sexual misconduct, no false speech, and no consumption of intoxicants.

4. The first part of the *Commentary on the Ullambana Sutra* says, "The human vehicle means that the three refuges and five precepts carry sentient beings across the three miserable planes of existence to

be born in the human path." The human vehicle signifies the means of transportation that human beings travel in; that is to say, it is the means of transportation or the conditions required for coming to the human realm. There is also the means of transportation for going to the heavens, which is called the heavenly vehicle. The conditions required for becoming shravakas and pratyekabuddhas are the two lesser vehicles, while those required for becoming bodhisattvas are called the greater vehicle. The supreme means of transportation is the buddha vehicle. One achieves buddhahood by cultivating the Buddhadharma, which includes five levels, the lowest one being the human and heavenly vehicle, which takes the three refuges, five precepts, and ten virtues. That is to say, taking the three refuges, upholding the five precepts, and cultivating the ten virtues enable one to be born in the human (and heavenly) realm(s).

5. Chapter three of the *Introduction to the Buddhadharma* by Master Yinshun says that the human realm has four superior features: encountering both suffering and happiness in the environment, knowing shame, having wisdom, and persevering. Only when one is equipped with these conditions can one be a human. Hence, there is the saying that it is rare to be born with a human form. In addition, because only the human form can be the best instrument for spiritual practice, it is all the more precious.

What Is a Pure Land?

A pure land is where the buddhas, bodhisattvas, and other sages live. It is a world that is achieved by the merit of a buddha, and it can also be a world that is achieved by the power of a buddha's vows. It differs from our world in that it is an environment without illness, vexations, and sufferings. However, because the accomplishments of their spiritual practice are different, the pure lands they build are different too. Likewise, in a pure land, what the buddhas build differs from that of the ordinary people. Therefore, the pure lands are classified into four levels:

1. The land the Dharma Body inhabits, which is perpetual and omnipresent. It is formless, yet there is not a single form that is not found in this pure land.

2. The land of the Reward Body (Skt. *Sambhogakaya*), which is a buddha's body of merit; a buddha's merit can be shared by the bodhisattvas in the sagehood, and can enable them to continue in the buddha's pure land to accomplish the paths of a buddha and a bodhisattva.

3. The pure land of the buddha of the Transformation Body (Skt. *Nirmanakaya*) who has come to deliver ordinary people. The world of ours is also a pure land—if we follow the Buddhist teachings or come into contact with the Buddhadharma, we will feel that the pure land is right in front of us. Of course, there are also buddha-lands that are the worlds where one may take rebirth after death, yet the pure buddha-land where ordinary people inhabit is also the land of the transformation body.

4. The land where ordinary beings and sages dwell together. Even if we go to the Western, Eastern, or any other Pure Land, we are still ordinary people. Although one can see many bodhisattvas, arhats, and buddhas there, even in the same place, the pure land that bodhisattvas perceive is different from the pure land that ordinary people perceive. This is called the land where ordinary beings and sages dwell together.

Types of Pure Lands

Based on the sutras, there are four types of pure lands.

1. The mind-only pure lands: the *Vimalakirti Sutra* says, "As one's mind is pure, the buddha-land will be pure too." This means that if one's mind is pure, the world one perceives will also be pure. This pure mind signifies that the mind is free of vexations, and that there is only the light of wisdom and no darkness of vexations. At such a time the world one perceives is a pure land; even though one might find oneself in a hell, if one's mind is free of vexations, the hell will also become a pure land. Therefore, with the change of one's thoughts, the world will be completely different too. If one's mind is full of vexations, then the world one perceives will also become a hell. If one's mind can be enlightened and become detached, what one perceives will be a pure land. The saying, "transforming flames into red lotuses, and transforming red lotuses into flames," signifies that as long as one's thoughts change, the world will change along the way.

2. The pure lands in other parts of the universe: the pure lands of the buddhas in the ten directions, among which Amitabha Buddha's Western Pure Land of Utmost Bliss is closely related and most dear to our world.

3. The pure lands in the heavenly realms: this refers to the Tushita Heaven in the heavens of the realm of desire, including the inner court and outer court. The outer court is inhabited by ordinary people, and the inner court is the place where the future Maitreya Buddha gives his teachings to sentient beings.

4. The pure lands on earth: this can be seen at several places. One such land will manifest when Maitreya comes to the human realm to achieve buddhahood. A second one can be seen at the Uttarakuru Continent in the northern part of Mt. Sumeru. This continent is currently a pure land on earth, but it is a pity that there is still no means of transportation for people to go visit. Therefore, it is better

for us to endeavor to build in this world a pure land on earth.

The construction of a pure land on earth and an ideal representation of it can be found in the chapter, "Responding to the Time" in fascicle 3 of the *Lotus Sutra* (Chn. *Zheng fahua jing*), "People are equal and happy, with noble, awe-inspiring deportment. All their activities are pure, and what they establish is secure and stable. The grains are abundant and cheap, the population is vast, flourishing with a great population of men and women, and all sorts of necessities are fully provided."

In our world today, we feel uneasy, worried, and insecure. And we also have a sense of lack and insufficiency; what we want to obtain cannot be obtained easily, while there are so many things that we do not want to have. Therefore, this is not a pure land. However, is it possible for us to build this world into a pure land? The answer is yes. If it were not possible, Shakyamuni Buddha would not have appeared in the human world. Did a pure land ever appear in the human world in the past? Yes, some are the pure lands perceived by individuals, namely, the mind-only pure land. Others are the pure lands that are established by a family or the people of a certain area or region.

Why Build a Pure Land on Earth?

The causal basis is that the Buddha achieved buddhahood in the human realm, and after achieving it, gave teachings mainly to humanity. In addition, among all sentient beings, it is only possible for human beings to cultivate the path and achieve buddhahood. Therefore, since we are here in the human realm and have encountered the Buddhadharma, we should of course start out by building a pure land on earth. Moreover, the cultivation of the Buddhadharma starts with the foundation of human beings; only then can one attain buddhahood. Therefore, if we have not played our role well as humans, there exists no possibility for us to become buddhas.

We have said that by receiving the three refuges, upholding the five precepts, and practicing the ten virtues one can be born in the human path and heavenly path. However, does this mean that people who do these things can only be born in the heavens or in the human realm? No, if they have not heard and cultivated the Buddhadharma, they can only go to the human realm or heavens because they cannot attain liberation. If, having heard the Buddhadharma, they realize the teachings of no-self and emptiness, they will be able to go beyond the three realms and enter the Buddha path.

The Buddhist principles of spiritual practice all have their respective levels. The first level teaches us not to create evil causes and fall into hells; therefore, in order not to fall into hells, we do not create evil karma. The second level is to cultivate good deeds because that enables one to be born in the human realm and heavens; thus, we will not do bad things. These teachings are all given to people with self-centered orientation. As sentient beings are all selfish and self-centered, they will remove evils and cultivate virtues for the sake of their own interests. This is the basic level of Buddhardharma. It is the teaching to the human and heavenly vehicle, which tells us that after the heavenly blessings are exhausted, one will fall to lower realms again, so the heavenly blessings are unreliable.

Therefore, when one practices with a self-centered, selfish mentality, one's karmic rewards will be limited, and the time for one to enjoy the blessings will be limited. If one does not practice for oneself only, but rather for delivering all sentient beings universally without seeking karmic rewards and repayment, and one keeps practicing perpetually, then one will absolutely attain buddhahood.

From the above we know that the practice methods have the same basis whether the path is: (1) obtaining limited lifespan and karmic blessings by taking rebirth as humans and heavenly beings, (2) seeking liberation, (3) achieving buddhahood. However, the mentalities and concepts that one cherishes are different for each path.

How to Build a Pure Land on Earth

A pure land on earth can be built in two directions, one being material construction and the other being spiritual development. We can carry out the former by endeavoring in the aspect of science and technology, and carry out the latter by endeavoring in the aspect of the faith in and the practice of the Buddhadharma. From the Buddhist standpoint, whether there is material construction or not, or whether it is a large- or small-scale construction is not important. What matters most is the spiritual development. Let me ask you: if an insatiably greedy person has a house, would he want to have a second and a third one? I think that people would not reject having a lot of money. If a person has possessed all the material requirements in the family, would the person feel that he or she is living in a pure land?

Once a lay believer drove me to visit his home—a beautiful villa with a big court. Entering the house, I saw the room was so elaborately furnished that one seemed to be in the Western Pure Land.

I said, "You must be very happy living here!"

He answered, "Master, if I were happy living here, I would not have invited you to come. I have to change my phone number every half a month, and the lock of my gate has been changed several times. The security and burglary-proof system have often been damaged. I'm very troubled living here, and I'm ready to move to another house."

It looked like the Western Pure Land to me, and I might have said, "Would you let me have the house?" So I told him, "The problem doesn't lie in the outside, but in the fact that you feel empty and lack security in your mind. Suppose you could regard your business and properties all as temporary and transient, and think that it is good to have them but there is no harm if you don't have them. Then I believe you would feel secure, and find your house a very nice place."

But he told me, "Master, you don't know what the world is like at all. In our world today, you may want to be a nice person and may be able to let go of things, but other people aren't able to let go of you! You may have a detached attitude, but others aren't detached! So, even if I think that it doesn't matter if all my things are lost tonight, the problems remain unsolved. There are people who are keen about kidnapping, targeting only those who drive a fancy car, or who are entrepreneurs. With a society like this, even if I can let go, they're unable to let go!"

Recently I met another lay practitioner and her family that lived in a nice house. One night a gang of five or six people broke into her house. They tied up the family and began to ransack the house. The lady had taken refuge with me not long ago, and at that time, I taught her: when you run into any trouble with no one to help you, someone will come to your rescue, namely, Guanyin Bodhisattva. So just recite Guanyin's name. Therefore, when the gang broke in she recited "Guanyin Bodhisattva" in a loud voice.

Then the robbers said, "Stop that reciting. We're also Buddhists!"

Later they stole the cash, without taking away other things or injuring her family members. After being robbed, they hurried to move to another house. She told me about the incident, and I said,

"Oh, you don't have to move from your house! They have come once, and they also know that you recite Guanyin's name. Besides, they're Buddhists too. So they won't come again. Even if they come again, as long as you often recite Guanyin Bodhisattva's name and practice with faith, you'll be safe."

When we follow the Buddhist teachings and practice in this way, as well as advise people to take the three refuges and uphold the five precepts, the buddhas, the bodhisattvas, and the virtuous deities who protect the Dharma will protect us. The construction of a pure land on earth requires that each one of us start from within; everyone must harbor a mind for doing good deeds, rather than have a selfish mindset. Next, each of us should take care of our whole family and wish that all our family members can be safe and practice Buddhism. Then we should further enable all those who are related to us to recite the Buddha's name, do good works, and be free of selfishness. If we can begin within ourselves and reach out to our families and further to communities, our world will gradually turn into a pure land.

If we can all do good deeds with our bodies, speak good words with our mouths, and think of good thoughts with our minds, engaging in wholesome bodily, verbal, and mental actions, a pure land will be right before us. Even if we cannot see it in the daytime, we would be able to see it at night in the dreams.

Chan: Thus Come, Thus Gone

Kaohsiung Chiang Kai-shek Cultural Center, Taiwan, August 18, 1990.

Many people think that the teachings of Chan and Pure Land schools are thoroughly different. Actually, there is no conflict. Since ancient times, the masters have given plenty of explanations: those who recite the Buddha's name with a concentrated, single-pointedness of mind can be reborn in the Western Pure Land, and this is due to the vow of Amitabha Buddha and their own powers of concentration. If Chan practitioners are able to illuminate their mind and see their nature, then their mind will be pure, and the land in which they live will also be pure. Therefore, there is no real need to separate the teachings of Chan from that of Pure Land. I not only teach people to use the methods of Chan, but I also encourage people to recite the Buddha's name.

What Is Chan?

Here are some views on the question, "What is Chan?"

A Calm, Stable, Harmonious Way of Life

Generally, we live with an unstable mindset in an unsteady environment. Because our mind is not calm and stable, the way we live, speak and behave is also not stable, leading to a lack of harmonious and joyful atmosphere between us and other people. Living in harmony means that everyone cares for, and looks after one another. If, in our mind there is no conflict between the previous and the next thought, as well as between our past and our present moment; and if we can get along with one another with a caring heart, how, then, can we not be happy?

An Open, Forgiving, and All-embracing Way for Living with Wisdom
When interacting with people, we find it most unpleasant when our minds are not open and cheerful. Not being open and cheerful is being closed-minded, separating oneself from others so that one is unable to communicate with them. We are closed-minded when we feel the need to protect and seek security for oneself, so as not to suffer harm or loss when interacting with others. The more closed-minded we are, the more we cannot communicate with people, and the greater our loss. Only with an open and cheerful mind can we get along with everyone, encounter favorable situations all around, and enjoy smooth sailing.

Very few people are willing to forgive others; rather, they find it easier to forgive themselves. That is to say, they cannot be compassionate to, and accepting of others. The more narrow-minded the person is, the more they are unable to put down self-attachment and be reluctant to give of themselves. People like this suffer great pain in their heart. They have no friends, and receive no help from others. Even if people want to help them, they will be afraid. So, Chan practice helps us to open up our mind and embrace everyone and everything, just as an ocean takes in each and every thing, whether they are big fish, small fish, or even poisonous fish. The ocean will not reject any creatures that seek habitation in it.

A Life Principle that Accords with Law, Reason, and Empathy
Some people place great emphasis on empathy, others on reason; still others emphasize the law. These attitudes are all attached and

biased; the best attitude is to handle a situation with empathy when empathy is called for, with reason when reason is required, and with the law when the law should be applied. In general, ordinary empathy involves self-interest, and is therefore impure; whereas selfless empathy is compassion, which is pure and clear. Reason should be good, but to reason about each and every thing makes us tense and uneasy, demanding that in all situations, "everyone has their own task, and no one will be spared." This is treating people like machines, with no room for flexible and expedient action. Therefore, we should handle things with reason with regard to the general principle and our own matters, and handle with empathy the minor issues concerning other people's problems. If we act to the contrary, only applying reason when dealing with other people, while only applying empathy when dealing with ourselves, it would be a problem. So whether empathy or reason should be applied depends on how important the situation is.

Now, what about law? The law is not necessarily reasonable, nor is it identical to empathy. The law is the rules that the public observes together. It can be amended, but when most people think it necessary to apply the law, then we should abide by it. However, many today pursue unreasonable or illegal gains. By unreasonable we mean that they want to get something for nothing, without putting in their own effort or paying the price. If illegally securing any gain, they nonetheless commit acts not allowed by the general public.

Once an officer from the Coast Guard told me that many fishing boats sail offshore to buy fish from the fishermen of Mainland China, and take them back to sell in the Taiwanese market. This is not legally permitted, yet the fishermen thought that they spend less time by buying fish from Mainland China, at lower cost and with higher profit, so why not just go ahead and do it? In addition, they save energy for the country, and earn more profit. So they hoped that the law could be amended. With regard to such a reasonable yet unlawful case, should we observe the law, or follow reason?

From the Buddhist perspective, we look at things in terms of causes and conditions, as well as cause and effect. If the general public thinks that the law should be amended, and if the law indeed causes the public loss now and brings no benefit in the future, and also fails to safeguard their security, then it is indeed necessary to modify the law. That is what we mean by "arising from causes and conditions." On the contrary, if just a small minority secures the gain in the short term, while a great majority suffers damage in the long term, then they should not do it, but should abide by the law. For example, smuggling guns brings exorbitant profits, but with everyone having a smuggled gun, it would certainly cause a terrible impact on Taiwanese society.

The ancients pointed out that what people pursue most is none other than merit, fame, gain, and status. Merit is achievement and credit; gain is money and fortune; fame is reputation; and status is social position. If one's pursuits accord with the law, reason, and empathy, it is encouraged by Buddhadharma. Nevertheless, we should take other human beings into account, as well as all sentient beings. If everyone thought only about themselves, what a chaos society would become! At that time, can we still enjoy safety and stability? Therefore, one will not achieve happiness by separating oneself from society. The benefits obtained at the expense of other people will definitely not be reliable and secure.

Many people prefer to reap profits without sowing good causes, wishing for unearned fortune or windfalls, not knowing that such behavior causes harm to themselves and society. From the Buddhist perspective, it goes against the law of causality. Without sowing good causes, they expect good effects; this will not instill a constructive influence for themselves or society. Therefore, it is best to seek benefits for all humanity, to work for all sentient beings, not longing for selfish gains or windfalls.

Then, some seek fame, trying to make everyone know about them through mass media, or all other available ways. Some even think that if they can't have a long-lasting good reputation, they should at least have a bad reputation that will be long remembered. As a result they not only fail to benefit themselves, but also cause harm to many. So, we should seek to be remembered for our good work, not fleeting, empty fame. And, while it is good to be remembered for our true achievement and good work, it is best to do good work without seeking fame at all.

Society is full of examples of people seeking quick gain and achievement. In Taiwan and abroad, I am often asked whether there are speedy ways to help people attain instant enlightenment. I tell them, "So far I have not discovered any such method, and if I did, I would put it to my own use first." Someone came to me for help when he fell sick, and I advised him to see a doctor.

He said, "It is because the doctors cannot heal me that I have come to Shifu. Shifu, you're an accomplished master. Surely you could help me."

I replied, "Sorry, but I also have to go to a doctor when I am ill."

He asked, "So, is spiritual practice of no use?"

I said, "It's useful. Others who fall sick feel they have bad luck, and they want to recover quickly, while feeling resentful and complaining about the suffering. As for me, I go to a doctor when I am ill, not bothering about how long it will take to get over my illness. When I haven't recovered, I think that it is karmic retribution; and when I recover, I think that the karmic retribution is gone." Not feeling bitter in the mind when the body is ill, that is one benefit and effect of Dharma practice.

When practicing the Dharma, we should regard the process as the goal, so that we won't regress from our aspiration for the Path. That is the spirit of "mind yourself plowing the field, but not the harvest." As long as we work hard, we will naturally be able to reap the harvest. However, if you expect to harvest too soon or too much, there will surely be problems.

The Content of Chan Is "Thus Come"

Chan is the method for achieving buddhahood. Observing the precepts, practicing concentration, and cultivating wisdom are all ways to achieve buddhahood.

Upholding the Precepts

The spirit of upholding the precepts is to benefit us as well as others. Do not be constrained by the clauses of the precepts and make your life too difficult in order to keep the precepts. Once I was sweeping the ground, and accidentally swept away many ants. Someone chastised me: "Shifu! How can you be so unkind! The ants have died from your sweeping."

I said, "Amituofo! Would *you* sweep then?"

He said, "The ants will also die when *I* sweep."

I asked him, "So, should we move into a new house?"

One day, the Buddha went with his disciples to a practice hall, which had not been inhabited and cleaned for a long time. The bathing pool teemed with the larvae of mosquitoes so the monks dared not bathe in it. They asked the Buddha how to deal with this situation. The Buddha told them to clean the pool. Hearing the monks worry about killing the larvae, the Buddha said, "I'm not asking you to kill the insects, but to clean the pool." This means that their purpose is to clean the pool instead of killing the insects in anger or hatred, so it does not count as breaking the precepts.

This shows that what the precepts require is for us not to do anything that does not accord with the principle of compassion and wisdom, and to actively do everything that accords with this principle. Otherwise, we would have broken the precepts.

Concentration and Wisdom

Some people think that concentration (meditative concentration) is all about "indulging in bliss like an old monk" sitting there doing nothing. That is why some people do not want others to disturb them when they are cultivating concentration. Practicing this way, these people eventually become extremely selfish. Afraid of being disturbed when meditating, they seclude themselves from society. Having achieved meditative concentration, they are attached to its bliss. They want to escape from reality and renounce the world. If this is not selfishness, what else could it be?

In reality, the concentration of Chan is none other than wisdom: concentration is wisdom, and wisdom is concentration. Wisdom is having a clear mind, with clear thinking and discernment; it means not judging or coping from a self-centered standpoint. Therefore, concentration is by no means just sitting still or escaping reality. The true meaning of concentration is to engage in spiritual practice, and to keep the precepts in a calm, stable, and harmonious body and mind. Wisdom is guiding oneself to observe the precepts; it is cultivating concentration with an open, generous, understanding, and selfless mind.

A Chinese doctor told me that, having read lots of Buddhist books, he intellectually and conceptually knew how he should act, and yet he did not always act accordingly. When greed, anger, or jealousy arose, he was not aware; and he often felt upset when he became aware later. Why was it so hard for him to keep his mind under control? This is because he seldom took time to practice concentration. Cultivating concentration includes meditating, prostrating, reciting the Buddha's name, and reciting the sutras. If you persistently and regularly engaged in these practices for some time, your mind will gradually become calm and stable, and you would not easily be influenced by the environment and become emotional.

Generally speaking, observing the precepts and practicing concentration are in the scope of cultivating compassion, while wisdom is in the scope of gaining liberation and freedom. If we are emotionally stable, open-minded, and generous, we will naturally exert an influence of stability on ourselves and others.

What Is "Thus Come" Is Also "Thus Gone"

The *Diamond Sutra* says, "The Tathagata does not come from anywhere, nor does he depart to anywhere." "Tathagata" is one of the ten honorifics of the Buddha, and means "neither comes nor goes." Before passing away, Venerable Master Guangqin said, "There's neither coming nor going, and nothing has happened at all." Many have valued this saying as a highly inspiring aphorism. It has the same meaning as the above-mentioned phrase from the *Diamond Sutra*, which elaborates the same wonder in a different way.

What does "thus come and thus gone" mean? For example, you

bought some stocks yesterday; the price goes way up, so you become rich overnight. The next day the stocks fall sharply and you turn into a poor man. Has the money come after all? It seems to have come, bringing you a big fortune, but where has it gone in the end? That money was not meant for you. This is called "thus-come and thus-gone." There is no need to be excited when it comes, or to feel upset when it is gone, because this is all very normal and common.

People in our world feel afflicted or distressed because they fail to clearly see the people and things they encounter. That is why they are deluded and called "ordinary people," and why they have the afflictions. We usually take false things to be true, and take unreal things as something permanent. We become attached to the people and things related to us; we are concerned about which is mine, which is more or less, which has come or gone, which has arisen or perished, and so on. All these attachments cause our mind to generate vexations.

According to Buddhism, phenomena arise from causes and conditions, and succeed one another in cycles of cause and effect; they are ever-changing and impermanent. "Causes and conditions" means that many factors come together to produce a result; so the presence or absence of any phenomena is created by different factors that come together. People often misinterpret the term "impermanence" as being passive and pessimistic, but it is actually the opposite. Impermanence means that change and evolution happen continuously. In other words, nothing can remain unchanged. So impermanence has a positive meaning: it inspires us to strive incessantly. When times are bad isn't impermanence or change a good thing? When times are good, things change and become impermanent, but we don't need to feel upset; as long as we keep working hard, good luck will still eventually come again. And we don't need to grieve or despair when misfortunes befall us, because they will not last forever.

In fascicle 16 of *The Compendium of the Five Lamps* (Chn. *Wudeng huiyuan*), Chan Master Baizhao Gui said, "Birds flying in the sky are unaware that the sky is their home, and the fish swimming in the water forget that water concerns their lives." The birds soar in the boundless sky and are not separated from the sky; they do not worry whether they need to occupy some room in the sky because the sky is expansive enough. Also, the fish in the water do not think of water as something important and begin to worry, in spite of the fact that water is a necessity for them. If we can take this attitude and live our life positively and diligently, without worrying or troubling over many things, we would definitely enjoy a happy life.

Chan: Freedom and Liberation

Sha Tin City Hall, Hong Kong, October 18, 1990

There is liberation of the body and there is liberation of the mind. If we were in prison, our body would be confined, and it would be liberated after we were released. However, for a Buddhist practitioner, liberation of the mind transcends liberation of the body; if we had no vexations and no attachments, we would be free even if we were in prison. Someone once mentioned to me that a certain person might go to jail, and people told him, "This is a chance for you to go into solitary retreat." I said, "For someone who was enlightened, being in prison could be a chance to practice, but for someone else it could just mean sitting in captivity." After I was on solitary retreat in the mountains for six years, someone asked me if it was a formidable experience. I said, "If I had been in jail, yes; but this was a solitary retreat, so I felt quite at ease." One difference between being in prison and being on solitary retreat is whether one's mind is free.

Liberation Depends on the Mind

When the fourteen-year-old monk Daoxin met Third Patriarch Sengcan, he said, "Master, please have compassion and teach me how to gain liberation." Sengcan asked him, "Who is preventing you from becoming liberated?" The young monk answered, "No one." The Third Patriarch asked, "Then why do you need to ask for liberation?" Upon hearing this Daoxin gained realization. So, were you enlightened upon hearing this story? If not, who was holding you back? If you did not gain realization, perhaps it was because you weren't asking for it. People may think they are not enlightened because something is holding them back. But if one reflected carefully, they will realize that there is no one in the way but themselves. So perhaps like Daoxin, one can get enlightened upon realizing this. Daoxin's situation is called "falling into one's own trap." There is a saying, "Under the heavens nothing really matters; still the ignorant worry themselves sick."

A Chan Master said, "Seeing, hearing, feeling, and knowing are all causes of the cycle of birth and death." But he also said, "Seeing, hearing, feeling, and knowing are the roots of liberation." Seeing, hearing, and feeling means perceiving with our sense organs; knowing means understanding with our mind. So, if we use our senses and our mind to discriminate among things, believing them to be real and clinging to them, they become the causes for continuing the cycle of birth and death. However, if you could perceive objectively what you see, hear, feel, and know without counting your gains and losses, then you have secured the ground for liberation. When you inject the sense of self into your affairs, then that gives rise to troubles; when you discard any sense of gain or loss, liberation is possible.

Once when the Buddha and his disciple Ananda went out for alms, Ananda saw some gold coins under a tree. Ananda said, "World Honored One, look at that pile of gold coins." The Buddha said, "No, that is a poisonous snake. Don't look at it." Later, a man passed by, picked up the gold coins, and ran off with them. At that time, the police were looking for the thief who had stolen the gold, so the escaping thief threw the coins under the tree. But the innocent man who picked up the gold was caught and punished, just as if he had been the robber. This story says that if you are attracted to something that looks like gold, it could turn out to be a poisonous snake, but if you see it as a poisonous snake, you will keep out of harm's way.

Perceiving the Emptiness of Phenomena

The opening of the *Heart Sutra* says, "The bodhisattva Avalokiteshvara, while coursing in deep prajnaparamita, perceived that all five *skandhas* are empty, thereby transcending all suffering." These lines say that to be liberated, one should be like Avalokiteshvara, the Bodhisattva of Compassion. So, when Avalokiteshvara manifests very deep wisdom and perceives the emptiness of all phenomena, all sufferings are transcended. "Coursing in deep prajnaparamita" means using deep wisdom to help deliver sentient beings from suffering. What is deep prajnaparamita? In the *Platform Sutra*, the Sixth Patriarch Huineng expounded the *Mahaprajnaparamita Sutra*, saying, "Mahaprajnaparamita is the great wisdom to reach the opposite shore of the sea of existence." In other words, to be liberated from birth and death, one must accomplish the great (maha) perfection (paramita) of wisdom (prajna).

After practicing Buddhadharma for a while and listening to lectures about liberation and freedom, some people feel very frustrated if they have not gained realization. They forget that it takes a very long time to evolve from being an ordinary person to being a buddha. And some people like to talk about the deepest Dharma—the Dharma of the buddhas and bodhisattvas—but not so much about Dharma for ordinary people. When the teaching is pitched too high, it can discourage people because it can be too difficult to accomplish. In this situation, the more some people study Buddhadharma, the more frustrated they can become. But if we realistically apply standards appropriate to ordinary human beings, if we use Dharma as our guide and strive to accomplish what ordinary humans can, this wisdom can lead us to the other shore. There being different levels of freedom and different levels of liberation, most people cannot expect to be liberated from everything all at once, and feel free in every place. This must be achieved gradually.

Freedom of the Mind and Freedom of the Body

Freedom of the body means being able to move without obstruction; freedom of the mind means being free from vexations. If one only cultivates freedom of the body, it is possible to gain supernatural powers and manifest transformation abilities. But for ordinary people, supernatural powers are limited and transient. Until one has attained buddhahood, there is no true freedom of the body; one will experience birth and death. Thus, supernatural powers are not enough to lead one to liberation. When one's perceptions are based on greed, anger, ignorance, pride, and suspicion, and so on, the world becomes full of problems; when one perceives the world through wisdom, the mind becomes unobstructed and free.

There are different levels of sentient beings and different levels of freedom. Ordinary people are perplexed and cannot be liberated in the Buddhist sense, and they remain not free. On the other hand, Buddhist sages who have gained liberation enjoy everlasting freedom. Ordinary sentient beings can apply Buddhist concepts to guide and regulate their lives and resolve light vexations, but it is more complex for heavy vexations. Some have high expectations, hoping that upon hearing the Dharma, their minds will become free. Some who have deep vexations say they are the happy, but soon afterwards their eyes may fill with tears. Is this true freedom?

Someone born in prison, who knows nothing about the outside world, may think prison is not such a bad place, but someone who is put there by force knows that being in jail is not being free. Similarly, some people, upon learning Buddhadharma, realize for the first time that they are not free. It is very precious that we can experience the Dharma in this way.

Those who are averse to life, death, pain, and worldly suffering, and who yearn to enter nirvana can only attain limited liberation. True freedom comes in not fearing life and death, and not being bound by the cycle of birth and death. Thus, we should not strive for limited liberation but for the great freedom of the buddhas and bodhisattvas. Only buddhas and bodhisattvas can be fearless in the face of life, death, and suffering, without themselves suffering. Kshitigarbha (Earth Treasury) Bodhisattva said, "Who will descend into hell to deliver sentient beings if I don't?" So he vowed "not to achieve buddhahood until all hells are empty." Willingly going to realms of suffering to deliver sentient beings while being able to enter and leave freely, that is true freedom. By contrast, ordinary sentient beings are restricted to places according to their karma, and are unable to come and go as they wish. Therefore, they are not truly free.

Freedom and States of Enlightenment

While liberation and freedom are states of enlightenment, ignorance and enlightenment are relative. People abiding in ignorance are not enlightened, but truly enlightened people do not abide in enlightenment. That is because when there is attachment to being enlightened, there is no true freedom. Ordinary people abide in the concept of "I," which includes "me" and "mine." When they analyze the "I," they may find that the "me" part is non-existent, but the "mine" part still exists. In the first place, the body is "my body" but it is not "me." As for "my money," "my house," etc., these are all "mine."

Since there is no real "me" that could be pointed out or be felt, it is ignorance to think of what is "mine" as "me."

I once met a retired businessman who said, "I am now liberated and free." I asked, "How are you liberated and free?" He said, "I passed on all my duties and properties to my son, so now I own nothing!" I asked him, "Is your son still yours?" He said, "Of course my son is mine, nobody can take that away." I said, "If your son is still yours, how you can you really be liberated and free?" If there is still something belonging to "me," one still abides in ignorance.

If an enlightened practitioner abides in the idea of being liberated, that is not great liberation. The true freedom of the path of the buddhas and bodhisattvas is in having no idea of self, nor any idea of being liberated. The *Diamond Sutra* asserts, "No self, no others, no sentient beings." This does not mean one should not act in the world, but that one should use compassion and wisdom to help any sentient being, unconditionally. This is true freedom.

Delusion and Enlightenment

There is a saying that goes, "Do not linger at the place where there is the Buddha," and another saying that goes, "Move on quickly at the place where there is no Buddha." Two Buddhists were on a pilgrimage, one of them was not enlightened; the other was. One day, they passed a temple and the first one said, "There must be a Buddha in the temple, let's go in and pay our respects." The other one said, "Since the Buddha is already there, let's not waste time and just move on." Another time, they passed a deserted temple, and the first one said, "There is no Buddha in there, so we should go in and pay our respects." The second one said, "We are on a pilgrimage; since there is no Buddha there let's just move on."

Why move on when the Buddha is there and also move on when there is no Buddha there? Because if the Buddha is not already in your mind you will not find him anywhere outside. If you cannot see the Buddha within and only see the Buddha outside, that is not the real Buddha. Just move on quickly and continue practicing. If you truly know liberation and freedom, the Buddha is everywhere and nowhere.

Seeming Liberation

The Chinese phrase "seeming liberation" refers to the liberation practices of ordinary people. It means using what we understand of the Dharma to help us relieve vexation, and the more we practice, the more we can help ourselves. One example is the use of malas—prayer beads. *Why use prayer beads?* It is used for counting with our hand when reciting the Buddha's name. *What is the use of counting when we recite the Buddha's name?* When our thoughts wander, as long as our fingers are moving, that reminds us that we were reciting the Buddha's name; so we can continue. *What is the use of reciting the Buddha's name?* Some recite the Buddha's name to be reborn in the Pure Land of Ultimate Bliss, for disaster mitigation, or for peace of mind. Actually, reciting the Buddha's name is for calming the mind and eliminating vexations. *Do we recite with the mind or with the mouth?* There are two useful sayings: "Reciting the Buddha's names is not a matter for the mouth," and "meditating is not a matter of training the legs." So we use the mind when we recite the Buddha's name. The Chinese character for "recite" (*nian*) means the "present mind." The present mind is the mind that is reciting the Buddha's name, and that is how to recite the Buddha's name. And when we meditate, we also use our mind instead of merely training our legs.

Using prayer beads, reciting mantras—any proper Buddhist method of practice can lead to liberation. Since the mind has vexations, one way to calm the mind is to recite the Buddha's name. When we encounter hardship, we can recite the names of bodhisattvas. People have obtained spiritual responses through reciting the names of the buddhas and bodhisattvas. However, reciting the names of buddhas and bodhisattvas is useful even if there are no spiritual responses. A woman came to me for advice about her misbehaving husband, and I gave her the mantra of Cundi (Mother of the Buddhas) Bodhisattva (Chn. *Zhunti Pusa*) to recite. Later on, she thanked me for giving her the mantra, as it helped her a lot. I asked if her husband was no longer misbehaving. She said, "He still misbehaves but I dedicated myself to taking care of my family, and now at least we have peace in the family."

When we practice with faith, there can be liberation, at least on the personal level; how much depends on how deep our practice is. For ordinary people, one cannot reach ultimate liberation all at once, so we call it seeming liberation.

Progressive Liberation and Ultimate Liberation

On the other hand, for bodhisattvas, it is called liberation and freedom through progressive realization. Progressive realization means that one doesn't attain permanent, thorough liberation all at once simply through one experience of liberation. There are levels of liberation. Lower levels of bodhisattvas attain shallower levels of liberation, while higher levels of bodhisattvas attain deeper levels of liberation. Thus, through gradual practice one can eventually attain buddhahood. Only when one attains buddhahood can one's liberation and freedom be everlasting, complete and perfect, and ultimate.

For people who wish to practice the Mahayana path to buddhahood, one begins by entering the bodhisattva path. This path is both gradual and progressive, so one should not be impractical and overly ambitious; one cannot become a buddha overnight. Although Mahayana Buddhism has the concept of sudden enlightenment, it requires long and gradual practice. So what appears to be sudden is actually the result of long practice. Chan and Zen talk about gradual and sudden enlightenment, but the two are actually the same. So, how then does one best practice Chan? The best way is by seeing Chan as daily life. Especially for ordinary practitioners, it is very important to experience Dharma with the mundane body and mind. Chan is not mystical and elusive; as long as one is mindful in daily life, Chan is everywhere.

Chan: Ordinary Body and Ordinary Mind

Sha Tin Town Hall, Hong Kong, October 19, 1990

"Ordinary body and ordinary mind" is the state of ordinary people, but it also refers to the body and mind of accomplished practitioners who have practiced for some time.

A Wholesome Body

It is normal for people to be ill in both body and the mind. Humans inherit their physical body from parents who are not completely healthy themselves; therefore, at the time of birth, any baby is born with a potential for sickness.

Once I was walking on the street with a medical doctor. He greeted two oncoming persons, and introduced them to me as his patients. Afterwards, I wondered how they could be patients, since they didn't seem ill at all. When I asked him what illness they had, the doctor said, "Well, from the perspective of a doctor, any person that comes to me for help is my patient. Although they may seem fine to you, they are still ill in some way." From that day on, I have been convinced that all people are patients from the standpoint of a medical doctor. Even though some may have seen the doctor, the root cause of their disease has not yet been eliminated; while some others may not have been detected ill, the cause of a disease might be latent.

Since there are no people in the world who don't have the potential for illness, then it is normal to have illness. And since it is normal we should accept it and need not harbor dread, fear, or begrudge being sick. This is the case with the physical body, and so it is with the mind. Since birth we are never satisfied in our minds, and this is because we have a mindset of either pursuing or rejecting what there is in this world—the mindset of craving and aversion. We tend to pursue and attach to nice things, while escaping and rejecting what we dislike.

Once, a mother asked me, "Does Buddhism believe that human nature is fundamentally good, such as the Confucian sage Mencius believed?"

I asked in return, "So you mean the human nature is fundamentally bad, instead?"

She replied, "Buddhism says that every person has buddha-nature and indeed, every sentient being has buddha-nature. That means human nature is fundamentally good. But I am confused because I have two kids, and the first has always been bad-tempered and greedy. If there is something not to his satisfaction he acts violently, crying and screaming. This makes me feel that he might be reborn from the realm of ashuras (demigods) or pretas (hungry ghosts). When the second child was born, I was expecting him to be better, but it turned out that he is worse than his elder brother. Raising those two is really harsh work. I give them a lot of love only to receive little nice response; whatever I do, they are not happy. I am so angry that I start to spank them, and scold them. But this only makes them hate me, and dislike me more. So from my children I find that human nature should be fundamentally bad."

I told her that human nature is not about good or bad; rather, since time without beginning, we have carried with us multitudes of afflictions, one life after another. That's why after birth, before receiving school education, a person's character says something about human nature, which is to have a mind of affliction. We were born into this world with afflictions; therefore, the mind manifests naturally, as it is.

A philanthropist from Hong Kong told me that he did not do any good deeds for the first half of his life. I think it is typical that he never thought of doing good deeds during his youth. But now he acknowledges he didn't do any good deeds when he was young. But back then, did he consider himself as someone who did not do anything good or was not a good person? If he had considered himself not as a good person, that might actually be a good deed in its own right. If he considered himself not bad and therefore need not do any good deeds, and later only as a philanthropist realized that he was not generous when young, then by this standard, who is a good person, the younger or the older?

The sickness we are talking about refers to physical and mental illness; together, these two kinds of sickness make us uncomfortable. If we realize that this is the state of body and mind of ordinary people, we will be more tolerant, sympathetic, considerate, and compassionate in treating our family or people we interact with. As the sayings go, "Misery loves company" and "We are all in the same boat." We are all sick in a way, and it is normal that sick people look after each other and help each other. If we treat all other people as healthy and only see ourselves as sick, this may pose a problem in that we will want others to forgive us, while not forgiving others.

So we should realize that everyone suffers from both physical and psychological illness. Whatever people do that may offend us or let down on society we should feel sympathy and pity for them. This is exactly the Buddhist spirit of compassion.

Those who begin spiritual practice start with an ordinary body and mind. Because they are now engaged in practice, their body and mind will evolve, bringing forth a more wholesome body and peaceful mind. Even while suffering from physical illness, they tend to be calm and stable. They will not be disturbed by their illness, anxious and agitated like ants on a hot pan. Some sick people blindly go to all kinds of doctors and take all kinds of medicines. This is like a ship with many captains, which will only create unease. Many people are very concerned about taking care of their body, but caring for the body too much will only make it worse. When one engages in spiritual practice, this is the way in principle: eat plain food, with good nutrition; eat less, with better intake; no refined food, but chew well and swallow slowly before you take another bite; eat moderately instead of irregularly or eating too much. This will ensure a peaceful body.

A Tranquil Mind

A tranquil mind arises through cultivation and practice, and enables the mind to remain tranquil. The first method is to use mindful breathing when you are angry or very agitated. By being mindful of your breath going in and out your nostrils, your mind will calm down gradually. For example, before giving a speech, you can ease your nerves by taking a couple of deep breaths, which is also a basic way to practice meditative absorption.

Another method is to redirect emotions by diverting one's focus of attention, for example, reciting the name of Amitabha Buddha or Avalokiteshvara Bodhisattva (Guanyin Pusa). This will pacify an agitated mind. When something aggravates or irritates us, reciting "Amitabha Buddha" even once will ease our agitation, and one does not need to be Buddhist. Do not think that reciting Amitabha Buddha's name only serves to help one gain rebirth to the Western

Pure Land, and nothing else. So, we can use these methods of transforming the emotions to ease our mental problems. This is in itself practice and a method that can be applied in daily life.

Somebody told me that when he gets angry he swears, and this would cool off his anger. So he asked me if reciting the Buddha's name brings out the same effect as swearing. I said it's not the same: by using profanity you will only feel angrier inside. Beside, swearing or yelling at people will make them angry too. With both parties becoming angrier, the situation will only get worse. Whereas, when you recite Amitabha Buddha's name, the other party will take it that you are repenting and therefore their anger will go away. So isn't it very useful?

Every Day Is a Good Day
What is the state of body and mind of a practitioner who has achieved a certain level of practice? The expression, "Every day is a good day" describes it well. For ordinary people like us, the emotions we experience in a week is like the weather—three rainy days, two windy days and two sunny days mixed with clouds. How can everyday be a good day? This expression originated when Chan Master Yunmen (ca. 862-949) asked his disciples, "What happened before the middle of the month I won't ask you. But please tell me the situation after that." Since none of his disciples was able to answer the question, he answered it himself, "Every day is a good day."

When we meet people we often say, "How are you?" or "How have you been?" These are common greetings to show our concern whether people are doing fine. Can we actually do really well every single day, without ever catching a cold or flu, suffering a headache, tripping over a stone, scraping our skin lifting things? I should think such mishaps do happen. Since they do happen, how can every day be a good day?

A Dharma teacher I know cut his finger while chopping wood and it was bleeding heavily. I asked him, "Are you alright?" He said, "I'm fine." I said, "You have nearly chopped half of your finger off, how can you be fine? Shall I help you?" He said, "It's alright. I am paying off my karmic debts. Perhaps I slaughtered a pig or an ox in a past life, so now I chopped off half of my finger to pay off my karmic debt. From now on I'll be alright."

When we encounter disasters and difficulties can we still call it a good day? Yes, we can. Our body may suffer, or we may come under criticism or attack, but as long as our state of mind is normal and peaceful, isn't that tantamount to every day being a good day?

The Body and Mind of Modern People

Once I met a young person who inadvertently stepped on the foot of an old man standing next to him. Astonished, the young person immediately turned around and ran away. The old man, however, managed to catch up with him and stopped him. At first I thought probably they were going to have a fight. But then the old man grabbed the young person and simply said, "Don't be afraid! I'm so sorry, that my foot startled you."

Stressful Body and Mind

What are the states of body and mind of today's people? First of all there is stress on the body and mind. Our sense of time is too short, our sense of space too small, and the interaction among people too frequent; all these make the connections among people more distant. Normally, the more we are in touch with others, the better the relationship with them, but in reality it is just the opposite. Why is that? In the past people lived in a simpler environment, so their relationship was more about care and concern for each other. Today, people have more contact with others and live an overly hectic life, so they end up not knowing whom to care for; therefore, they stop caring for others. What are people nowadays concerned about the most? About themselves! In what way are they concerned about themselves? By being defensive, guarding against any harm or loss that can be possibly brought about by the people they encounter. Otherwise, they contrive to reap gains and benefits from people. In this way, we live in stress, taking the people we meet as thieves, enemies. Even worse, we frighten ourselves, only adding more stress to ourselves.

A couple and their child came to the Chan Meditation Center in New York. Having not seen them for a long time, I asked them how they were doing. He said, "Shifu, let's not talk about it—life is not easy, being human! For months we have been living a tense, hectic life. So today we are here to seek some peace and quiet." I thought they were probably going to stay for a while—meditate or do Buddha-name recitation, or something. Instead I saw the man having his family burn some incense, prostrate to the Buddha, and then they were ready to leave. So I stopped them and said, "Wait a minute! Aren't you here to find some peace of mind? Why are you so tense? You came here hoping to relax your mind, and enjoy some peace of mind. Yet right here you are still so tense. Now you are here, you are supposed to find peace of mind. You should calm your mind." Aren't there lots of such examples like this?

Tension Due to Material Comforts
Besides tension due to mental stress, there is tension from

material stimuli—whatever we see, hear, eat, etc. These stimuli are everywhere—temptations of all kinds and sorts, which can be bewildering and confusing. This is a phenomenon not seen in past societies. For example, a lay disciple of mine was very troubled about a criminal gang that targeted people who owned Mercedes cars and blackmailed them for ransom. He asked me, "What should I do with my car?" I said, "Sell it." He said, "No, I can't. Otherwise I would have no car to get around." I said, "Then take taxi instead." But he said, "I can't take taxi; it will be so inconvenient." This tells us how material comforts also create unease for us. This person was afraid to drive his Mercedes around, yet he couldn't do without it for his daily life. So, material comforts sometimes bring unintended consequences, and prevent us from truly enjoying the sense of safety and security.

The Spiritual Void

The third body-mind state of modern life is the spiritual void. People with abundant material goods do not necessarily live happily or peacefully. When a person feels empty inside, he constantly feels threatened and tends to be dissatisfied. A spiritual void is like a feather in the air or duckweed in a pond, floating and drifting without a certain place to settle down, or something on which to rely. You might have heard the saying, "Money makes the mare go," meaning that money means status; status means power, and power is something you can rely on. This is a philosophy especially common among modern people. But, is having money the best safeguard for security? In fact, the pursuit of money, power, and status leads to nothing more than exhaustion.

People who enjoy power and status fear losing them, and their loss entails much more agony than never having had them. Therefore, people with little or no power and status pursue them, but when they lose them, they suffer a great deal. The abundance of material comfort is why people nowadays suffer spiritual void more seriously than before. The more abundant the material comforts, the poorer our spiritual life becomes.

People of the current generation are most pitiful. For example, if I had not become a monk I would probably have felt that I am pitiful or worse, that I had better die than live. Because when I am in Taiwan, people there look at me as someone from Mainland China; when I went to Japan, they regarded me as a Chinese; when I was in the United States, Americans thought of me as an Asian; when I was back visiting China, they referred to me as a "Taiwanese fellow countryman." Now I really have no idea where I am from! Fortunately a monastic is one who leaves home but is also at home everywhere; otherwise I would have become a "wanderer in the world."

I am certainly not a wanderer in the world, being my own master wherever I go. What people say does not affect me. So leaving home to become a monastic is good, because, as the phrase "thus come and thus gone" says, wherever I go, wherever I am, I am comfortable in taking that place as my own place. Whenever conditions require me to leave, I leave for another place. Wherever I go I can always make myself comfortable and settled. Practicing in this way, we will be able to free our mind from fear.

Feeling Lost

Feeling lost also represents another problem for today's people—one feels lost in their environment, and one also feels lost in the "time of the generation" as well. We can also say that one is positioned at the intersection of the time and the environment, not knowing which direction is home or where the safe shore is.

Someone asked me, "Master, who asked you to become a monastic?"

I said, "My master did."

Then he asked again, "Did you want to become a monastic then? Have you ever regretted it?"

I said, "Actually, I had no previous idea whether I should become a monk or not. At that time, someone asked me to become a monk, and so I did. After becoming a monk I also felt that I was born to be a monk. So I have never questioned whether becoming a monk was right or wrong. Just like that, I have since been treading on this path. And maybe because I have quite favorable causes and conditions, there has been little temptation from the environment. So I feel pretty fine being a monk."

I knew that being a monk would probably be the only thing for me; aside from being a monk, I don't think I would be good for other professions. However, many people don't understand themselves, and have no idea which way to turn. Facing many crossroads in their life time, they often don't know what to choose or where to go. That explains why, for example, the Wong Tai Sin Temple in Hong Kong and the Matsu temples in Taiwan are always popular and flooded with their devotees. Besides, there are also many fortune tellers who do really good business. This is because many people have lost their way, not knowing what to do. They simply seek advice by praying to deities, drawing lots, dissecting the written Chinese characters, and going fortune-telling. Especially in our time, there are still people who are utterly superstitious. This is all due to loss of self-confidence; as a result, people eventually rely on luck and seek help in blind faith.

It is not easy to develop the kind of self-confidence that is based on self-understanding. We can use two approaches to derive self-understanding and self-confidence. First, we use Buddhist concepts to lead and guide ourselves. Second, we need a well-balanced body and mind. If we have confidence in ourselves we will have faith in the Three Jewels; in return, by believing in the Three Jewels we will develop more understanding of ourselves. So, Buddhist practice helps us discover our weaknesses first, and then know our own strengths, and which among the methods is the most fundamental and provides the essential functions.

Therefore, Chan enables us to achieve three goals: a healthy body, a balanced mind, and spiritual elevation. After developing a healthy body and mind, we move further into healthy spirituality, which means we become wiser and more objective. The more objective one is the richer their spiritual life, and the greater their spiritual energy. So, I hope that all of you have the opportunity to learn Chan practice and its methods.

Chan: Carrying Water and Firewood

Chuang Yen Monastery, New York, December 8, 1990
(Additional text written at the Chan Meditation Center, New York)

Chan is an inner world of the mind that is hard to describe; it is a subjective experience that only those who have had it can understand. One may try to explain Chan to those who have not experienced it, using language, words, and concepts, but it would be like a blind man trying to size up an elephant or a duck hearing thunder, not knowing its true meaning. As it is said, "Only the person who drinks the water knows how cold or warm it is." When we introduce Chan, we can only try to make it known in the manner of a painter adding clouds to enhance the image of the moon. We introduce the moon by illuminating the clouds, without pointing out the moon directly. Today I will introduce the content and phenomena of Chan through eight sub-themes around the topic Chan: Carrying Water and Chopping Firewood, as designated by lay believer Zhang Hongyang, who convened this lecture series at Chuang Yen Monastery, for a two-hour exploration.

Chan Exists Pervasively

Since Chan is an inner experience that defies verbal description or explanation, it is not a phenomenon with substance or form, but it may also be all the phenomena that you can encounter, discover, or perceive. In other words, if one has not experienced Chan, then whatever one says about it is not right. If one has already experienced Chan, then it is pervasive—it *is* everywhere and can be *found* everywhere. By pervasive we mean each and every distinct individual, actually existent phenomenon in the universe. For example, you are not I; a human being is not an ox; water is not fire; the east is not the west; upside is not downside. And if you analyze each individual thing in the greatest detail, you will find that there are even more individual phenomena that exist. Buddhism calls this "the myriad dharmas" or "all dharmas." Each dharma has its boundary, definition, and property. When facing all phenomena (all dharmas), one who has experienced Chan enlightenment will be clearly and distinctly aware of the minutest details of them at one glance, each in good order. That is, one reflects them as they truly are. The record of sayings of Chan patriarchs evidences this.

1. Chan Master Guifeng Zongmi (780-841) said, "When the mirror is clear, it reflects all different images distinctly. When the mind is pure, it responds universally to all with miraculous powers. The images are like those of a magnificent buddha-land, and miraculous powers are applied to teach and transform sentient beings." These words mean that after attaining enlightenment, one's mind will be very calm and peaceful: like the surface of a lake without a ripple, or that of a mirror without even the tiniest defilement of dust; one's mind can reflect all things in the surroundings without any subtle variance, and is said to react to all as they really are.

Why? Because there is not a matter or thing in one's mind, which is open, unobstructed, vast, and bright, as well as absolutely objective; thus, one can respond to and deal with all things appropriately. The myriad, innumerable phenomena that appear in one's mind—whether beautiful or ugly, good or bad, rain or sunshine, complete or lacking—all are nothing but the magnificence of the direct and circumstantial reward of a buddha-land. One teaches and transforms countless sentient beings as the conditions arise while remaining unobstructed in the mind. Because one is free and at ease, this is called the "wondrous function of miraculous powers."

2. Li Ao (772-841) asked Yaoshan Weiyan (745-828), "What is Dao (the Way)?" The Master replied, "Cloud in sky, water in jar." This passage is an anecdote about Li Ao, the student of Han Yu (768-824), the great Confucian scholar. Also a great scholar, Li one day visited Chan Master Weiyan and asked, "What is Dao?" This question was because Dao differed in its meaning among Confucianism, Daoism, and other schools of thought in ancient China; their general understanding was that "the metaphysical is Dao, while the physical is *qi* (vital energy)." And Lao Zi said, "The Dao that can be spoken is not a constant Dao." These all describe Dao as not something concrete, but an abstract concept, or even a kind of intangible, elusive existence.

Li Ao, of course, knew that the Dao as mentioned in Buddhism refers to bodhi, and includes not only the guiding principle and the methods, but also the experience realized in spiritual practice. Li Ao wanted to know how the enlightened and eminent monk, Weiyan, would reply about the meaning of the Dao. The Chan master's answer was very simple: When in the sky, it is cloud; when in the jar, it is water; they are the same essence, but appear as different phenomena, clear and distinct, without confusion. Water may become the cloud and vice versa—in the sky it is cloud, in the jar it is water. By the same token, a person's state differs according to the situation, and this should be very distinct—this is Dao. Do not think of Dao as so profound, so uncanny and so mysterious; Dao is the world as seen from the standpoint of Chan.

3. Master Hongzhi Zhengjue (1091-1157) said, "Not being

oblivious, one sees everything clearly. Readily available, it is everywhere." After attaining enlightenment, one clearly and distinctly sees all variety of things and all phenomena–without taking one as two or three as one—while not being confused and losing one's direction because of intricate and complex phenomena. So, this state of mind is described as being "readily available everywhere." It may be called the Dao, or the Buddha, or whatever, and it is the enlightened state of Chan.

Chan Is the Unity of the Internal and the External

The unity of the internal and the external means the totality is harmonious. There are three parts to this: First, whether we meditate, do massage, practice Daoist breathing, or do Indian yoga, we may cause our *qi* to circulate freely in its channels, so that we feel the ease and peace that comes from the *unity of body and mind*. Second, through sitting meditation, absorbed contemplation, prayer, and other methods, we may experience the unity of the environment outside and inside the mind. This is the manifestation of *unity with the universe*. Third, practicing meditative concentration, we focus on a method so that gradually, our thought-stream is the same from one thought to the next, without any wandering. This is concentration, where we are one-pointedly concentrated on one object or one thought. This is achieving *unity of the mind within*.

When a Chan master encounters the external world in daily life, the level of attainment he or she displays should [at least] be that of unity of the internal and the external. This is why many philosophers and religious leaders think that, though descriptions of the Way or Path may differ, the *experience* of Way should be the same in West and East. In fact, from the standpoint of Chan, these experiences can be shallow or deep at varying levels. This is because the unity of the mind as well as the level that even goes beyond unity cannot be expressed by words, and there is no need to debate. I will now cite three examples.

1. Someone asked Shitou Xiqian (700-790), "What is the meaning of Bodhidharma coming from the West?" Shitou answered, "Go ask the pillar in the courtyard." "Bodhidharma coming from the West" refers to Bodhidharma, the First Patriarch of the Chan School, who came to China (ca. 527 C.E.) from India to transmit Chan. What was transmitted? What is Chan? Can it be explained? Can we witness it? Common knowledge tells us that Chan is a teaching of the mind, so transmitting it requires a "meeting of minds." This means that the true Chan cannot be expressed or described through language or phenomena. However, Master Shitou told his disciple to go ask the pillar outside. A pillar is inanimate and cannot give you any answer. Nevertheless, for an enlightened Chan master, the inner experience is no other than the outer environment. The insentient pillar, the mind within, the inherent buddha, Bodhidharma from India, Chan master Shitou; all these—in front of you right now—are one and the same, equal and not separate. So the Master says, "You better go ask the pillar, not Shitou."

2. A monk asked Niutou Huizhong (682-769): "What is buddha-mind?" The master replied, "It is the wall and the rubble." The monk asked again, "Since an insentient object has the nature of mind, does it know how to speak the Dharma?" The master replied, "It speaks profusely all the time without a moment's pause." People generally think that buddha-mind exists only in sentient beings; in addition, that buddha-mind is one's pure mind—not mixed up or chaotic— that it is the mind of great wisdom and great compassion. However, from the standpoint of an enlightened Chan practitioner, to know the

buddha-mind, one does not explain it with theory; one elucidates it with a mind in which the world within and the world without are united. So the master said that buddha-mind could also be found in a wall, broken bricks, and smashed tile. The monk still failed to understand: "Since inanimate objects all possess the true mind or pure self-nature of a buddha, aren't they the same as the buddhas? So, do they know how to speak the Dharma to deliver sentient beings?" The Chan master answered affirmatively: "These inanimate things not only speak the Dharma, but also do so vigorously, zealously, and dynamically. They constantly speak the Dharma, never stopping for a moment,"

This is freer and more liberal than the common viewpoint in which the Buddha attained enlightenment and discovered that all sentient beings, without exception, possess the wisdom and merit of a buddha. However, as a Chan master sees it, not only sentient beings are such, but all phenomena—animals, plants, minerals—all are of one essence with the buddhas. This is how one experiences the unity of the internal and the external: as long as one realizes the buddha within one's mind, none of the dharmas outside is not also buddha.

3. A monk asked Dongshan Liangjie (807-869): "What is a buddha?" The master replied, "Three catties of hemp" (about 4 pounds). Another monk asked: "What is a buddha?" The master replied, "A dried piece of shit."

These two *gong'ans* (Jpn. *koans*) are very well known in Chan history, with different people interpreting them in different ways. Normally, a Buddhist would not take an inanimate plant as a buddha, much less describe a buddha as dried shit. However, when we see all phenomena as the unity of the internal and the external—ordinary beings as equal to sages, all dharmas as one integral suchness—we would realize that only the buddha as seen by Master Dongshan is true: all things are buddha and buddha exists everywhere. Does such a buddha exist as one body or countless bodies? In fact, since a buddha has countless bodies, this is saying that everywhere exists a buddha, and nowhere exists a buddha. When there is unity there is no difference, and there is also no question of buddha or no buddha.

Chan Is the Ease of the Mind Within

The experience of Chan enlightenment is subjective, and the perception of liberation is a matter of the mind within. A mind that is confined by or attached to something will be turned by the environment. When it is the contrary, one will attain liberation. Therefore, the Chan School places special emphasis on training the mind, which is also called "training against the demons"; and the purpose of training against the demons is to "single out the buddha." The effort put into Chan practice is to calm the mind; as long as there is concern or worry, the mind will not be calm. Only when there is no mind to be applied can there be no mind to be calmed—this is true liberation. Liberated people may be imprisoned, or even shackled, with the executioner's ax at their neck, but they can still talk and laugh cheerfully. This is the ease within the mind that belongs to that level of spirituality; it is not something that can be shared or savored by those yet to attain realization. Now let me illustrate this with some examples in the Chan School.

1. In his verse, *Faith in Mind*, the Third Patriarch Sengcan (?-606) says, "Neither love nor hate, and one clearly understands." Most people love good fortune and hate adversity; they call those who follow their wishes good people, and those who oppose them, bad people. For unscrupulous or petty men, joy, anger, love, hate, and

other emotions are written on their face and always visible. Cultured people of noble character do not openly show love or hate, but inwardly, are unable to remain unmoved; so, in their mind, they are not free or at ease. The Sixth Patriarch Huineng's (638-713) *Platform Sutra* tells us that if we think of neither good nor evil, we will see our "original face." This original face is the same root we share with all buddhas. This turns vexation into wisdom, so the Third Patriarch called it "clearly understanding." And as the *Heart Sutra* says, it is "having no obstruction in the mind." So what does one clearly understand? It is to discover that as long as one's mind is liberated, one will perceive that all things turn out to be the best.

2. In his *Song of Mind*, Niutou Farong (594-657) said, "Not doing anything, it manifests naturally, bright and quiescent." The arhats—the sages of the Theravada tradition—have cut off all vexations, and therefore are said to have "accomplished all that needs to be accomplished." In their minds there is not anything they want to do, nor is there anything they do not want to do. Thus, deep in their mind, they experience the brightness arising from quiescence, and since it is bright and always quiescent, they realize the buddha of their self-nature.

3. In the *Reply to the Crown Prince's Question about the Essence of the Mind* of Qingliang Chengguan (738-839), it says, "Each successive thought in the mind can be that of buddha. There is no mind that is not buddha-mind. The path can be attained everywhere. There is not one particle of dust which is not the buddha-land." These four phrases signify that each and every thought in the mind is, without exception, buddha-mind. Viewed with buddha-mind, each and every infinitesimal space is nonetheless the pure buddha-land. If the mind can be free and at ease, then it is buddha-mind; seeing

the world with a free and peaceful mind is none other than seeing buddha-land. Whether the external world is good or bad, favorable or adverse, it is all the same for that person. This is a purely subjective state of liberation, but do not misunderstand; it is not self-hypnosis or self-deception—it is as real as water to a thirsty person, or food to one who is famished.

4. The *Record of Sayings* of Dahui Zonggao (1089-1163) says, "In order to empty the myriad dharmas, first purify one's own mind. When one's mind is pure, all conditions will come to rest." When the mind clings to any one thing, it is not empty, and one has vexations. How can we keep our mind from clinging to anything, and from being moved by the environment? Chan Master Zonggao tells us to just purify our mind first; and there are many ways to purify the mind. In his *Record of Sayings*, Dahui often taught people to investigate the *huatou*, "*wu*" (nothingness). If one investigates this *huatou* [and raises the "great ball of doubt,"] at the moment of shattering the doubt, one illuminates one's mind and sees buddha-nature; one will find that one's nature is inherently pure. At such a time, all the dharmas outside the mind—whether pure or impure, good or bad, virtuous or evil—will have no power whatsoever to affect you. The saying, "the eight winds of circumstance are unable to move you," aptly describes the state of mind that has attained this freedom and ease.

Chan Is the Wisdom of No-self
The "no-self," "no-form," and "no-mind" as mentioned in Chan all refer to wisdom. The "no" does not mean non-existent, but refers to the self-liberation of a mind that does not abide in anything. It has no attachment to the self but the function of wisdom. Manifesting wisdom inwardly is liberation, manifesting wisdom outwardly is

compassion. If one has only departed from self-attachment but cannot bring forth compassion, it is definitely not true liberation. Liberation is wisdom and compassion is bodhi-mind. The two relate like the wings of a bird, or the wheels of a cart; they have to develop in parallel, without lacking either one of them. Let me give two examples.

1. In the *Two Entrances and Four Practices* of Bodhidharma, it says, "The sutras say, 'The Dharma is devoid of sentient beings, as it departs from the contamination of sentient beings. The Dharma is devoid of the self, as it departs from the contamination of the self.'" And it says, "(As) the essence of the Dharma is free of miserliness, one gives body, life, and material possessions generously, without stinting." It also says, "One works to transform sentient beings in accordance to phenomena, but does not cling to forms. This is cultivating oneself, but it can also benefit others, and can also ennoble the bodhi path. As it is with the perfection (*paramita*) of giving, so is it with the five other perfections."

This passage denotes that enlightened, liberated people are free of [attachment to] the ideas of people, self, sentient beings, and lifespan as mentioned in the *Diamond Sutra*. That is to say, one will not generate vexations because of the "self," "sentient beings," and so on; this is called "departing from the contamination of self," and "departing from the contamination of sentient beings." However, one will not abandon delivering sentient beings because of one's own liberation. On the contrary, one will give all one has even more actively; only then can one manifest the selfless and unstinted wisdom and compassion. Therefore, one must practice before attaining enlightenment, and one still has to practice after attaining it. Generating bodhi-mind is the preparation before attaining enlightenment, for one to deliver sentient beings universally. Then, after attaining enlightenment, the core practice of a bodhisattva is to cultivate the Six Paramitas.

2. Yangshan Huiji (807-883) asked Weishan Lingyou (771-853): "When hundreds of thousands of external objects come before you all at once, what would you do?" Weishan said, "What is blue is not yellow, and what is long is not short. All dharmas dwell in their own places respectively, and have nothing to do with me."

The sutras say, "The dharmas dwell in their respective places, and are naturally so." This means that all dharmas, or all things, have their respective phenomena and scopes, without the slightest disorder. Their harmonious unity does not hinder other phenomena from existing individually. If we see all phenomena in the world with the eyes of wisdom, each phenomenon has its own position. So Master Weishan asserted that what is blue is not yellow, and what is long is not short. Even if myriads or millions of situations simultaneously appear in front of you, you will not confuse them or mix them up, mistaking one for another, and you will also not be affected or deluded by them; one will handle things as they should be handled, and respond properly to different problems in different ways.

Chan Is Life without Attachment

The phenomenon of life can be recognized as the continuation in one lifetime, of numerous past lifetimes and eons. Through their karma, the life of ordinary people is just drifting with the stream, caught in ceaseless births and deaths; whereas, with the power of their compassionate vows, the lives of sages and bodhisattvas are coming and going in the boundless ocean of samsara, while delivering countless sentient beings. Ordinary beings have no other alternative than to experience life and death, while for bodhisattvas, it is natural. Ordinary beings have come to undergo sufferings and troubles, whereas bodhisattvas have come to save others from suffering and troubles. The essential difference lies in whether or not one harbors attachments in one's mind.

Chan practitioners who have already attained enlightenment have no attachment in their mind, so they are not concerned about the matter of birth and death, nor are they concerned about no-birth or no-death. Because one has realized no-self, who is it that cycles through birth and death, since there is not even the self? Because they have realized no-form, they have neither the form of samsara nor that of nirvana. For them there is neither self nor dharmas; therefore, they are able to dwell neither in samsara nor in nirvana. This is the great liberation and the great nirvana. This is also the reason why great Chan masters do not worry about the issue of their own birth and death. Now let me cite two instances.

1. When visiting Huineng for the first time, Yongjia Xuanjue (665-713) said, "The matter of birth and death is great, and impermanence is so rapid and swift." Thereupon Huineng told him, "Then why not relate to the birthless and realize that there is no swiftness?" The *Song of Enlightenment* by Yongjia says: "In dreams there clearly exist the six realms of samsara; upon awakening the great universe is completely empty." It further says, "Continuing rounds of birth and death; samsara prolonged without interruption. Since sudden enlightenment, I understand the unborn, thus I have no concern for honor or shame." This passage tells us that before Huineng's words, Yongjia was still attached to the issue of birth and death. If one does not put an end to the cycle of samsara, once impermanence—namely, death—catches up, where would one

go after all? What an important and terrible thing it is! Huineng told Yongjia that he need not be afraid of samsara, nor worry about the impermanence of life, and that as long as he realized that birth is no-birth, and what is fleeting is not fleeting, then samsara is put to an end, and impermanence is gone. After hearing this teaching, Yongjia resolved for himself the important matter of samsara, and said that in times of delusion, it is like dreaming, while after attaining enlightenment, it is like waking up. In dreams there are births and deaths; upon awakening the world is empty. No-birth signifies no attachment, as well as not generating vexations, which means that one does not give rise to discrimination. One who fears samsara will seek nirvana. To dislike suffering and long for happiness is nothing but attachment. If the mind has no attachment, then one will not care that samsara is frightful, nor think that one should hold on to nirvana. This is the attitude toward life of those who have awakened to Chan.

2. Dazhu Huihai (d.u.), the disciple of Mazu Daoyi (709-788, or 688-763), said, "To seek the great nirvana is the karma of samsara, so is the action of rejecting impurity and seeking purity." "There is originally no binding, so there is no need to seek liberation. Just apply and act straightforwardly. That is the unsurpassed universality and equality."

The meaning of this passage is very clear. Originally, nirvana and samsara, purity and impurity, and binding and untying are all relative. Only from samsara does one know there is nirvana; only from impurity does one know there is purity; and only from bondage does one know there is liberation. Therefore, one who seeks nirvana is definitely in samsara; one who seeks purity is definitely in impurity; and one who seeks liberation is definitely in bondage. One should have no attachment in one's mind, neither fearing samsara nor seeking nirvana, neither detesting impurity nor delighting in purity, neither feeling bondage nor feeling the need for liberation; only then is it the realization of Chan life, which is lively, dynamic, free, and at ease, without any worry or concern.

Chan Life Is Vivacious and Dynamic

Chan is neither religion nor philosophy, but a kind of outlook, style, and way of life. However, Chan life is different from the life of ordinary people; a Chan practitioner does not seek, display, or reject things for oneself, nor does one feel joyful in good circumstances, or troubled in bad; one only needs to live each day like everyone else, doing what should be done and not doing what shouldn't be, doing what can be done and not doing what cannot. Engaging in society is neither for oneself nor for others, but simply to fulfill one's duties. The principle is that Chan mind neither drifts with the environment, nor departs from it. When the mind does not move with the environment, that is the power of Chan concentration; when the mind does not depart from the environment, that is the function of wisdom, quiescent yet illuminating, illuminating yet quiescent. Being quiescent, it departs from forms and is thus free of them; capable of illumination, Chan mind makes flexible use of everything in daily life, without becoming vulgar or vexed—this is the effect of wisdom. Ordinary people become disoriented if their minds move, and close-minded if their minds are stilled—that is not the life of a Chan practitioner. Now let me cite two examples as follows:

1. In the *Platform Sutra*, it says, "It is not the wind that is moving, and it is not the flag that is moving. It is your minds that are moving." When Master Huineng sojourned to Faxing Monastery

in Guangzhou, he saw two monks arguing about a flag in front of the monastery—one saying it was the wind that moved, the other that it was the flag, each arguing for his own stand. According to the *Platform Sutra,* Master Huineng told them, "It is neither the wind nor the flag that moves; it is your mind that moves."

To know that the objects in the environment are moving is common sense, and it is not wrong. If one goes deeper in one's investigation, one realizes that it is people's mind that is aware of external objects moving; this is not wrong, either. If one insists that it is the flag or the wind that moves, one will give rise to vexations. Thus, the moving of ordinary people's minds is called "discrimination and attachment" because they have definite views of their own; their mind dwells [unyieldingly] on something, and so loses the lively, free spirit. The mind of those who have attained Chan enlightenment will move just the same, but their mind does not dwell on anything, and is free from attachment, so it is the illuminating function of wisdom. Because the mind is free of obstructions, it is lively, dynamic, and free.

2. The verse on "Formlessness" in the *Platform Sutra* says, "Buddhadharma exists in the world, and enlightenment is inseparable from the world." And it says, "In the dark house of vexations, one must always give rise to the sunny light of wisdom." We find many similar ideas in the records of Chan. Yet, many misunderstand the spirit of Chan, and misconstrue Buddhism as passive, escapist, and world-weary. Indeed, many who study Buddhism or Chan do display such mentalities. But in truth, Chan is absolutely positive; it is engaged in the world and works to improve it. It is not just a theory or belief, but encourages a lively, free, down-to-earth life. As long as we can practice Chan and put aside impulses to love or

hate when meeting fortune or adversity, we can be free, at ease, and in peace. Therefore, Buddharma is right for daily life; but to seek Buddhadharma by avoiding daily life is to look for hair on a turtle or horns on a rabbit—there is no such thing. For a practitioner who has not attained enlightenment, as long as they know they are not enlightened, they will be close to enlightenment. Once they find that reality is originally "just so" and put down all attachment to longing or detesting, that will manifest in an enlightened state. This shows that delusion and enlightenment live next door to each other, and are even two names of one thing. Wisdom arises from vexations, and is applied to vexations. If we are willy-nilly, over-scrupulous, tentative, craving this and disliking that, then we will find obstructions everywhere. If, becoming inured to the unusual, and knowing they are vexations, we neither reject nor accept them, wisdom is right here and now, and we are free and at ease with whatever we encounter.

Chan Is Carrying Water and Firewood

What people today get paid for their work is called salary or *xinshui* in Chinese. *Xinshui* translated literally means "firewood and water," which comes from an allusion. It refers to the literati and governmental officials during ancient times who lived simply and frugally, as the salary given by the imperial court was only enough to buy firewood to boil the water, not enough to pay for staple and non-staple food. That is why payment for work is called "firewood and water." The life of Chan practitioners of ancient times was much simpler than that of the literati. They were not provided even with firewood and water, and had to live in a self-supporting manner. Therefore, everyone had to labor as part of the routine daily schedule; there was always the "work in the hillside fields," which involved carrying water and firewood.

In Chan writings, we find lay practitioner Pang Yun (?-808) saying: "In carrying water and firewood there are miraculous powers and wondrous functions." This saying reflected the life of enlightened Chan practitioners. In other words, for Chan practitioners, there are opportunities for Chan investigation everywhere in daily life, and the subtleties of Chan can be found in everything, when interacting with people and dealing with matters.

Everyday life *is* Chan. In today's society, besides living the family life, people also have their work environment and their social milieu. The work environment includes vocations related to industry, commerce, agriculture, and military, official, and teaching jobs, as well as professions with no fixed office hours such as religion, culture, entertainment, catering services, and other livelihoods. This is not at all like the simple life of Chan practitioners of ancient times, which involved only the daily monastic routine from morning till evening—eating, sleeping, and walking, as well as work in the kitchen and on the farm. Therefore, in the records of Chan, we often find that the masters applied their wisdom pervasively and flexibly in their daily life. Following are some examples.

1. Youyuan, a *vinaya* master, asked Dazhu Huihai (a disciple of Mazu Daoyi), "Master, when engaging in spiritual practice, do you make an effort?" The Master replied, "Yes, I make an effort." The vinaya master asked again, "How do you make an effort?" The Master replied, "I eat when I'm hungry, and sleep when I'm tired."

2. A monk asked Weishan Lingyou, "Master, what is your teaching about the Dharma?" The Master said, "A bowl of rice gruel."

3. A monk asked Zhaozhou Congshen (778-897), "I'm an ignorant learner. Could you please teach me something?" The Master

asked, "Have you eaten your gruel?" The monk answered, "Yes, I have." The Master said, "Then go wash your bowl."

4. Huangbo Xiyun (?-850) once said, "Eating day in and day out, I have never bitten a grain of rice. Walking day in and day out, I have never stepped on a piece of land."

All four examples mentioned above talk about eating; one of them talks about sleeping, and another talks about walking. As a matter of fact, these things represent what we do in daily life: walking, standing, sitting, and lying down, as well as things regarding food, clothes, inhabitation, and transportation, which are our everyday activities. Unenlightened people think of the Path as something very lofty and very remote, like a Confucian sage who said, "When I watch it, it is in front of me, but suddenly it is at my back." And he further said, "The more I look up at it, the higher it becomes; the more I drill it, the harder it becomes." Usually, the Path that Chan practitioners experience is not so mysterious. As long as one departs from anger, craving, and self-centered value judgment regarding everything, then that is the Path; it is enlightenment, liberation, and wisdom. In sum, Chan is not separate from practical life.

Two years ago, a lay Buddhist gave me a box of huge, purple grapes as a gift. After making an offering of it to the Buddha, he insisted that I eat the grapes in his presence. I took a bite, and it tasted very fresh and delicious, with suitable sweetness and also strong, fresh fragrance. So I said several times that it was delicious. Seeing this, a disciple of mine who was standing by me said, "Look, the Master eats with great pleasure." The lay Buddhist at the side was very glad upon seeing this. Till the third day, that disciple left all the grapes for me to eat, and the lay Buddhist brought me two more boxes. Then I said, "I'm not going to open a wine brewery, so why do you give me so many grapes?"

The two followers, one a monastic, the other a layperson, said in unison, "Shifu, why did you enjoy it the other day, but dislike it today?" I smiled at them and sighing, said, "That it is delicious is a fact, but one doesn't need to be greedy." I then told them, "As far as practitioners are concerned, they should also follow common reasoning, have common sense, and normal value judgment. However, if they become greedy for something good and angry at something bad, then their minds have deviated from the Path.

Chan Is neither South nor North, neither East nor West

Chan cannot be described or explained in language, words, or thinking; it is a teaching "not based on words or language, pointing directly to the human mind, a separate transmission outside the scriptures." Whatever is past, present, or future, as well as front and back, right and left, up and down are delineations in time and space with marks or symbols. They do not have absolute meanings, nor represent something substantial. However, if we depart from these ideas, the universe would become a void concept. It all depends on how we experience them: when the experience is right, then all are right; when it is wrong, then all are wrong. We can find quite a few examples for this in the *gong'ans* of Chan. That is to say, the Chan mind does not depart from the experience of time and space, nor does it cling to them.

1. The *Platform Sutra* records that [as a youth] Huineng went to see the Fifth Patriarch, Hongren, saying that he had come from the south. The Fifth Patriarch then asked, "What do you seek?" Huineng replied, "To become a buddha." Hongren said, "You are from Lingnan (today's Guangdong) and a barbarian. How can you become

a buddha?" Huineng answered, "People may live in the south or the north, but buddha-nature makes no such distinctions."

2. In another story, Zhaozhou Congshen taught the Dharma in the north. When he saw a monk who newly arrived, he asked, "Where do you come from?" The monk answered, "From the South." The Master said, "All the Buddhadharma can be found in the South; why do you come here?" The monk answered, "How can Buddhadharma be differentiated between south and north?" Sighing, the Master said, "Just a simpleton shouldering a plank."

The two dialogues above seem to show different levels of understanding. In the first instance, Huineng thought that people are differentiated as to southern or northern, but from the viewpoint of buddha-nature, there is no south and north. The monk in the second instance saw no differentiation of Buddhadharma in the south and north, and Chan Master Zhaozhou called him "a simpleton shouldering a plank." As a matter of fact, in order to test disciples, enlightened Chan masters sometimes talk about things like the "south and north." Their purpose is to beat around the bush (teach by indirection), to eliminate attachment and obstruction in the learners' mind, rather than discussing the south, north, east, and west. If one could get the point right there it could become a trigger for Chan enlightenment.

3. Xitang Zhizang (735-814), a disciple of Mazu Daoyi, paid a visit to the Imperial Master Huizhong (677-775). The latter asked, "What Dharma does Eminent Master Mazu teach?" Zhizang walked from the east side to the west side and then stood there. The Huizhong said, "Is that all? Anything else?" Zhizang then moved to the east side and stood there. Master Huizhong then said, "That belongs to Master Mazu. What about you, my dear friend?" Chan

Master Zhizang said, "I've already presented it to you, Venerable Master."

In this *gong'an*, there are a host and a guest exchanging questions and responses, vividly and dramatically, in a lively, free, and easy manner. Speaking amounts to remaining wordless, and vice versa. The Dharma of Master Mazu can only be appreciated with the mind instead of with the mouth or with gestures. The four postures of walking, standing, sitting, and lying down, as well as any single point in space/time, are all correct when one of them is correct, or are all mistaken when one of them is mistaken. Therefore, it is correct to go east to west, and also correct to go west to east; this manifests unconstraint flexibility, and freedom. If your mind is infatuated or attached to something, you will be hindered no matter what you encounter, and you will get stuck wherever you go. Whether you believe in and practice Buddhism, this breadth of mind of enlightened Chan practitioners is something you must know and should learn. This will make your life richer, more cheerful, as well as more down-to-earth and freer.

Chan: Human Consciousness

Brooklyn College, City University of New York, November 8, 1990

Today, I will introduce some concepts about the activities and functions of human consciousness from the point of view of Chan Buddhism. I will cover three key points: the Buddhist analysis of human consciousness; the Chan view of human consciousness; and how to deal with the problems of consciousness.

Buddhist Analysis of Human Consciousness

Buddhism classifies consciousness into three interrelated aspects: mind, thought, and cognition (Skt., *citta-mano-vijnana*). The states of the mind include "true mind" and "false mind": the false mind is afflicted with vexations, while the true mind is wisdom. False mind consists of the activities of ordinary human consciousness; these activities are subjective and characterized by judgments or ideas about our interests, gains, and losses, and so on; being illusory, they are vexations. Only when we become free of the functions of ordinary consciousness and we perceive the environment and phenomena as they really are—without adding subjective views and judgments—will the mind be true; only then can we call it wisdom. After we are free from the self-center and subjective judgments, and we remain in the purely objective state, then it can be called wisdom, or true mind. Whether the mind is in a true or false state, the psychological activities are the same; the difference is whether the mind is functioning with or without a self-center.

The false mind includes "thought," which contains the mental functions of discrimination and attachment, as well as "consciousness," which has no discriminating function, although it is the main feature—or fundamental essence—of sentience in living beings. Together, they are "thought consciousness" and "base consciousness." Generally, common sense or psychology only admits that humankind and higher level animals such as elephants, horses, oxen, monkeys, and dogs, etc., have the functions of consciousness, and deny that lower animal forms, such as caterpillars and earthworms, etc., also have these functions. However, Buddhism holds that all animate life has the functions or capacity for consciousness. The higher level animals possess discriminating consciousness, as well as the base consciousness that sustains continuing life. Although the lower level animals do not have thought consciousness, they indeed possess base consciousness; otherwise, they would not possess lives that transmigrate in samsara.

The main purpose of Buddhism is to help human beings transform themselves, to help them be rid of false mind and retain true mind. It is also to help people engage in spiritual practice to cut off vexations and realize bodhi, thus transforming the ordinary functions of consciousness into wisdom. It is to help people be rid of the thought consciousness and the base consciousness and only keep the true mind of wisdom, so they may attain liberation, and no longer be affected by the power of karma. To experience true mind, which manifests as wisdom, is to attain enlightenment.

Buddhism classifies consciousness into base consciousness and thought consciousness, affirming that base consciousness is innate in humans and animate life, even at the lowest levels, while thought consciousness derives from base consciousness. Thus, from the standpoint of base consciousness, all sentient beings are equal. Therefore, Buddhist compassion is not limited to saving humankind, but also rendering help to all sentient beings.

Chan Buddhist View of Consciousness

Normally, the Chan tradition does not use the term "consciousness," instead, using "mind." The buddha-mind they speak of refers to the true mind of wisdom, while the mind of ordinary sentient beings refers to the false mind of vexations. The purpose of Chan is to illuminate the mind and see "the nature." What mind does one illuminate? What nature does one see? One illuminates the true mind, and sees buddha-nature. Since the mind of sentient beings has consciousness of self as well as the interests of the self, it cannot be objective. Therefore, it is in the dark. Illuminated mind is the wisdom that is revealed after one breaks away from self-centeredness; namely, it is the true mind. Only after the true mind is revealed can one see buddha-nature, which is inherent in every person, and possessed by all sentient beings.

Rather than speaking of "consciousness" or "thought," the Chan records and discourses mostly refer to "mind," whether it is of false mind or true mind. Before one has begun to practice, the mind is unsettled and anxious—it has vexations. Discovering that one has vexations, one would hope to obtain help through spiritual practice. In Chan, this spiritual practice is called calming the mind, resting the mind, clearing the mind, or contemplating the mind, which all aim to deal with the false mind. There is the term "beginner's mind," which refers to the initial aspiration, the initial generation of the mind of bodhi, or awakening. Thus, bodhi-mind is the true mind, illuminated with the light of wisdom.

Those who understand Chan know whether the mind that Chan masters speak of is the mind of wisdom or the mind of delusion.

Indeed, in the process of spiritual practice it is the false mind, while the aim of spiritual practice is the true mind. Thus, regardless of whether it refers to the basis, the process, or the purpose, Chan expresses it with just the one word: mind.

However, Western psychology employs the term "consciousness," and thus does not explain mind in the Buddhist context that covers the whole mental process. It is hard to explain "true mind" and "base consciousness" from the viewpoint of Western psychology, or indeed, of most people. Consider that the mental activities of people with wisdom are also called "consciousness." When those who have attained liberation perceive things as they truly are, with the genuine wisdom of unselfishness and no-self, it is very ambiguous to still call this activity consciousness. If one insists on calling both the wisdom of liberated people and the vexations of ordinary people the same as the functions of consciousness, then it would be better to label them as "pure consciousness" and "impure consciousness."

The Problems of Consciousness

Ordinarily, people deal with personal issues by trying to understand the problems and analyzing them. In contrast, Chan Buddhism teaches us that only by putting down our problems can we truly solve them. How do we put down personal problems? The preliminary method is to consider other people's welfare more than your own. When you help others solve their problems, it is being compassionate. Where does compassion come from? It arises from the mind of bodhi. To generate bodhi-mind, first let go of selfish desires, and work to relieve sentient beings from suffering. When you strive to help sentient beings to become free from suffering and attain happiness, your own problems will disappear at the same time. The gradual lessening and lightening of self-centeredness is precisely removing false mind and illuminating true mind, thus transforming vexations into wisdom.

When treating a patient, a psychotherapist may ask many questions. After the patients talk with the psychotherapist for some time, they may feel their problems resolved. However, they will come again several days later. A patient with serious problems may have to be treated for several decades, and would still need to see a psychotherapist. Chan teachers do not need to know so much about their students. If they know where their students' main problems lie, a Chan teacher does not need to know at all the background of the problems. Sometimes, all it takes is to give them a few words or a couple of phrases, and their problems could be solved. So it takes less effort.

When we employ the principles of Chan to handle a problem, as long as we have correct concepts and are clear about the principles, we will more or less be able to help ourselves, and help others as well. We do not necessarily have to tackle the person's problem head-on. Rather, it is best to let the person with a problem face it on his or her own, or simply let that person ignore the problem. These are the principles.

How do we face a problem? It is to tell ourselves that whatever matter or phenomenon occurs, there are always definite causes for it. We do not need to investigate the causes, nor do we spend the time to investigate the causes. Only to face it and improve it is the most direct and most important thing. If we still fail to solve the problem by facing it, or it is impossible for us to solve it, then we simply leave it alone. This way, when the problem is left alone and unsettled, it will eventually be settled. Without being resolved, it is actually resolved.

Therefore, when the ancient patriarchs of Chan received their disciples, they asked and responded to questions. Often, they rendered seemingly unrelated answers, or simply gave no answer at all, or acted with bodily gestures to help their disciples attain realization.

Once, a Chan master was visited by a monk who, seeking the Dharma, pushed the master's door open. The master immediately closed the door. The monk did this three times, and each time the master shut the door on the monk. The fourth time, the monk pushed the door open very rapidly. Once more, the master shut the door, but so swiftly that it broke the monk's leg. [When this happened, the monk attained realization.] Originally the monk wanted a method for achieving enlightenment, but after his leg was broken he no longer had any questions.

Here is a story about Chan Master Mazu and one of his disciples. One day, a monk asked Mazu, "Master, please tell me what Bodhidharma brought to China from the West." Mazu replied, "I'm not in a mood for a talk today. Go ask Dharma brother Zhizang!" When the monk asked Zhizang, the latter said, "I have a headache today. Just go and ask Dharma brother Huaihai!" So the monk asked Huaihai, and the latter said, "That's something beyond me, so you had better go and ask Master Mazu!" When the monk went back to Master Mazu, the master scolded him: "You blockhead! Zhizang's hair is white, and Huaihai's hair is black." In this way the monk realized self-nature, and the issue was settled.

Chan has two approaches to help people resolve their problems: one is to free oneself from continuous thoughts, and the other is to cultivate contemplation. The two examples mentioned above are methods of freeing oneself from thinking; they are the "sudden" approach that does not rely on words and language. That is to say, there is no need to gain experience, knowledge, thought, and study, but to just—right here and now—not be bound by notions of time and space, by shaking off the barriers of consciousness of self, to become as it were, stark naked and unveiled. At that time, we are "without any obstruction in the mind." This, then, is "pointing directly to people's mind, not relying on words and language."

The contemplation approach adopts the method of focusing consciousness on a phrase, a matter, a point, or a thought. For instance, when contemplating the breath, we pay attention to the breath coming in and going out; or when counting the breath we focus on the current number; or we can just watch the rise and fall of the abdomen. When using recitation, we focus on the holy name of a buddha or bodhisattva. We can also contemplate how a human body goes from death to decay, how it keeps changing until just a bleached skeleton remains, and how there are finally no more bones, with only white light remaining. Using these methods of contemplation, one can quiet one's vexations and purify one's consciousness gradually, so that wisdom will manifest.

Clearly, Chan differs from the therapy methods of psychology or psychiatry. However, people with a mental disorder or psychological problem can still use sitting meditation as an auxiliary treatment. However, they must not expect to achieve enlightenment while receiving the treatment of their problems, as that could trigger additional problems.

Chan: Mental Health

San Francisco General Hospital, October 25, 1990

Buddhadharma Is the Cure for Mental Illness

Buddhism originated in India and began with Shakyamuni Buddha addressing the question of illness in human beings. We can say that humans are born with illness, for at the time of birth, they are already afflicted. People without any illness have yet to be born; and if they were born without illness, they would have to wait until they die to be again free from illness. This is because in the process of living, illness and pain—physical or mental—will happen. The Buddha said that when you are physically ill, go to a doctor; but when you are suffering from mental illness, Buddhadharma is the cure. However, the healthier one's mind is, the less physical illness one will have, and the less the body will feel sick. Therefore, in the Buddha's deliverance of the world he placed more importance in saving people's mind than in saving their body.

When one's mental illness is completely cured, that is called liberation. Having a healthy body and an unhealthy mind, one will suffer more than if one were just physically ill. On the other hand, if the body is sick while the mind remains healthy, the illness can be bearable. So, while the Buddha taught about both physical and mental suffering, he gave more importance to the mental side.

Physical illness can be painful but not necessarily suffering, while mental illness is always suffering. Therefore, Buddhadharma is not meant for eliminating physical pain—like an injection of anesthesia—

but for relieving mental suffering.

The Cause of Suffering

From the perspective of Buddhism there are two kinds of causes of suffering: ignorance since time without beginning, and afflictions arising due to the law of cause and effect.

The Result of Ignorance from Time without Beginning

Western religions talk about the time when the world was first created, and Western philosophy and science speculate on the beginning of the universe. But it is not very easy to answer the question: "When did it all really begin?" For this reason, Buddhism speaks of time without beginning—it is like a circle where there may be a beginning, but you cannot locate it because every point on the circle can be the place of origin. So, Buddhism says that suffering has existed since time without beginning, and its origin is ignorance in the minds of sentient beings.

Affliction as a Cycle of Cause and Effect

From the perspective of causation, a condition beforehand causes a result afterwards, and the result becomes another cause, bringing out another result. As time moves along, through our actions we incessantly create the causes for the future results. In our life, there are three kinds of affliction: those having to do with the environment, with relationships, and with internal conflicts.

1. *Affliction coming from the environment*: San Francisco is a nice place, with thin mist, cool wind, and a bay view to enjoy. However, it can be cold and hot here too. Many people regard San Francisco as a "heaven on Earth," but still, people living here are not exempt from

sickness either. Just now when I was in the car, a lay practitioner was sneezing. I asked her, "Why are you sick?" She said, "I'm not sick. I am just allergic to cold air." I thought people living in heaven never get sick, and now in such a nice place like San Francisco there are also people who get sick, and we are now speaking at this hospital. In this place, as it is elsewhere, no matter how lovely the weather, how refreshing the air, people still get sick. From time to time, there are horrible earthquakes and drought. As elsewhere, sometimes there are toxins in some foods too.

2. *Affliction coming from interpersonal relationship in society*: Human relations also cause us afflictions, but then who brings the most affliction? Many people would think it is their enemies, but that is not necessarily the case. It can very likely be your husband, wife, or children; it may well be your family rather than your enemies that argues with you the most. Apart from our family and relatives, we also meet people, well acquainted or not, and we develop relationships with them. Some may help us, while others may create troubles for us; sometimes they bring us help, sometimes they bring us trouble. Living among them, you feel there is constant competition.

Yesterday I gave a talk at a great American university and someone told me that the academic circles there were most murky, and they often engage in fierce struggles. Normally we would assume that scholars are people of great learning, excellent thought, and smart brains, and so they should be considerate and help each other instead of fighting. But very often, the more knowledgeable people are, the fiercer they struggle with each other. On a common intellectual level, people struggle for power, fame, and profit; on a higher intellectual level, people struggle for ideas, thoughts, and views, having no wish to compromise at all. This phenomenon is the same everywhere. As long as there are people, there will be competition. You look down on me, and I would appear to be prouder than you. I ask you, have you ever found people competing with you? And have you ever competed with others? The answer to both questions is most likely, yes. Charles Darwin said, "Evolution is the law of the survival of the fittest." However, this represents the nature of animals, not the nature of humans, least of all does it represent buddha-nature. So this competitive attitude brings affliction to human beings.

3. *Affliction comes from our inner struggle of the emotions*: Our biggest enemy is not someone from the outside but ourselves, because we constantly change our mind and ideas. When we feel regret or pride for what happened yesterday, we give rise to afflictive emotions. Very often, because we need to weigh and prioritize the pros and cons, the complexity of relationships, issues of how big, how many, how high, how much further, we find it hard to reach a decision. Very often, when we consider gain and loss, right and wrong, positive and negative, we waver and find it difficult to make up our mind, and this is most painful. Moreover, we may think there are no problems in our minds, yet we get angry and upset all the time. I once asked a person: "Why do you have so many troubles and afflictions?" He simply replied, "I don't have troubles and afflictions myself; it is other people that are causing me troubles and afflictions." In fact, it is because people like this have problems themselves, that they have problems in their relationships.

Yesterday, I was in a car with four people who were talking very loudly, and they talked a lot. One of them said to me, "I am really sorry Master, that we have been so loud." I said, "You are loud but that has nothing to do with me." Indeed, they were loud, and I heard them all very clearly. However, since their conversation had nothing to do with me, the noise itself didn't really matter. This morning, one of them told me, "Some people really cannot stand noise. When they hear us making noise, they feel annoyed and angry." On the surface, this may seem like a trouble from outside, but actually it is their own problem.

Five Causes of Affliction

From the Buddhist perspective, there are five causes of mental afflictions, which are called the "five hindrances." They are desire, anger, ignorance, arrogance, and doubt. When affliction arises in us, we should reflect on its source. By doing so, the affliction in question will then diminish relatively. When we realize that we are afflicted by craving, then its magnitude will naturally lessen. When anger afflicts you, if you can sit back, reflect, and become aware that you are angry—so angry that you feel utter pain—then ask yourself, "Why am I asking for suffering and looking for trouble?" Then your agony or hatred will be alleviated. Look into your mind as the source of your affliction instead of looking outwards at the environment. Instead of focusing on the problem tell yourself, "There is no need to be so afflicted."

When your affliction arises because of your foolish actions, if you can realize that you are being foolish, your agony and affliction will diminish relatively. When you can say to yourself, "I am so foolish," that means you realize that you created your own affliction, and it will alleviate naturally. We can apply the same principle to arrogance. Arrogance may not seem to be an affliction, but the actual root of arrogance is the sense of inferiority. Arrogance results from a lack of confidence, which in turn comes from a lack of the sense of security, so it is also an affliction.

Furthermore, doubt can bring agony; because of doubt, we are unable to make decisions, we do not believe in ourselves, and we lack the mental capacity to trust others. Therefore, we are suspicious and lack faith in things, people, and ourselves; we waver and are undetermined. This way we have much agony and affliction. If you realize that doubt will only bring you affliction, think this: "Since I hope to accomplish this goal, I should believe that it is the best and right thing to do, so I should stop doubting." Then you will really go ahead with it. Some people, even after they decide to get married, still have doubts, "We are getting married, but will we divorce some day? Will my other half abandon me? Has my spouse lied to me, even before we are married?" If you have such suspicions about your other half, and you suffer greatly even before the wedding, it will be very difficult to maintain a harmonious and happy family. Originally, you do not intend to get divorced, but because doubt and heavy suspicion, you will end up getting divorced very soon.

When you have doubts, tell yourself, "If I really have doubts about him, then I may as well keep away from him. But if I decide to marry him then I should accept him and trust him." Otherwise it would like knowing there are tigers in the mountains and still heading in that direction —which would be simply asking for trouble. What would be the point? Nonetheless, it is impossible not to have any doubt at all; it is normal to have some doubt. In other words, it is normal for ordinary people to have the sickness of doubt.

The Causes of Mental Imbalance

From a Buddhist perspective, I want to discuss five causes for mental imbalance.

Pursuit and Resistance without Considering one's own Capability

Pursuit and resistance means that one is greedy and unable to satisfy one's desires without ever measuring one's own abilities. One hopes to unreasonably escape and ignorantly resist the unavoidable and irresistible reality without first considering one's own capabilities. This tendency is more or less common to every individual, especially young people, who tend to think they have the ability to "make it," and that they have a strong potential. They think that they can undertake whatever other people undertake, and acquire whatever other people acquire. Once they encounter unexpected setbacks or adversity, they stubbornly persist in the struggle, yet they are doomed to fail because they lack the ability and strength.

Expanding and Conquering without Being Satisfied

A trait common to humans is the hope to extend one's horizons. People wish to exert their influence by means of their own ideas and actions, expanding themselves without limit. Some people fight for fame, hoping to catch the notice of the world. Some people fight for power, aspiring to conquer others and the whole world. And some people fight for wealth, wishing to become a billionaire, or the richest among the richest. Even in a family setting, we can also find situations where the wife wants to dominate the husband, or the other way around. People oppose each other and are unwilling to compromise; such situations happen so often among individuals, groups, society, nations, and ethnic groups; examples like this can go on and on.

Pride and Arrogance

When people achieve success, they tend to be proud and arrogant. Pride and arrogance are not easily separable, and they are not in line with humility. With humility comes tolerance and with tolerance comes vastness. Overly proud, one becomes pompous, which not only hurts oneself but also others.

Complaining about and Blaming Others

It is rare to meet people who can summon the courage and continue to work hard when they encounter defeat or failure. Most people would feel discouraged, disheartened, and tend to complain and blame others, not understanding that there must be reasons behind their own encounters and experiences in life. Not believing the law of cause and effect, and merely blaming and cursing others do not make things better.

Doubt and Fear

People having heavy doubt and suspicion definitely lack the sense of security.

How to Maintain Mental Balance

How can people maintain mental balance? For ordinary people, mental illness can be addressed in three ways: one way is to deceive oneself by saying, "I am not suffering from any illness." But this merely shows unwillingness to face the facts and seek help from a psychotherapist; this is a pitiful mindset. A second way is to acknowledge the illness and admit the imbalanced state of mind. But then, one may think that they can help themself through control and suppression of their emotions. The result might be that the longer the suppression, the more serious the problem, which is also very pitiful.

A third way to maintain emotional balance is to consult a psychiatrist, who will explore your problems with you, to diagnose and guide you towards resolving your situation, and sometimes medication is prescribed to relieve symptoms. Although this might help, it is only partial, and it helps only for a while. Doctors can only know a part of you, and the same is true for yourself. Without first knowing what illness you suffer from, a doctor will not have a complete idea of its cause either. After relieving and releasing the problem, it may seem to have been solved; however, you may find after some time that the problem is still there. That is why some people, having seen their psychiatrists for years, still need to keep visiting them. Treating such patients so frequently, these psychiatrists may eventually suffer from mental illness themselves.

How Chan Buddhism Cures Mental Illness

Applying Buddhist Concepts as an Approach

I will give some examples of how Chan Buddhist concepts can address mental illness and pain.

1. *Cause and effect*: The Buddhist concept of cause and effect (karma) is a religious belief, but it also reflects the reality that in life, whatever we do will cause a response, and lead to a result. As a matter of faith, we believe that we had a life before this life, another prior to that, and countless lives before that. And after this life, there will be a next life. Without gaining liberation, we will experience countless and innumerable subsequent lives. We may find much of the result of what we are experiencing unfair. The "unfairness" we encounter in this life is a result from what we did in past lives. If we can embrace this faith and concept, then whatever we encounter that cannot be overcome, solved, or rejected, we can face and accept with a sense of ease, without being adversely affected.

2. *Causes and conditions*: All phenomena arise because of the

coming together of many different causes and conditions, and they perish, also due to many different causes and conditions. Therefore, whenever we experience success, there is no need to be too excited and proud. Our achievements do not only depend on the effort of a single person, but also upon the coming together of many different causes and conditions, including time, space, and people. By the same token, when we encounter adversity and unfavorable situations, there is no need to be too upset. As a philosopher once said, "The darkest hour is just before the dawn." The arising and perishing of any phenomenon reflects the arising and perishing of its causes and conditions, so why feel upset or excited about it? If one can keep a peaceful and tranquil mind, one will enjoy good health and longevity.

3. *Compassion*: Ordinary people hope to be treated with compassion, but sometimes forget to treat others with compassion. After doing something wrong, most people would hope to be forgiven: "Please do not judge me against the standards of a sage!" But when others make a mistake, they tend to be relentlessly unforgiving: "You are supposed to do this right. Why are you doing it wrong?" This is lacking compassion. Compassion encompasses four principles: harmonizing one's own inner conflicts; having sympathy for people's ignorance; forgiving other people's mistakes; and caring about other people's pain and suffering. Especially important is to harmonize one's own inner conflicts. To have a peaceful and stable mind, one must act in accord with the law of cause and effect, as well as with causes and conditions. Only by having peace of mind is one really able to care for others with genuine compassion. If you sympathize with, forgive, and care for others, you can be assured to have a rather healthy mind.

Methods of Practice as an Approach

Here are two examples of methods that can be used to for mental balance.

1. *Buddha-name recitation*: Buddha-name recitation serves two purposes: first, when one recites the Buddha's name in order to gain rebirth in Amitabha Buddha's Pure Land, one may have hope in a permanent future and let go of one's troubles. Second, one will be able to transform one's mental problems: when the mind is out of balance, redirecting it to reciting and concentrating on a buddha's name helps to put aside the issue that is causing imbalance. Therefore I often encourage people: "When you are on the verge of losing your temper and scolding someone, instead, recite the name of Amitabha Buddha." The idea is to leave the problem to Amitabha Buddha.

2. *Sitting meditation*: The different methods of Chan meditation concentrate the scattered, unbalanced mind and stabilize it; as a result, scattered thoughts will disappear and mindfulness will persist. This is called entering concentration. In such a state of mind, you will not be afflicted by any other person or matter. Depending on the level of your concentration, you can further realize the wisdom of no-self, and that is enlightenment. With enlightenment, you can be sure to have a rather healthy mind. However, there is small enlightenment and big enlightenment. With small enlightenment, one may be free of problems in one's mind during the enlightenment, but once the state has passed, one will likely have problems again. Nonetheless, having experienced enlightenment, one will have a better idea how to deal with those problems. Therefore, small enlightenment is better than no enlightenment at all.

Chan: Peace Within and Without

Ukiah Sarwa Dharma, Laytonville, California, October 29, 1990.

Within and without the Mind

When we look inward and examine our mind, we often find that it reflects the external environment rather than the mind within. So, is the internal in opposition to the external? From the Buddhist perspective, the internal and the external are unified, not in opposition. As long as the mind within is pure and peaceful, the external world we see will also be pure and peaceful. However, most people feel greatly afflicted because there are many contradictions and conflicts between their mind within and the world without. If we could apply the Buddhist concepts and its methods of practice to harmonize the inside and the outside, then our body and mind would naturally become peaceful, happy, and at ease.

The Inner and Outer Worlds in Buddhist Perspective

The Buddhist Views of the Universe and of Life

Buddhism looks upon the universe as something created by the mind's inner activities. The outside world is a reflection of what the mind has created in the past because karma arises from the mind, and all phenomena are only the manifestation of mind. The small world of an individual is manifested by their own karma, and the external world arises due to the collective karma of all sentient beings. With ignorance and mental defilement as root causes, there arise the life and universe as a result. Vexations resulting from ignorance since time without beginning cause people to give rise to mental and physical conduct. The conduct of body and mind then bring about subsequent lives and existences. Upon obtaining a new life and existence, we again create new conducts of body and mind, without cease. This is owing to the fundamental instincts of aversion to suffering and seeking happiness. In this way—with cause leading to effect, and effect further giving rise to cause—life after life comes into being. This is the cycle of past, present, and future lives. These life phenomena originate from the ignorance and vexations within our mind. Due to inner vexations, people cannot remain at peace and as a result, the world outside also cannot be peaceful.

Buddhist Teaching of Internal and External Unity
A difference between ordinary beings and sages is that the mind of an ordinary being is impure with all sorts of defilements, while the mind of a sage is pure and undefiled. Ordinary beings perceive the world as impure because their minds are contaminated, whereas Buddhism perceives the world as the Mind Dharma of the spiritual aspect and the form dharma of the material aspect. Life and the universe are composed of mind dharma and form dharma. The mind dharma of spiritual aspect is the more essential because the mind is the dynamic power of life within, while the external aspect is the phenomenon of life. Between mind and form (the spiritual and the material), the phenomena of the universe and life come into being.

We have to rely on the spirit inside to be able to recognize the material world outside. Without the spirit, the material world does not exist for us. If we hope for world peace, then every one of us has to be at peace within. Most people only long for world peace without being able to attain peace within. In that case, there won't be peace in the world. Some people wish for world peace and therefore detest war; this indicates that their minds are not at peace. Two people argued with each other: one maintained that peace required no war; the other claimed that only with war can peace be achieved. When the dispute got vehement, the one who stood for war asked the other, "Since you stand for peace, why argue with me? Arguing goes against peace." People like this can be found everywhere.

To Reach Inner and Outer Harmony
The Reality That the World Is Full of Suffering

1. Our world is full of suffering caused by conflicts between the individual and the natural and the social environments. We witness conflicts between people: children fighting with parents, relatives and friends opposing, or even struggling against each other. This is very common. Have you ever seen married couples that never quarreled? When a married couple wrangles, they will blame each other for causing so much pain. A wife who often argues with her husband feels very troubled and came to me. When I asked her why she felt so troubled, she replied, "I don't have troubles myself. It's my husband who has brought me so much trouble."

2. The contradiction and conflict within the self manifest in several ways:

(1) Conflicts between giving and taking, gain and loss: when we have to make a choice between two equally important things we are always uncertain which one to choose, and after deciding we still worry about the gains or losses. One day, a student of mine asked me whether she should get married. I replied, "Fine. But why ask me?" She said, "I have three boyfriends, all very nice guys. I don't know which one I should marry. So, I came to ask for your advice." I

suggested that she chose one out of the three and bring him to see me. The next day, she brought this one boyfriend to see me. I told her immediately, "He's the best one." She answered, "But you haven't seen the other two. They're also very nice guys." I said, "Well, how about drawing lots to decide? But you should know that there must be a reason why you brought this one here first." So she ended up marrying the boyfriend she brought to see me.

(2) Conflicts between reason and emotion: most people usually handle other people's matters with reason, but handle their own with emotion. This is the reason why we say that those closely involved cannot see things as clearly as those outside. A renowned doctor always asked another doctor to treat his son when the son falls ill. Someone asked the doctor, "Since you're a famous doctor, why couldn't you treat your own son?" The doctor answered, "Just because he's my son, I'm afraid that I may fail to give him a diagnosis and treatment in a rational way, so that serious consequences may result. Other doctors don't have the ties of family affection to my son, so they'll be cool to rationally give my son a correct diagnosis and treatment." This shows that if we handle things with emotion, it is often easy to end up making mistakes.

(3) In the ordinary mind there are always conflicts between the previous and the subsequent thoughts: the thought of yesterday may change today. What we deem right yesterday may be regarded as wrong today; what we decide on today may have to be changed tomorrow. Some people change their mind so often that they begin to doubt their own decisions. With an unstable mind like this, one's life will also lack stability.

(4) A sense of loss of purpose and blind pursuits: a young man was always angry in my presence. So I asked him, "Why are you always

angry?" He answered, "This world has turned crazy! I'd just made a plan for something yesterday, and the circumstances already changed today, so that I can never catch up with the world. That's why I'm so angry." This person has no principled goal, and simply drifts with the currents of the environment, chasing after things blindly. When he finds the east better today, he goes east; when he finds the west better tomorrow, he hurriedly moves westward. Fleeting temptations in the environment cause his mind to be unsettled and chaotic, and he ends up losing stability and a sense of security.

Departing from Suffering and Attaining Happiness
This means inner and outer tranquility and peace.

Using Buddhist ideas to guide ourselves in our thoughts.

(1) The concept of cause and effect: all the good and bad things that we encounter have their causes; if they are not the causes we created in this life then they are causes we created in countless past lives. So we don't need to be proud when something good happens, or to feel annoyed or bitter when we undergo something bad. To promptly make an effort for improvement and progress is the best decision. Bodhidharma, the first patriarch of the Chan School, said: First, when we are confronted with adversity, we should accept the retribution due to karma. Since adversities arise from the causes we created in the past, we should accept the negative consequences now, just as when our hands are dirty, it is foolish to complain or argue about how they got dirty—we should just wash them. Second, when good things happen, we should accord with causes and conditions. Since positive results derive from the causes we created in the past, it is natural to accept positive results now. It is like withdrawing money from our own savings account; it would be foolish to think with great

joy that we got an unearned fortune.

(2) The concept of causes and conditions: nothing in the world can be achieved by one individual alone; everything arises from the combination of various factors. Once, the boss of a big company told me proudly, "There are thirty thousand employees in my company, and they all rely on me for their livelihood." I asked him, "If all your employees refused to work for you, or if you could not find enough qualified employees, would your company still exist?" This boss is an example of failing to understand the concept of causes and conditions. The environment in which we live arises from the coming together of various causes and conditions. As causes and conditions ceaselessly change, the resulting phenomena constantly change as well. So both favorable and unfavorable things are impermanent. Either way, there is no need to feel overly joyful or sorrowful. What is really important is to keep striving in a wholesome direction.

Achieving Inner Peace through Practice

There are many methods of practice, such as reciting the sutras or mantras, prostration, and chanting the holy name of a buddha or bodhisattva. Generally speaking, however, it is easiest for us to achieve inner peace through meditation. When doing sitting meditation, we should first have a correct sitting posture and use the breathing method to allow the whole body to become relaxed. We should use the method of harmonizing the mind to bring the scattered mind to concentration; from the concentrated mind we practice further, and advance to the unified mind where previous and subsequent thoughts are unified. So, there are three levels in the progress of reaching the unified mind:

(1) The unification of body and mind: at this time you are no

longer aware of the existence of your own body, and you feel very relaxed and easy.

(2) The unification of the inner and outer worlds: when you reach this state, you feel that the external environment is one with your body and mind. The grandest does not lie outside, and the most profound does not lie inside; at this moment, mind and environment are integrated into oneness—you and the universe are of the same root, you are one with all things. In this state, your mind is broad and all-inclusive, with a feeling of benevolence for all people and all beings. When you have this kind of experience, there is no distinction between good and bad, beautiful and ugly, in everything you perceive. Moreover, they are all so very lovely to you.

(3) The unification of the previous and subsequent thoughts: when you reach this state, the sense of time and the concept of space no longer exist because you perceive no difference between the previous and the next moments; this is what we call "entering samadhi." While immersed in concentration, there is no distinction between body, mind, world, time, and space for you, except the immediate, actual existence. For you, the whole universe is just an existence in its totality. After one comes out of concentration, one will still feel the unification of inner and outer for a period of time.

The Method of Investigating Chan
The Teaching of Vimalakirti
The *Vimalakirti Sutra* says, "As sentient beings are brought to spiritual maturity, a pure buddha-land is established." And it further says, "As our minds become pure, the pure buddha-land is realized." If we vow to help all sentient beings, we won't have enemies or adversaries, and as a result we will achieve both inner serenity and world peace. If one

does everything not for one's own sake, but for the sake of sentient beings, one will give rise to a compassionate mind. Those who have a compassionate mind will definitely accord with wisdom, and those who have wisdom will definitely accord with liberation, which makes them feel free and at ease.

The buddhas perceive our world as originally pure, and see all sentient beings as equals. When the minds of sentient beings are not calm, pure, but filled with defilements, they perceive the world as not tranquil and impure; and they also see sentient beings as unequal.

The Chan Method to Calm the Mind

The Chan School says, "The investigation of Chan is not a matter of training the legs." In other words, it is not necessary to just rely on sitting meditation to investigate Chan, and also that enlightenment doesn't always result from spiritual cultivation. As long as the mind has become settled and peaceful, all problems can be solved easily.

Before he became the Second Patriarch of the Chan School, Huike went to see First Patriarch Bodhidharma, and asked the master to help him pacify his mind. Bodhidharma said, "Bring me your mind, and I'll pacify it for you." Huike tried to find his mind but could not. Bodhidharma then said, "There, I've already pacified your mind for you." The mind is no other than our thoughts. Examining every single thought, we find that it either belongs to the past or to the future. The past is already gone and the future has yet to come, so we can never find the present thought.

Master Niutou Farong and the Fifth Patriarch Hongren practiced under the same master, the Fourth Patriarch, Daoxin. [Before he knew Niutou, Daoxin was sojourning, and he encountered Niutou, who was meditating in a cave.] When Daoxin asked Niutou what he was doing, the latter said he was contemplating his mind. Daoxin asked him, "Who is contemplating the mind? What mind is there [to be contemplated]?" Like Huike before him, Niutou could not find his mind either. Later on, Niutou did become enlightened when Daoxin spoke the Dharma to him.

In his *Platform Sutra*, Huineng said, "Not concerned about likes or dislikes, I sleep with my legs stretched out." When likes and dislikes do not concern you any more, you can stretch your legs far out and have a good sleep. This, however, does not mean that an enlightened person has nothing to do, but that there is nothing in his mind to bother him. For instance, Chan Master Yunyan asked the Eminent Master Baizhang, "For whom do you busy yourself all day long?" Baizhang replied, "I have nothing to do, so I busy myself solely for those who need my help."

If we can use Buddhist concepts and practice methods to calm and settle our mind, we would perceive the external world as definitely peaceful too. And we should further endeavor to help other people, enabling those who have karmic affinities with Buddhist teachings to achieve tranquility and peace, within and without. That way, the strife and discords in our world will lessen.

Chan: You, I, They

Kaohsiung Girls' Senior High School, Taiwan, March 7, 1988

After he became enlightened, a Chan master was so joyful that he danced gleefully. Someone asked him, "Why are you so joyful?" He replied, "It's only now I know that my nostrils point downwards."

One difference between unenlightened and enlightened people is that the former have discriminations, attachments, and vexations, as well as ideas of "you, I, and they." These are terms of reference that arise when we interact with people. The "I," in the center, being the core, is entangled among the "you" in the front and the "they" in the back. However, the crux of all problems is in the "I." In contrast, the *Diamond Sutra* says, "There is no form of self, of others, of sentient beings, or of a life span." In other words, you, I, and they do not exist.

Shakyamuni Buddha silently transmitted the wondrous mind of nirvana to Venerable Mahakashyapa, his foremost disciple, when before a large assembly, the Buddha held up a flower, and Mahakashyapa said nothing but just smiled. Tradition has it that Bodhidharma, the first patriarch of the Chan School, meditated facing a wall at the Shaolin Monastery of Mount Song for nine years without speaking. These stories illustrate that the true Chan cannot be put into words. Although what is expressed in words is by no means Chan, we still need to use language to introduce what Chan is.

What Is Chan?

Chan is Buddhadharma. The Chan that I understand is the teachings that Shyakyamuni Buddha spoke, and is a true expression of the doctrines of Buddhism. Yet, by using the method of Chan, one may derive experiences and benefits very directly and rapidly. Chan is not something to be talked about, but to be personally experienced—if it is only to be talked about with words, it is definitely not Chan.

Shortly before entering parinirvana, Shakyamuni Buddha said that although he spoke the Dharma for forty-nine years, he had never uttered a single word. In other words, the true Dharma is unspeakable. What can be expressed in words are just expedient teachings. When I point to the moon, my finger points to the truth of the moon being there, but my finger is not the moon itself. Similarly, if there were no expedient teachings to guide people to grasp the Buddhadharma, they would not be able to derive benefits from it.

Chan Is Separate from Words, Language, and Symbols

The Buddhadharma is inconceivable and unspeakable. "Inconceivable" means it is impossible to imagine with the reasoning mind; "unspeakable" means that it cannot be introduced, discussed, or explained with language. Even if you use billions of words, you would still not express Buddadharma in its completeness. Therefore, Chan patriarchs had a saying: "Speak a word, and you are way off the mark." They also said, "The moment you open your mouth, you're wrong. The moment you generate a thought, you've deviated from it." As long as one says any single thing, it is wrong.

A Chan disciple who, before getting enlightened, asked his master, "What is Buddhadharma?" The master would answer with words like, "a turnip in Nanjing," or "a robe made in Qing Province."

Another disciple asked, "What is Chan?"

His master said, "Have you eaten yet?"

The disciple replied, "Not yet." Having taken a meal, he came to ask again, "What is Chan?"

The master asked, "Have you washed your bowl and chopsticks?"

The disciple answered, "Not yet."

The Master said, "Go wash them!"

Having washed his utensils, the disciple came and asked again, "What is Chan?"

Everyone does their daily routine of putting on clothes, eating meals, washing dishes, sleeping, and so on. In doing these things, if there is a mind of attachment to the self, then everything one perceives is not Chan; but if one puts down attachment to the self, everything is Chan.

Chan Is of the World, yet Separate from the World

Buddhadharma tells us that the world is illusory, but because we do not understand this, we give rise to all kinds of attachment, and generate numerous vexations. The Buddha taught that while humans cannot avoid birth, aging, sickness, and death, we can use Buddhadharma to teach people how to resolve the sufferings of birth, aging, sickness, and death, and thus become free. The pervasiveness of suffering has resulted in great misunderstanding, as some people come to loathe birth and death, thinking that by committing suicide and escaping from the world, one can be rid of suffering. In fact, not only does this not rid oneself of suffering, but adds suffering to suffering.

The method for relieving suffering that the Buddha taught is Buddhadharma. By removing the attachments in our mind and eliminating the vexations, we will not be afraid of the cycle of birth and death. Only then is it liberation and departure from suffering. The Sixth Patriarch's *Platform Sutra* says, "Buddhadharma is found in the world; and enlightenment is not separate from the world. If one departs from the world to pursue bodhi, it's just like trying to find a hare with horns." Therefore, departing from the world does not amount to departing from the sea of suffering. There will not be any Buddhadharma to be sought if one departs from the world.

In this world, there are people who forget their own difficulties and suffering, instead, setting their mind on alleviating the suffering and hardships of sentient beings. These are people who cultivate the bodhisattva path; they also suffer, starve, are harmed, insulted, or mistreated; however, sentient beings rely on and trust them. To help sentient beings depart from suffering and obtain happiness, bodhisattvas are not self-centered, nor do they feel that they are suffering. Therefore, one who generates bodhi-mind perceives the world differently from those who do not follow Buddhist teachings.

Buddhadharma and worldly dharmas are neither integrated nor separate, neither existent nor non-existent, and neither identical nor different. A bodhisattva knows suffering but does not perceive it as suffering. However, suffering does in fact exist in the world. To ordinary people, worldly dharmas and Buddhadharma are experienced as separate, but for bodhisattvas who have generated bodhi-mind, whatever worldly dharmas they encounter are not apart from Buddhadharma.

"You, I, and They" Are Worldly Dharmas

"Worldly" refers to the phenomena of time and space. Time goes from the past to the present, and extends to the future; it is the cycle of cause and effect, and the uninterrupted continuation of cause and effect. Space is a boundlessly vast realm from which arise mutual relations among people, things, and objects. These relations are inconceivably complex in terms of cause and effect, as well as in terms of causes and conditions.

Some lay Buddhists tell me things like, "What did I do in the past lives so that I suffer so much in this life? In my family, spouses and children have conflict and wrangle with each other; in society, unpleasant things arise between me and my relatives, friends, colleagues, and classmates. What evils had I done after all?"

I tell them, "The retribution that you receive now all result from the fact that you had done the same things to other people in the past. From time without beginning, due to greed, anger, ignorance, and blind impulses, you created the evil karmas of killing, stealing, sexual misconduct, and speaking falsehood. The evil karmas become mutually entangled one lifetime after another, so that the causes and effects are complicated and inconceivable, and the causes and conditions are also inconceivable."

Therefore, as long as we practice Buddhadharma, and put down the self-centered "I," if we can dissolve the boundaries between "you, I, and they," then gradually, our evil karmas will diminish, our vexations will decrease, and our suffering will lessen. When we are not so vexed with suffering, we will not feel as if we are receiving retribution, and this world will be just like a buddha's pure land. Since the environment has changed with our mind, we see people as good, and all things that occur will be good. This way, whether we find ourselves in a buddha-land, in the human realm, or in the hells, we will always remain calm and composed. To be thus is Chan.

"You, I, and They" Is Chan

Shakyamuni Buddha appeared in the world to deliver sentient beings, but people in this world have attachments, vexations, and suffering; that is why they need and value the Buddhadharma. According to the sutras, in the continent of Uttarakuru on the north side of Mount Sumeru, people obtain food and clothes as they wish, effortlessly. Moreover, they live a long life; but there is no Buddhadharma there. The sutras also say, "In the heavens of the desire realm, the beings there have the heavenly blessings and feel no suffering, and they do not need the Buddhadharma, so they have no idea of spiritual practice. Since they have no opportunities to practice, it is impossible for them to achieve buddhahood. In contrast, in the human realm, sentient beings—"you, I, and they"—experience suffering. As a result buddhas are able to practice and achieve buddhahood, the pure lands of buddhas can be established, and bodhisattvas and arhats engage in deliverance and teaching. This benefits themselves and people. Although the "I" is not something to be considered good, without it, we would not know to learn and practice Buddhism. Therefore, spiritual practice should begin with the "I."

Vexation Is the Source for Generating Wisdom

The *Platform Sutra* says, "Within the dark house of the afflictions, one should continually give rise to the sun of wisdom. The false comes, and afflictions arrive; the correct comes, and the afflictions are eliminated." We follow Buddhism in order to remove vexations and attain wisdom. Nevertheless, we should not detest vexations. Without vexations, we would not seek wisdom, or know what wisdom is. When we become aware that our current vexations are vexations, they are not so vexing any more. However, only through practice can we become aware of our vexations. A practitioner should be alert at all times to the undercurrents of vexation that arise and perish, and pay attention so as not be affected by them.

Someone said to me, "When I meditate, I often have wandering thoughts, and among them, there often appear bad thoughts. And bad thoughts also emerge when I recite the sutras or the Buddha's name. Instead of doing something good ain't I committing more wrongdoing?"

I told him, "Your karma is diminishing, your vexations are lessening, and your wisdom is growing gradually. That's why you can become aware that you have generated deluded thoughts when reciting the sutras or the Buddha's names." Only when we have pure, right mindfulness can we discover that we have the erroneous thoughts caused by vexations. Practitioners need not fear having vexations, wandering thoughts, or erroneous thoughts. With our self as the center that takes control, when we become aware of erroneous thoughts, the erroneous thoughts do not exist any more. Vexations definitely have their objects, which are either "you" or "them." No matter whether the "you" and "them" are things or people, if there are no "you" or "them," it is impossible for us to have vexations. Therefore, when we become aware of vexations emerging, we should thank the people, things, and objects that cause us to generate vexations, because they are helping us to practice.

Chan Is Non-discriminating Mind

The saying "vexation is Chan" refers to the fact that one has already been practicing or has already generated wisdom. Because of wisdom, we know that we have vexations; this is Chan. If we do not practice, we won't know that we have vexations, and wisdom will not arise. In that case, vexations would remain vexations.

The Sixth Patriarch's *Platform Sutra* says: "Allowing neither false nor correct to be used. In purity, one arrives at the remainderless. Bodhi fundamentally is the self-nature. Activate the mind, and all is false. Purify the mind within the false. Always be on the right path and you will be free of the three hindrances."

Huineng is describing the state after enlightenment. If we deeply cultivate worldly meditative practice until we achieve unity of body and mind—where there is no longer "you, I, and they"—then that is worldly concentration. Although the mind of vexation does not emerge, the "I" still exists somewhere between "being" and "non-being." If we become aware of "non-being," this means there is still a trace of "being." When we are conscious of the unity of all things, this means there is still a trace of "non-being" that is distinct from the "I."

The Chan enlightenment of Buddhadharma differs from worldly concentration in that in Chan enlightenment, one is clearly aware of the "you, I, and them," rather than being "blind" to them. However, one does not have the relative mind of attachment.

Seeking wisdom and eliminating vexations are causes for increasing vexations, because there is an "I" that seeks wisdom and wants to eliminate vexations. The Chan method is to dissolve this "I," clearing it away completely; only then is it the manifestation of wisdom. Hence, whether we generate a pure mind or a vexed mind, they are all deluded mind.

Therefore, if practitioners do not loathe the mind of vexation, then the mind of vexations will diminish little by little. The saying that vexation is bodhi, and nirvana is samsara gives practitioners the guidance that one should not pursue bodhi, nor should one reject vexations; if we know that we have vexations, then we are practicing; and we also know that vexations themselves are the cause for generating bodhi.

Chan: Many, One, and Nothingness

Kaohsiung Girls' Senior High School, Taiwan, March 8, 1988.

Today, I will talk about the concepts of many, one, and nothingness from the Chan point of view. "Many" means innumerable; "one" means all beings are a unity; "nothingness" means that there is not a thing in front of one, and being without attachments.

Chan Is All Dharmas

"All dharmas" refers to all existent phenomena; in contemporary terms they are all the natural, physical, psychological, and physiological objects and events that exist. All that we can see with eyes, hear with ears, make contact with the body, or think with the mind, are dharmas. Dharma (with upper case "D") also refers to the laws or principles whose operation results in all varieties of phenomena, and of the activities of people, things, and matter.

Chan is the Buddhadharma, and it is not separate from worldly dharmas. The Buddhadharma teaches people to experience all dharmas by living in a solid, grounded way, purifying their minds, so that they will awaken to the fact that all dharmas arise from causes and conditions, and therefore, are fleeting and changing. Knowing that all dharmas derive from causes and conditions, we should strive unremittingly to improve ourselves and our environment with a vigorous spirit. We also strive to improve causes and conditions and engage in spiritual practice so that buddhahood is attainable. Therefore, rather than being passive, Buddhism is quite proactive and engaged in making changes through diligent work.

Dharmas can be illusory dharmas or true dharmas. Illusory dharmas refer to "many" and "dual" dharmas that result from changing conditions in space and time. Through causation, these dharmas form the myriad kinds of phenomena. Because we do not fully recognize that phenomena arise from causes and conditions and are forever changing, we think that phenomena are enduring. Therefore, by pursuing, possessing, and rejecting, we give rise to "the many." If we know that all dharmas are illusory, it would be easy to see through their emptiness, let go of them, and give them away. In this way, we would not be bothered by, escape from, or attach to phenomena—we would return to our true nature.

In some religions and philosophies, truth consists of certain principles or deities that remain forever unchanged. However, Buddhism regards what are called "truth" or "God" as still attachments. Buddhadharma says that "there is not a single dharma to be obtained," and that no matter whether it is truth, true God, or any dharma, none is real, and all belong to people's delusion and attachment.

However, to practice Buddhadharma or Chan, we still must begin from a standpoint of delusion and the discrimination of "many." From there we make progress through stages to unification of the internal and external, and then we will be able to reach the level of "non-being" (empty of self). There is a famous Chan saying: "All dharmas return to one; to where does the one return?" That all dharmas return to one is a religious experience and a philosophical theory as well. "All dharmas" is physical and concrete while "returning to one" is metaphysical—oneness is the common ground to which religions and philosophies return.

Religious devotees see phenomena as the creations of gods, and these phenomena would still return to gods eventually. Philosophers see all physical and concrete things as all appearing from the cosmic principles or laws. Since all things and matters are inseparable from the cosmic principles or laws, they are unified phenomena.

However, there seems to be a paradox in the reasoning of philosophers and religious devotees. Since there is one, there must be two; in other words, oneness cannot exist independently. For example, when we draw a circle on the blackboard to represent unity, this "one" does not exist independently, but the blackboard and the circle together are actually two. If God is unity then where does this unity exist? If the principle is oneness, then where does this oneness exist? It exists in opposition to non-being, and since this opposition is dualistic, we have two, not one.

Chan: One Is No Other than Many

Someone asked Chan Master Zhaozhou, "All dharmas return to one; where does one return to?" Zhaozhou replied, "I had a robe made in Qingzhou which weighs 7 jins (about 3.5 kilograms)." Master Zhaozhou's new robe was of course a dharma, and his answer signified that no phenomenon is separate from oneness—all dharmas are precisely one, and one also comes from all dharmas. The Daoists say, "One generates two, two generates three, and three generates all things." What does "one generates two" mean? In fact, one is generated from two and is not perfect. Oneness is inseparable from the many; it is the same as all dharmas.

Unless one is a religious devotee or philosopher, it would seem unsociable, eccentric, and too abstract if one tries to find the truth of "oneness" or Godhead behind phenomena. However, Chan only teaches us to live as ordinary people, do what people do, and say what people say.

Chan: Many Are No Other than One

Master Zhaozhou once entered the Chan Hall to expound the Dharma and made three remarks. First, he said: "A gold buddha trespasses no furnace, a wooden buddha trespasses no fire, and a clay-made buddha trespasses no water, whereas the true Buddha sits inside." Whether a buddha statue is made of gold, wood, or clay, it stands for the Buddha. A buddha statue is a medium for spiritual practice in which one pays homage or makes offerings. When one's practices reach a certain level one realizes that all dharmas are not real, and that the true buddha is not without but within—a pure mind is buddha. When one reaches this level, it is to return to oneness from the myriad dharmas, from the external to the buddha-nature within. However, if we are attached to the idea that there is a buddha-nature or pure mind then it is still a vexation.

Zhaozhou's second remark was: "Bodhi, nirvana, true suchness, and buddha-nature are all clothes that cover the body." Zhaozhou is saying that buddha-nature, bodhi, and nirvana are also vexations, just like having to wear clothes. If true suchness and buddha-nature are like clothes then what is our body? If bodhi and nirvana are still vexations then what is there that has no vexations?

Buddhists wish to be liberated from the cycle of birth and death, realize bodhi, awaken the buddha-nature, and enter into nirvana. But if one clings to ideas of true suchness or buddha-nature, this is attachment as well as greed; one has not departed from "returning to the one from the many" and to "return to non-being from the one." Therefore, even those reaching the highest religious level of returning to the truth or Godhead have yet to attain liberation. As for philosophy, reaching the state of returning to the ultimate idea is not liberation either, and there is still attachment.

Zhaozhou's third remark was: "Existing on the ground of true principle, where is there a place to attach to? When the one-mind does not arise, all dharmas are without fault." "One-mind" refers to the thought that is unified, unchanging, always in the same state. When one-mind is no longer generated, then there is no-thought; only when there is no-thought does one depart from illusion and achieve true liberation. Therefore, those who harbor the idea that they are liberated, or are on the way to liberation, have yet to truly attain liberation.

It is not easy to attain even one-mind. To go beyond one-mind is to have not even a single thought, and those who do have great freedom and great wisdom. Such people live amidst myriad dharmas, see myriad dharmas, and act in accordance with myriad dharmas, yet they are not hindered, and do not generate even a single thought.

Chan Is Not Many, Not One, and Not Nothingness

In the beginning stage of practice, people sometimes see a vision of the Buddha while reciting his name or prostrating to him, but even this is already quite difficult. The purpose of the Pure Land School is to "see" the Buddha, and one may also see a variety of forms while practicing Chan. The *Diamond Sutra* says, "Each and every form is an illusion." Therefore, when you see visions during the process of practice, do not attach to them.

Chan Master Zhaozhou said, "Do not dwell in a place where there are buddhas; hasten from a place where there is no buddha." Whether there are buddhas or not, we should not be attached to them. Most people tend to think of buddhas as being in the temples,

Buddha halls, or in the Western Pure Land. Buddha statues in the temples or Buddha halls are images, not real buddhas. It is also an expediency to speak of buddhas residing in the Western Pure Land. A passage of the *Amitabha Sutra* reads, "At dawn, beings in the Pure Land always hold within their clothing numerous wondrous flowers to make offerings to ten thousand billion buddhas in other lands, and then return to their own land within the time of a meal." What we call the Western Pure Land of Utmost Bliss is not necessarily in the west of the buddha-lands. Rather, it shows that all lands are in the Western Pure Land of Utmost Bliss and are not separated from that place. Sentient beings who have not yet attained great liberation rely on the power of Amitabha Buddha's vows to guide them towards rebirth in the Western Pure Land.

One buddha is no other than all buddhas. Depending on their various vows, buddhas dwell in their respective lands as expedient means for helping and transforming sentient beings, but there are not really such worlds. Although there are not really the lands of buddhas, we cannot flatly deny that there is no Western Pure Land and no buddhas. Therefore, whether we are attached to all the buddhas in the ten directions or to the one buddha essence, none of them are real. For those who are attached to the ideas of "many" and "one," it is like having obtained the Buddha's robes but not the Buddha's body.

In the sutras that introduce Avalokiteshvara Bodhisattva (Chn. *Guanyin Pusa*) are accounts that after Amitabha Buddha passes into parinirvana, Avalokiteshvara will become a buddha in the Western Pure Land of Utmost Bliss. This shows that when Amitabha Buddha's vows and conditions for delivering sentient beings are fulfilled, the Western Pure Land will not necessarily continue. There would be no difference from the Heavens of other religions if one attaches to the permanent existence of the Western Pure Land. People holding an eternalist view err in attaching to the existence of an eternal buddha, or of all buddhas in the ten directions. On the other hand, the view that there is no Western Pure Land, and no such thing as one or all buddhas in the ten directions, is neither Buddhadharma or Chan. Rather, it is the nihilistic view of atheism and non-buddhist schools of thought.

Whether we attach to the existence or non-existence of buddhas or buddha-lands, either view is mistaken and vexation. However, those beginning the Buddhist path should believe in the buddhas and buddha-lands. When they have reached a certain level of practice with vexations gradually diminished, attachments to existence or non-existence as well as vexations, should all be let go. Only then can they illuminate the mind and see their nature.

Chan Is Giving Rise to the Mind without Abiding

The *Diamond Sutra* says, "Without abiding in anything, give rise to mind." No-abiding is having no attachment, either to the many, to the one, or to nothingness. The world perceived by those who have not practiced, or who have just begun to practice, is "the many." As for those who have practiced to a considerable degree, they are at the level of oneness.

As far as religion is concerned, when those who cultivate worldly concentration attain oneness, it is at least one of the four formless concentrations (of the formless realm). Within the unified state there are three levels: unity of body and mind, unity of the internal and the external, and the unity of time and space. When we reach the unity of body and mind we feel that the body and mind do not exist anymore, and vexations are gone. When we reach the unification of the internal and external, the "self" is unified with people, things, and matters without. We would then generate a loving heart towards all people and even plants, which is universal love and benevolence for all humanity and all beings. When we reach the unification of time and space, time and space do not exist for us. The unification of time and space includes these four states: limitless space, limitless consciousness, nothingness, and neither thought nor no-thought.

For practitioners, compassion is of three kinds: compassion based on awareness of the suffering of sentient beings, compassion based on awareness of the true nature of phenomena, and unconditional compassion. When our practice reaches the state of all dharmas returning to one, we would have the compassionate aspiration to share the same body with all sentient beings, and vow to deliver all sentient beings. Next, we attain the compassion conditioned by dharmas. Finally, being able let go of even oneness is the great bodhisattva's unconditional compassion.

Someone once told me that they had attained liberation and enlightenment. I will not comment on whether this person was actually liberated or enlightened; what is important is whether one still has attachments. Being attached to vexations is to abide in them, and being attached to enlightenment and liberation is also to abide in vexations. "Non-abiding" means having no attachments and no vexations; it is the true liberation. Those who have truly attained liberation have no attachments in the mind and still generate the mind of wisdom; they deliver sentient beings as conditions arise and teach according to people's spiritual capacities.

A famous Chan patriarch said, "I eat when hungry and sleep when tired." This shows that enlightened people still lead an ordinary life as ordinary people, and will not do something unconventional or act in eccentric or strange ways.

Chan Master Zhaozhou had a saying: "A bright pearl on the palm shows a foreigner when a foreigner comes, and shows a Chinese when a Chinese comes." The bright pearl itself is not tinged with subjectivity. The mind is likened to a bright pearl; the pure mind holds no preconceived ideas when teaching sentient beings, and gives sentient beings different kinds of relief according to their needs. Zhaozhou also said, "When people of the highest attainment come, I receive them while sitting on the Chan dais; when people of the intermediate attainment come, I receive them by coming down from the Chan dais; and when people of the low attainment come, I greet them at the monastery's front gate." Those with superior spiritual capacity have steadfast faith in the Three Jewels; those with secondary spiritual capacity understand the Buddhadharma, but have insufficient faith; and those with inferior spiritual capacity have no understandings of the Three Jewels. We receive and teach them in different ways to strengthen their faith or to make them joyful and uphold the Three Jewels.

The Practice of Chan

The Sixth Patriarch's *Platform Sutra* says, "Chan teaching has no-thought as the principle, no-form as the essence, and non-abiding as the foundation." When the mind is not contaminated by external factors and not affected by the external environment, one reaches the state of no-thought. Being detached from all external forms is no-form. A monk asked Chan Master Zhaozhou, "Does a dog have buddha-nature?" The Chan master replied, "*Wu*" ("no" or "without"). The monastic asked again, "Beings from the highest buddhas to the lowest ants all have the buddha-nature. Why, then, doesn't a dog have it?" Having a consciousness which manifests their karma, sentient beings discriminate and attach; therefore, they think that buddha-nature is something that can be acquired. For those who have attained enlightenment, they are free of such attachments. In order to eliminate the questioner's attachment to the buddha-nature, the master replied, "No." The purpose of Chan practice lies in non-being, yet without being attached to non-being.

The Method of Chan Practice

According to a Chan proverb, there are three stages in practice. First, we see "mountains as mountains." For example, when we meditate, recite the Buddha's name or a mantra, or make prostrations to the Buddha, we go from a mind with numerous wandering thoughts flying around, to a mind concentrated on one point. The second stage is to see "mountains not as mountains." Here, we can investigate a *huatou* so as to give rise to a ball of doubt, and when we shatter that ball of doubt, we go from oneness to non-being. The third stage is to again see "mountains as mountains." We do not attach either to the one or to the many, and we also put down non-being; we return to the practical world and live like other ordinary people while delivering as many sentient beings as possible.

Discrimination and Non-discrimination

Nung Chan Monastery, Taiwan, January 31, 1988

Discrimination is the mental activity which makes it possible for us to know about the world and to act in it. Indeed, humanity would be in chaos if we were not able to discriminate between things and between acts. However, the Dharma teaches us to transform the mind of discrimination and attachment to a mind of non-discrimination and as a result, liberation. Afflictions arise from discrimination, and due to afflictions, we are in bondage to the cycle birth and death (samsara). As a result, we transmigrate through endless lifetimes. As we keep cycling in samsara, we become mutually indebted to sentient beings. Since time without beginning, we have created countless relationships with sentient beings, leading to feelings of both gratitude and resentment.

Some would think it is good to have relationships. Yes, it is good indeed if it is a good affinity, and even better if the affinity is formed through sharing of the Dharma. However, bad affinity is not good. Thus, the fact that we encounter one another, regardless of good or bad relations from the past, shows that we have affinity. Why would some people say, "Life always goes against our wishes"? This happens when we have created more bad affinity than good affinity. So, when people with bad affinity meet, most likely one would "push" and the other would "kick." But with some other people, you would help me, and I would thank you. This is because people use their discriminating mind to differentiate "good" from "bad" and because they form gratitude and resentment towards each other.

However, it is not necessarily bad to have a discriminating mind. The progress of civilization, the quality of life, and the betterment of the environment, all require self-interested discrimination to benefit self and others. To protect ourselves in the long term, and for our greater benefit, we must ensure the health and success of every person and of every matter that is relevant to us. This means that besides our own body and mind, the stake of every member and everything in our family, clan, society, nation, and the world are inseparable from us. We start from ourselves as the center, and gradually extend ourselves to benefit others, all human beings, and in the end, all sentient beings.

However, the goal of practicing Dharma is to achieve a mind free of discrimination. According to the *Diamond Sutra*, non-discrimination is the state where one does not harbor ideas of a self, of others, of sentient beings, or of a lifespan. Self, others and sentient beings, are concepts of existing in space, while lifespan is a concept of time experienced as a life cycle. Everything involving concepts of space and time is discrimination; discrimination gives rise to attachment, and with attachment we cannot be free from affliction. Attachments —whether big or small, partial or whole, to things nonexistent or existent, true or false—are all discriminations. The illusory thoughts existing within time and space and all their attachments, are none other than affliction itself.

The "self" results from an illusory mind differentiating between the "small self" and "big self." The self-centered ego is the small self, while the big self includes all human beings, extending to all sentient beings in the universe. Usually, the small self is regarded as selfishness; while the big self is regarded as universal love, or selflessness. Although the big self is mightier than the small self, it still is not separate from discriminative attachments; it is still within the mundane world of endless arising, perishing, and change. The big self is a concept for philosophers, artists, and spiritual practitioners—it is a kind of recognition and experience. But whether this big self is a material, mental, or spiritual phenomenon, it is still transient and illusory. Therefore the formlessness advocated by Buddhism–[that neither small self nor big self exists]—could help us go from discrimination and attachment to bliss and liberation.

Some practitioners may think they have achieved no-self, but at most have only released themselves from the small self and experienced the big self. Even though they have had the experience of "attaining oneness with everything in the universe," they are still in the three realms (desire, form, and formless) of discriminative attachment.

The no-self taught in the Dharma has two levels: one is the "emptiness of the self" of the arhat, in which one is liberated from the three realms and enters nirvana. Such beings have renounced the individual small self but cannot see the holistic big self. They perceive worldly phenomena as illusory, arising and perishing with causes and conditions; they view nirvana—the stage beyond the worldly that neither arises nor perishes—as the ultimate reality. They do not attach to the big self as self, but take the nirvana that neither arises nor ceases as the self. The second level is the "emptiness of all dharmas" as taught in the Mahayana school, which takes as ultimate reality neither worldly causes and conditions, nor the nirvana beyond the world.

From the standpoint of Mahayana Buddhism, the nirvana of the arhats is also not necessarily permanent. Although beings in nirvana are liberated from afflictions and from birth and death, they should still take a further step to evolve from the small vehicle to the great vehicle; that is, from the Hinayana view to that of the Mayahana. Only then may they attain the ultimate and achieve buddhahood. Therefore, Mahayana Buddhism teaches us that there is no need to avoid and fear the transmigration of birth and death in the three realms of existence. As long as one faces the reality of birth and death in the three realms without attachment, one can remain in the realm of birth and death without being trapped in ensuing afflictions. The ability of being in the cycle of birth and death without being afflicted by the sufferings of birth and death is true liberation.

One who has achieved buddhahood would not escape the world, meaning that "one neither abides in birth and death, nor in nirvana." This is what we call "the great nirvana." Not abiding in birth and death means one is not bonded to birth and death. Not abiding in nirvana means one can manifest freely in the birth-and-death environment of sentient beings. Thus, bodhisattvas are at once in the world as well as beyond it; they do not become bodhisattvas after escaping from reality. Great bodhisattvas are in the world without being afflicted by the world. After achieving buddhahood, they will be with all sentient beings in the Dharma Realm; as long as there is still a sentient being, they will be there.

Right Path and Evil Path

Zhong Xing Hall, Taichung, Taiwan, August 17, 1988

Today I want to discuss what Buddhism means by "the right path" and "the evil path." Is there an evil path in today's society? Please do not mistakenly think that "evil path" necessarily means something that is extremely bad. That is not necessarily the case. I will introduce today's topic under five headings: (1) definition of the path, (2) definition of the right path; (3) definition of the evil path; (4) clear distinctions of right and evil in various aspects, (5) non-duality versus clear distinction between right and evil.

Definition of "Path"

Common Meanings of "Path" in Chinese

At a simple level, a path is a road or passageway to walk or travel on, that is open to anyone. "Path" can also refer to a method, technique, and skill, with which one can serve others and make a living; that is what we call "livelihood." In Chinese philosophy, the Path refers to the source of all phenomena in the universe, which is termed "noumenon." It is also referred to as "god." In ancient Chinese texts there are many references to deities, and there are also references to "god" as the metaphysical principle of the path. What most people speak of as the "common principle" refers to a law that is constant and steady, and which represents a law of nature. Thus, in the philosophical sense, the Path (Way or Dao) is the source of all phenomena in the universe.

Path as Defined by Buddhist Philosophy

In Buddhism, the Path refers to the principle or method of cultivating spiritual practice. The Path may also refer to the results of spiritual practice, such as the completion of the path, accomplishing the bodhi-path [as a bodhisattva], realizing the bodhi-fruit through enlightenment, and buddhahood. The way and principle for spiritual practice is discussed in several Buddhist texts. As the *Great Treatise on the Perfection of Wisdom* (Skt. *Mahaprajnaparamita Shastra*) puts it, "The Path means a single path that leads all the way to nirvana." In the *Abhidharma Treatise* (Skt. *Abhidharmakosha*), the path means the way of nirvana—one can achieve nirvana with the methods and principles of practice.

The way to nirvana can be leveled in three stages: (1) that of the human and heavenly realms, (2) the two vehicles [of shravakas and *pratyekabuddhas*], and (3) the bodhisattva. Most people regard Buddhism as renouncing the world, thinking that the purpose of practicing Buddhism is to achieve nirvana and be liberated from birth and death. Actually, in terms of Theravada Buddhism, one cannot achieve nirvana by simply paying no mind to the human world. Furthermore, Mahayana Buddhism advocates transcending the world by engaging in the world. Indeed, transcending the world has to be based on first fulfilling human morality; only then can transcendence be achieved. It is impossible to enter nirvana without living up to society's standards for a human being.

Therefore, Buddhist practice must start with meeting the standards of humanity. After that, one achieves the higher standard of ascending to the heavenly realms, and beyond that, transcending to the level of leaving behind birth-and-death, and eventually, entering nirvana. Only when one has the ability to enter nirvana can one really practice the bodhisattva path in the most engaged manner. So, spiritual practice should begin within the human realm. Even when one has the ability to enter nirvana, one should still return to the human world to universally deliver sentient beings. That is the true purpose of Buddhism.

As mentioned in the *Great Treatise on the Perfection of Wisdom*, there are four kinds of path: the path of the human and heavenly realms, the path of two vehicles, the path of bodhisattva, and the path of a buddha. If one aspires to attain buddhahood one must start with and practice the bodhisattva path. However, this does not mean rejecting the Hinayana path. Hinayana cultivation must be based on the path of human and heavenly realms, which is the foundation for all the paths.

As humans, we are concerned about matters in the human world. However, there are many things in the human world that are undesirable and difficult to solve. Therefore, people admire the heavenly state, which is more prosperous and easeful than the human realm. Living in this human world, we care about things associated with humans, and it is natural and normal for people to long for heaven.

China was a nation highly developed in humanism, and Confucianism is centered on human matters. The Chinese traditionally have no objection to spirits and deities, but did not especially study them. Western societies also value human living, but there are wars, death, and various pains and sufferings in the human world; therefore people long for heaven. Both Eastern and Western societies are concerned about the issues of the human world; at most they may long for heaven. However, pursuits that go beyond attaining heaven are only found in Buddhism, which originated in India.

Today, we are mostly concerned with life in the real world, and not many people are really that interested in the prospect of ascending to heaven. Ideally, it is best that one has a joyful, happy, and satisfactory life, and then ascend to the heaven, or gain rebirth in the Pure Land. For Buddhists, this is a correct attitude. Indeed, the Buddha taught the Dharma to enable people to live a harmonious and peaceful life. Liberation from pain, suffering, and affliction should therefore start with life in this human world.

Since human life is most essential, we approach Buddhadharma from the standpoint of humanity. If one fails to live appropriately as a human, one will not be able to enter the Hinayana path. If one does not even want to cultivate human blessings in the present life, one will definitely not be able to ascend to the heaven, let alone enter the Hinayana path.

Definition of "Right Path"

The "right path" can be understood from the point of view of worldly knowledge and from the perspective of Buddhism.

Three Aspects of the Right Path in Worldly Knowledge

1. *Wholesome customs and habits*: that which benefits the public and brings peace and harmony to people is the right path.

2. *Philosophy based on reason*: a humanistic philosophy that treats people with dignity is the right path. Any philosophy that treats humans [and animals] as objects to be used and exploited, or as subjects to be governed and controlled, is not the right path.

3. *Religion advocating a loving heart*: a religion based on rationality shall encourage wholesome deeds. Therefore all rational religions should be the right path.

Right Path from the Buddhist Perspective

From the Buddhist perspective Right Path can be seen as methods of cultivation and principles for practicing.

1. *The path and methods of spiritual cultivation*: Worldly Dharma can be divided into three types: that which craves the world, that which renounces the world, and that which engages in the world. One who treads on the path of human and heavenly realms enjoys being in this world and longs to ascend to heaven to receive heavenly blessings; this attitude actually represents craving for worldly existence. When one is reluctant to leave behind the world while pursuing heavenly bliss, it is still craving. As we often say, wholesome deeds result in good karmic rewards and unwholesome deeds bring bad karmic retribution. Therefore, it is good to believe in the law of cause and effect for fear of karmic retribution. However, it is still craving to do good and create good karma in order to gain worldly blessings and heavenly bliss. But if one cultivates human and heavenly merit and abides by society's morals—without craving the world or the heavens—then one will indeed be deserving of heaven, and one will enter the level of transcending the world.

To transcend the world, one needs to practice the Eightfold Noble Path, which are the eight ways of living in accordance with Buddhadharma. They include the bodily, verbal, and mental aspects. That is, one should abstain from unwholesome speech, unwholesome actions, and unwholesome thoughts. One should not acquire livelihood by means that harm others and oneself. The most important thing is to have the right view. One's standard of behavior has to be based on Buddhadharma, namely, the Buddha's teachings.

A foundation of cultivating concentration and wisdom is also required. Many people regard sitting meditation as the only way to cultivate concentration, but reciting the Buddha's name, doing prostrations, and reciting sutras are also methods to cultivate concentration. However, reciting the Buddha's name with a scattered mind does not help one gain concentration; only by reciting the Buddha's name with an attentive mind can one achieve concentration. And only when the mind is stable and calm can one give rise to wisdom. The purpose of reading the sutras and studying Buddhadharma is to use the Buddha's wisdom to help our practice, so that we can generate wisdom and attain enlightenment. Only by attaining enlightenment can one transcend the three realms, leave behind birth-and-death, and enter nirvana.

In Buddhism, the purpose of truly transcending the world is to engage oneself in the world. Without transcending the world as a precondition, one cannot engage in the world truly and thoroughly. Therefore, a bodhisattva must transcend worldliness before committing to engaging in the world. This is transcending the world.

One must strive to free the mind from attachment, from craving for the world while still living among sentient beings and delivering them, without exception. This is the bodhisattva path and also the path to buddhahood, which is true and genuine engagement in the world.

2. *The principle of practice*: we practice Buddhadharma because we are not living freely, at ease and with satisfaction. Our environment, body, and mind bring us many afflictions and troubles. Therefore, we long for a solution to these problems, or what Buddhism refers to as the causes of our suffering. There are some people who, throughout their lives, never realize what suffering means, and think that there is not much suffering in this world. Nonetheless, most people find that their life—from birth to death—is filled with hardship and

difficulties. The other day I met a boy of nine and I asked him if he was happy. He said he was not happy. I asked him, "What is making you unhappy?" He said, "My mom scolds me; my brother bullies me; and my sister hits me."

I met a girl of 19 whose parents have very high social status and very good careers. They have a happy family and she is very much loved by her parents.

I asked her, "You must be very happy, aren't you? You have a nice car to ride, live in a fancy house, and get to enjoy great food. You have everything you want, don't you?"

But she said, "Master, I feel I am suffering a great deal."

I asked, "What are you suffering from?"

She said, "The most suffering is studying."

Then I told her, "Use your time well to study. When you finish your studies you'll be happy."

She said, "Not necessarily. I can see that my parents are still not happy, even though they no longer need to study."

I said, "Then stay unmarried. By not becoming a parent you will be happy."

But then she said, "But it must be lonesome, and painful to stay unmarried!"

A 19-year-old girl can already suffer so much! Do all of you here have pain and suffering? If you do, that is normal. Now if you were sitting here, listening to a boring lecture and you felt like leaving but you simply couldn't because the place is crowded with people, then you would feel agony at this time. Our life is filled with all kinds of suffering, so we need to learn the Buddhadharma, and use it to resolve our afflictions.

Why is there suffering? It is because in the past we created karma and therefore we are now receiving the karmic results. The problem is that after we receive retribution, we still continue to create karma. What we receive are karmic retribution and reward, with less reward than retribution. Marriage may bring happiness and divorce, suffering. But while most couples may stay married into old age, how many of them never had a fight or a quarrel throughout their marriage?

The causes of suffering are referred to as the accumulation of suffering. We can begin to release ourselves from suffering when we realize that all phenomena are impermanent and constantly changing, lacking a permanent self. If by practicing Buddhadharma we are able to realize no-self, we can then enter nirvana. Nirvana literally means "extinction of suffering;" it means freedom from suffering, leaving behind suffering. In order to eliminate suffering one needs to practice the Path. How does one practice the Path? One should uphold the precepts, practice concentration, and develop wisdom; through those means one may eliminate suffering and enter nirvana.

The Buddhist principles for explaining all phenomena are the law of cause and effect (karma) and the law of causes and conditions (dependent origination). The law of cause and effect looks at phenomena in terms of time. The succession of one thought by the next represents the relationship of cause and effect, and so does the relationship between one lifetime to the next. Some people take advantage of other people and try to gain something without making the effort. There are many ways to gain something without working for it—some people may steal, some may commit robbery, and some may resort to kidnapping. These people have no idea what the law of cause and effect means; they don't believe in causality at all, and tend to think they can simply gain by luck or chance.

In reality, there are fixed laws and principles in this world, and there are indeed causes and effects. There are always reasons why things happen to us—not a single thing can occur without a cause. Results in our current life that may not be explained reasonably will become understandable and clear to us with the perspective of the causality of three times of past, present, and future.

It is hard for people who do not believe in the law of cause and effect to accept in their hearts the standards of human morality. If one believes in cause and effect, one will naturally refrain from doing bad things, and instead work hard for one's future. The law of causes and conditions reveals various relationships derived from the interactions in time and space. In Chinese culture it is said that finding a partner in life is a matter of affinity—causes and conditions working together; but in fact no phenomena are exempt from causes and conditions. The meeting and parting of people, the success and failing of an undertaking, as well as the rising and perishing of any phenomenon, all result from the working together of various causes and conditions.

The line from the *Heart Sutra*, "form is precisely emptiness," represents the supreme law and principle in Buddhism. By "form is precisely emptiness" we mean that all phenomena are inherently empty because they arise as a result of causes and conditions working together. They arise because of causes and conditions, and perish because of causes and conditions. They appear when the causes and conditions come together, and vanish when the causes and conditions disperse. Therefore, all phenomena do exist as we see them, but they are actually perishing at the very moment we see them, because they are constantly changing.

This statement, all by itself, will create misconceptions that make people pessimistic: since all phenomena are empty, one might as well not do anything at all. So the rest of the line from the *Heart Sutra*—

"and emptiness is precisely form"—should also be added, so we get: "Form is precisely emptiness, and emptiness is precisely form." Empty as all phenomena are, they still consist of the relationships of causes and effects. There are many levels of cause and effect involved in this world, and they run in cycles within the three realms, incessantly. The law of causes and effects is itself never empty. "Emptiness is precisely form," indicates that emptiness is precisely existence—emptiness does not mean non-existence.

Definition of Wrong Path

Evil path can be defined in the worldly sense and from a Buddhist perspective.

The Wrong Path Defined in the Worldly Sense.
This can be further divided into evil crafts and cults.

1. *Evil crafts*: Some people use unethical means and superstition to bewilder people, to trick or cheat money out of them. There are folk religions that resort to evil crafts. I met a woman who told me that her friend took her to a shrine to seek divine guidance about her future. There she drank a cup of tea and suddenly she couldn't remember anything at all. Then she proceeded home, took her savings book to the bank, and withdrew some money. When she got home again she found that the money was gone. The woman herself withdrew the money out of her bank account. She then gave the money to somebody else, but she had no idea to whom. This is an example of the use of evil crafts.

2. *Evil cults*: There are theories propagated by cults that sound appealing and appear to be true, but are actually false. The ideas may seem correct and persuasive, making you want to become a convert

and believe that you will thereby gain welfare and happiness. But in fact it may cost you your job, your fortune, your family, and your health. This kind of evil cult can be found everywhere. Or, there are religions that combine the elements of evil crafts and cults. They have their own doctrines, amulets, language, and spells. They either give you some magic words or teach you to chant spells that cause you to lose your own personality, and begin to speak some seemingly correct ethical or moral concepts. Once you become a convert to this kind of religion you will not be able to get out of it easily, and will be subject to its control. If you want to leave, it will cost you great pain and a very big price.

Erroneous Path from the Perspective of Buddhism.
This can be divided into outer paths and erroneous views.

1. *Outer path*: One who follows an outer path seeks truth outside of one's own mind, such as when one prays to some god to grant a wish, or when one seeks help from nature. This kind of seeking or searching outside of the mind is referred to as "outer path." As the Buddha's verse in the *Diamond Sutra* puts it, "Those who attempt to see me in form, or seek me through sound are on the erroneous path, and therefore will not see the Tathagata." The meaning is that trying to seek liberation and the supreme Buddha Path through form and sound is the evil path and is far from the right path. The Buddha Path has nothing to do with external form, but it also requires one to be free from internal, mental forms to be on the genuine right path.

2. *Erroneous views*: Erroneous, or wrong views include not believing in the law of cause and effect, not believing in causes and conditions, and becoming attached to either eternalism or nihilism. All these are the erroneous path.

Clear Distinctions of Right and Wrong

There are clear distinctions of right and wrong from the points of view of religion and political bias, customs and habits, and Buddhist perspective.

Right and Wrong as Perceived by Religion and Political Bias

Judgment of right and wrong based on biased views is not reliable as it only possesses the ideology of either-friend-or-enemy, where people band together with those of similar inclination and attack the different, without actually differentiating right and wrong based on rational selection.

Right and Wrong as Perceived by Customs and Habits

In general, what accords with the customs and habits of a certain region is the right path; otherwise it is the wrong path. Buddhadharma cannot go against the local customs and habits of the region at the time, and discourages actions that are not in line with them. However, the Buddhadharma has the guiding and correcting function towards unwholesome customs.

Right and Wrong from the Perspective of Buddhism

From the standpoint of a Buddhist who has taken refuge, believing in the Three Jewels is the right path, and not believing in the Three Jewels is the wrong path. From the standpoint of the human and heavenly realm, upholding and practicing the five precepts and the ten virtues represents the right path, while committing the five offences and the ten evils represents the wrong path. From the perspective of a sage who has transcended the world, practicing the Eightfold Noble Path, seeking liberation from birth and death represents the right path, while the sentient beings in the Six Realms, who are attached to birth and death, are on the wrong path. From the standpoint of a bodhisattva, who is dedicated to delivering the world, practicing the Six Perfections (paramitas) and the "ten thousand meritorious deeds," and delivering sentient beings represents the right path, while only seeking self-liberation represents the wrong path.

Non-duality vs. Clear Distinction between Right and Wrong

From the Standpoint of a Buddha, Right and Wrong do not Exist

All dharmas are Buddhadharma, and all sentient beings are of the same nature as the buddhas. From the standpoint of a buddha, there is no such thing as right and wrong, there are no demons, and there is no buddha—they are all the same.

From the Standpoint of Ordinary Human Beings, Wrong and Right are Clearly Distinct

Not believing the law of cause and effect represents the wrong path; so does attachment, craving, hatred, ignorance, arrogance, and doubt, pride and pomposity, as well as pretending to be a sage while being in reality an ordinary human—these are all wrong paths. Therefore, we cannot say that any beliefs different from Buddhism are wrong paths; nor can we say there is no wrong path within Buddhism. As Buddhists we are sometimes on the right path and sometimes we stray from the correct path. However, from the perspective of a buddha, our views about right and wrong are all erroneous.

Transcending Time, Space, and Life

University of Massachusetts at Lowell, Massachusetts, November 11, 1988.
(Additional text added later by Master Sheng Yen.)

Time and Space

In Chinese, "time-and-space" (Chn. *yuzhou*), is a composite of "space" and "time," and it is synonymous with "cosmos." Space extends in the four compass directions, plus up and down; time extends from the ancient past to the present and into the distant future. In other words, the infinite extension of time and space together, we call cosmos. The time and space that are vertically and horizontally interwoven (Chn. *shijian*) are also a synonym for "the world." The temporal continuation of the past, present, and future is called "*shi*," traceable to the infinite past and into the limitless future. Generally, we take the lifespan of human beings as one generation (or one lifetime, *shi*), and in Chinese a period of twelve years is called *ji*, a unit for time. In modern times, another measure of time is the century, or 100 years. The spatial aspect is called *jian*, or dimension; it includes things too small to be seen in a microscope, as well as vastness that can only be fathomed by an astronomer. Based on this, the lines of time are combined with the points and planes of space to form the world, or *shijian*.

In Chinese, "time and space" is also synonymous with "activities." The movements of objects, the transformation of phenomena, the changes to matter, are all activities occurring in time and space. If we depart from time and space, then the phenomena of these activities will no longer exist. We can infer from this that if there is an eternal thing, it would definitely be unchanging and it would not occupy time and space. Using common sense, it follows that we can only perceive the present, and infer about the past and the future. However, such inferences are extremely limited; there is no way of knowing what the infinite past and the limitless future are like. Likewise, our knowledge of space is also extremely limited. The scope of space that we know by means of the activities of our human body and through scientific observation is extremely small. Therefore, we rely on religion and philosophy to resolve these issues. But this shifts the questions unsolvable by common sense to the realms of theism and philosophy without really solving them—the scope of the human body and the human mind is, after all, very limited.

For the Chinese "time and space" is also synonymous with "existence." All things that exist—whether physical, physiological, psychological, or even purely spiritual—have their phenomena and their symbols that cannot exist apart from time and space. Ordinary people think that only material phenomena occupy time and space, and that, since spirits are immaterial as well as formless, they do not belong to time and space. As a matter of fact, mental activities are definitely based on experiences and memories. And, experiences become memories when the images and impressions of things we have experienced become recorded in our brain as symbols, concepts, feelings, habits, and the like. Even purely spiritual entities, such as spirits, ghosts, deities, rely on the operation of material objects to manifest. The realm of spirits, in itself, cannot act or be displayed, and is nothing but forms of energy. And the power of such energy is manifested through material phenomena. Therefore, all things that have activities and exist, visible or invisible, are within the scope of time and space.

Moreover, time and space are a different name for "illusory existence." By illusory existence, we mean that phenomena exist but they do not possess substance; we also mean that while there are activities, they too are without substance. Existence can be classified into objective existence, subjective existence, and mind-only existence.

Objective existence refers to the world commonly shared by all sentient beings. Before the birth and death of an individual, whether there are activities of body and mind, the world always seems to have an objective entity that connects with the individual and actually exists separately. But in fact, this world as an objective entity is inseparable from our subjective world; the birth and death of any single person changes the objective world. The influence that each individual's behavior exerts on the whole world is not entirely obvious, but as long as one takes part in activities of body or mind, both the cultural and natural environment will be influenced. We can also say that with the emerging and vanishing of each individual in the journey of time, the world changes ceaselessly. Because the world is not permanently unchanging, it is called illusory existence.

Subjective existence is the world of the individual self that begins with birth and ends with death. This world of self is psychological but it is also based in reality. Whether in relation to the living environment or to our family and friends, when the self exists, others exist; when the self does not exist, others do not. The world was there before we were born, and it will be there after we die—it exists independently, though not separately, from us. However, this does not mean that when we die, the world of the self ceases to exist; in reality, the self has been undergoing constant change since the moment we were born. The cells and tissues of our body, our ethical relationships with family, our relationships in society, and the things in the natural environment, all undergo many changes at every instant. Our mental activities arise and perish from thought to thought, never pausing in the whole process from birth to death. Therefore, the existence of the individual is absolutely an illusory one, not a true or substantial existence.

"Mind-only" as "being" can be divided into the mind-only ("idealism") of Western philosophy and science, and the mind-only of Buddhism (not be confused with the Yogachara Mind-Only School). In Western philosophy, mind-only is a metaphysical concept, taking the highest idea as the "mind," in which mind is paramount, with three theoretical orientations (intellectualism, emotionalism, and voluntarism) that are actually connected to knowledge understood as "intuitive moral knowledge," or "principle" in the sense of a "nature's law" that Asians are familiar with. In science, mind-only is the analysis of mental activities, which entails investigations based on experiences and memories along with various explanations; its theoretical background is thus closely allied to philosophical materialism, with no investigation of pre-birth or post-death phenomena regarding the world or individuals.

The mind-only doctrine of Buddhism is spoken from the standpoint of the buddhas and bodhisattvas who have attained liberation. That is, all phenomena in the world are the things within the mind of the buddhas, as in the expression: "sentient beings are the sentient beings within the mind of all buddhas, and buddhas are the buddhas within the mind of sentient beings." This mind is the true suchness or the buddha–nature possessed in common by buddhas and sentient beings. The consciousness-only tenet is spoken from the standpoint of ordinary beings: since time without beginning, every sentient being gives rise to activities in the world of samsara, due to their ignorance and vexations. Due to these samsaric activities, there will be discrimination and attachments based on the views of self and others, thus creating karmas and receiving retributions. The karmic actions they create, whether virtuous, evil, or indeterminate, all have their force, which is called the karmic force or karmic seeds, namely, the karmic causes. The core that amasses the seeds and causes is called in Sanskrit, alaya, or "store consciousness." The alaya stores the seeds of a variety of karma, and when these seeds manifest, it is the manifestation of karmic results. Thus, whether it is the mind-only or consciousness-only tenet of Buddhism, they all explain the phenomena of all sentient beings' activities in the world; and all these phenomena change ceaselessly, being just transient, not lasting existence. Buddhism calls it "emptiness," or "all dharmas are empty without form," or the "empty nature."

The Buddhist Perspective of Time and Space

From the Buddhist perspective, one cannot speak of time without implying space, and vice versa. In Sanskrit, whenever time is mentioned, space is definitely implied, as in the expression, "a fixed or right point of time, a space of time." Although Buddhadharma speaks of transcending the world, it actually tries to explain the Dharma of transcendence by referring to mundane dharmas, but the true world-transcending Dharma cannot be expressed in words. Therefore, when mundane dharmas were expounded by the Buddha they became Buddhadharma. So, what is Buddhadharma? Its fundamental principles are the teaching of cause and effect and the teaching of causes and conditions. In reality, cause-and-effect and causes-and-conditions are not separate; they actually complement each other.

The successive relation from cause to effect is the aspect of time, while the dualistic relation of subject and object (so-called "host and guest") in phenomena is the aspect of space. Whether we speak of the successive relation in time or the dualistic relation in space, it all belongs to the teaching of causes and conditions. Causes and conditions mean that phenomena manifest as subject-object relations. For a given effect, there is only one subjective cause, while there can be few or many objective conditions. The causes and conditions may alter their relation of subject and object in the relativity of time-and-space; therefore causes and conditions are not separate from cause and effect, and vice versa.

Causes and conditions, as most people understand it refers only to relativity in terms of spatial position. For example, when saying that something is formed by many conditions they mean that the combination of many factors bring forth a certain phenomenon. In fact, the objects of Buddhism are human beings, not material things. Therefore, the causes and conditions mentioned in the earliest period—the past—do not refer to the dualistic relation between material phenomena in space, but rather to the successive relation between birth and death, taking the past, present, and future—as well as countless past and future times—as three infinitely extending periods of time.

Buddhism conceives of the phenomenon of the lifespan of a sentient being as having twelve phases. These phases encompass the past, present, and future, and are called the twelve links of dependent origination. They are: (1) ignorance, (2) volition, (3) consciousness, (4) name-and-form, (5) the six sense faculties, (6) contact, (7) sensation, (8) desire, (9) grasping, (10) becoming, (11) birth, and

(12) aging-and- death. Ignorance and volition belong to the past life; the eight following phases, consciousness through becoming, belong to the present life, and the last two phases, birth and aging-and-death, belong to the future life. Birth and aging-and-death of the future life contain the eight aspects of present life; the ignorance and volition of past life also contain the eight aspects of present life. Thus, the present depends on the past for its existence, and the future depends on the present for its existence. That is, there is the present because of the past, and there is the future because of the present.

The causal relations of the twelve links can be further elaborated: because of ignorance there is volition; because of volition there is consciousness; because of consciousness there is name-and-form; because of name-and-form there are the six sense faculties; and so on, up to becoming being the cause of birth, and there will also be aging-and-death. If this continues, it becomes the cycle of the three periods of time that goes on and on endlessly, with innumerable births and deaths. On the contrary, if there is no ignorance, there is no volition; if there is no volition there is no consciousness; if there is no consciousness, there is no name-and-form; if there is no name-and-form, there are no six sense faculties; and so on, up to if there is no birth, there is no aging-and-death. Liberation from the cause and effect of the three periods enables one to transcend the world; that is to say, transcending the scope of time and space. In order to reach transcendence, one requires the methods of practice. I will discuss this later.

The Buddhist perspective on time and space has evolved several times, beginning with Shakyamuni Buddha's fundamental teachings, to the sectarianism of early Buddhism, to the Madhyamaka and Yogachara of Mahayana, and so on. Early Buddhism took the *Agama*

Sutras as its basis, and used the phrase, "all activities are impermanent; all dharmas are selfless," to explain that things are not eternal in terms of time, and not really existent in terms of space. The activities mentioned here refer to the bodily and mental activities, mainly mental. Thoughts arise and perish moment by moment, so they are impermanent; between one thought and the next, there might be traces of the previous thought, but the present thought is not the next thought, so any single thought is transient. "All dharmas" refer to all phenomena existing in space, including words, languages, ideas, and concepts. Though there are relative connections among various phenomena, these phenomena interact and interrelate, one growing while the other declines, one increasing while the other decreases, without exception. What people regard as the "self" refers to nothing else, and has nothing else as its basis, but these phenomena. Now that we know all phenomena are changing unceasingly, how can we doubt that there is no true self in the phenomena of minds, activities, and material things?

Among the various sects of the Theravada tradition, the theories of the Sarvastivada achieved the most powerful development, and they also left the most writings. From fascicle 77 of the commentary, *Abhidharma-mahavibhasa-shastra*, we know that "in the Sarvastivada sect there are four great shastra masters who respectively established the different theories about the existence of the three periods of time. These four great shastra masters were Dharmatrata, Buddhadeva, Vasumitra, and Ghosha. The two former ones are masters of analogy who upheld the sutras, while the two latter ones are shastra masters of abhidharma who upheld the shastras. The meaning of *sarva* ("all") originates from the *Samyuktagama-sutra*, and refers to the six "internal" sense organs (eyes, ears, nose, tongue, body, and mind) in the bodies of sentient beings, and the six "external" sense objects (forms, sounds, smells, tastes, touch, and mental objects) in the environment in which they live. The concept of the three time periods being existent can often be found in the *Agamas*, with such expressions as: "*have* contemplated," "*is* contemplating," and "*will* contemplate;" as well as "*have* eliminated," "*is* eliminating," and "*will* eliminate." Thus, these ideas evolved into the concepts of "the real existence of the three periods of time, the permanent existence of the substance of dharmas," and "there being substance in the present, but no substance in the past and future."

This concept of the three times originally refers to the existence of the bodies of sentient beings and their environment, which belong to space. At the same time, one who follows Theravada path of liberation asserts the existence of time, with karma threading through past, present, and future. From this developed the theory of the real existence of the three times. Although their behaviors constantly change, sentient beings' essential nature remains the same; therefore, the theory claims that "the dharma substance permanently exists." However, a person's reception of retribution and their creation of karma all gather in the present, with the past already existing in the present and the future awaiting to be extended. Therefore, the theory claims that "there is substance in the present, but no substance in the past and the future." Furthermore, since the karma of conditioned dharmas created in the past is not lost, this concept developed into the three kinds of true unconditioned dharma by the Sarvastivada.

Fascicle 51 of the *Nyayanusara shastra* says, "As argued earlier, there are indeed the three time periods and the three kinds of true unconditioned dharma. Only then can one claim that all exist." The three kinds of unconditioned dharma are: (1) analytical cessation [of afflictions] (Skt. *pratisamkhya-nirodhasamskrta*), (2) non-analytical cessation (Skt. *apratisamkhya-nirodhasamskrta*), and (3) empty space (Skt. *akasasamskrta*). That is, it can be said that the mundane continues to exist when the supramundane is reached. However, the conditioned existence of the mundane is not separate from time and space, while the unconditioned existence of the supramundane does not occupy any position in time and space; it is beyond the scope of concepts and theories. There are also various perspectives of time and space in Mahayana Buddhism. Here we will introduce two of its systems as follows:

The Philosophy of Nagarjuna Bodhisattva

The verse in the chapter on "Contemplation on Time" from the *Madhyamika Shastra* by Nagarjuna Bodhisattva says, "If it is because of the past time that there are the future and the present, then the future and the present should exist in the past time…if there are no future and present in the past time, how can the future and present times exist because of the past?" Also: "Without the cause of the past time, there will be neither the future time nor the present time. Therefore, there are no two latter times." This means that if it is because of the past that there are the future and the present, then the future and the present should exist in the past. If there was no future and the present in the past, one cannot say that there are future and present because of the past. If it is not because of the past that there are the present and the future, then the future and the present also do not exist. This is to explain with the *Madhyamika Shastra* that time does not exist; if one wants to say that it exists, then it is a relative existence.

How do we know that it is relative? It is because we perceive the movement of material objects that we have the association that time exists. However, material objects are formed through the coming together of causes and conditions, and are changing every moment, so there are no true, unchanging material objects. This shows that time exists because of material objects, and that material objects exist because of causes and conditions. Since causes and conditions themselves are unreal dharmas, time and space do not really exist. So the chapter on "Contemplation on Time" has another verse that says, "There is time because of material things; apart from material things how can there be time? Material things do not even exist; how then, could there be time?" This is to thoroughly deny the reality of time and space.

The Philosophy of Vasubandhu Bodhisattva

Some of you may know that the Vasubandhu Bodhisattva first wrote the *Abhidharma-kosa-shastra* in the Theravada tradition, and later wrote the *Vimshatika-vijnapti-matrata-siddhi-shastra* in the Mahayana tradition. In the earlier shastra, he describes the operation of the 75 dharmas in time and space in terms of the four states: "arising, abiding, changing, and extinction." In the later shastra he explains the 100 dharmas in terms of fourteen states: "arising, abiding, aging, impermanence, continuity, distinction of good and evil causes, concomitance, instantaneousness, sequence, time, direction, number, combining nature, and non-combining nature." The earlier canon speaks of the three states of "arising, abiding, and extinction," while the later canon has a fourth state, "changing." However, this state evolved out of "abiding" in the three-state analysis (arising, abiding, extinction).

Between the arising and extinction of any phenomenon, there

is always a continuing process, whether of long or short duration. It may appear that there is no variation, but actually, the object changes unremittingly from the moment it is produced to the moment it is gone. The process, beginning with changes in quality, then to changes in quantity, then shape and form, until it eventually disappears entirely. As for the fourteen aspects of the dharmas, they all speak of the changes of dharmas in succession of time and in position of space. In fact, whether four aspects or fourteen aspects are mentioned, they are not definite but just a way of explaining the movement of all varieties of phenomena in time and space. The purpose of the Yogachara Consciousness-Only doctrine is to point out the transient existence of phenomena and their emptiness of substance in order to remove attachment among sentient beings.

The Buddhist Perspective of Life
Kinds of Life
Buddhism calls all for whom life has meaning sentient beings, and calls plants and minerals non-sentient beings. Being sentient means having an attachment to life. We may classify attachment to life into three biological levels: first, having the cells and nerves; second, having cells and nerves plus memory; and third, having cells, nerves, and memory plus thinking.

If living beings only have cells and tissues composed of cells [but lack a neural system]—such as microscopic creatures and plants—then they are called non-sentient beings because, though they have life, they have no attachment to life [in the Buddhist sense]. A living being must have neural structures to perceive pain; it must have memory to be afraid of pain; and it must have thoughts to know that pain can be avoided and to how to avoid it. Therefore, only with neural structures will it generate the attachment to life, though the degree of attachment can be strong or weak. Human beings have the strongest attachment to life because they are equipped with the highest ability to think. The next are higher-level animals, such as apes, elephants, dogs, horses, monkeys, birds, etc., which all have a certain degree of memory ability. Then the next are lower animals including insects, which have the functions of nerves, and therefore are called sentient beings.

The sentience, or feeling, that we speak of here is not just that of emotions, but covers three levels, namely, emotions, affections and noble sentiments. Only human beings have all three categories of feeling; higher animals only have emotions and affections; and lower animals only have emotions which refer to the instinctive impulses and desires. Confucius said, "The desire for food and sex is one's inherent nature." They are the natural operations that enable living beings to exist and continue ceaselessly, and also belong to the scope of sentience. Therefore, Buddhism calls them sentient beings.

Buddhadharma divides sentient life into the four phases of birth, aging, illness, and death. Buddhadharma also divides plants, which are non-sentient beings, and the physical environment in which sentient beings live, into the four phenomena of formation, existence, decay, and disappearance. Whether it is sentient beings or the environment on which they depend, everything is constantly changing and cycling; nothing remains permanently unchanging. This is the coming together of causes and conditions; when conditions come together, things arise; when conditions disperse, things perish.

The Origin of Life
From the Buddhist perspective, sentient beings are the main body

of lives, and non-sentient beings are what sentient beings depend on. Being born as the former is called "direct result," and the latter, "circumstantial result." Circumstantial result arises because of the direct result. If there were just the direct result but no circumstantial result, the phenomena of life cannot occur. In other words, if sentient beings do not have the living space and time for their activities, the phenomena of life cannot be established. We may compare circumstantial result to the house people live in, and direct result to the owner of the house. If there is no one to live there, the house would be unnecessary. Because there are people, it is necessary to build houses. In sum, Buddhism thinks that the world forms and exists for the sake of sentient beings' activities, being the result entailed by all varieties of karma they created since their past lives. Theism maintains that God creates all things and lets humankind control and manage them, while Buddhism says that all things in the world are entailed by the collective karma of each and every sentient being born onto this world.

So what is the origin of life? This is a very common question. Other religions say that life is the creation of God(s). If we further inquire as to who created God and why God created life, then we cannot avoid being trapped in unsolvable paradoxes. Without naming a creator, Buddhism maintains that sentient beings existed since time without beginning. Instead, Buddhism talks about how to solve problems that create suffering in sentient beings' lives, and how to attain liberation from suffering. For example, if someone is shot with a poisoned arrow, what is important is to pull out the arrow and cure the wound. If we were to stop and research who invented the arrow and how it was made, it would be meaningless to the person who got shot by the arrow.

1. *Viewing the origin of life from the standpoint of ordinary beings*: The first view regarding the origin of and continuation of life is to explain it in terms of conditioned arising based on karma and conditioned arising based on the *alaya*.

(1) Conditioned arising based on karma means that one reaps the result from the karma one creates. Sentient beings have desire owing to their attachment to life; therefore, they have the survival instinct, which develops into the inclination towards selfishness. Because of selfishness, there arise greed, anger, ignorance, arrogance, doubt, etc., which then generate the physical and verbal conducts of killing, stealing, sexual lusting, and telling lies. From the positive aspect, one will give rise to ethical and moral conduct in order to safeguard the security of one's family, race, nation, and human society. Generally speaking, acting out of selfishness is evil, while doing anything for the sake of one's family or even the whole human society is good. However, whether it is for the individual or for others, and whether it is good or evil, it is an attachment to life. All the conducts generated from attachment are called "karma with outflows," and will definitely lead to karmic result of another life. That is to say, amidst the karmic result of this life, one also continues to create a variety of good and evil karma, which becomes the cause for the result of future lives. This is conditioned arising based on karma. If one does not know how to attain liberation from the attachment to life, then one will take birth and die, one lifetime after another, endlessly.

(2) The conditioned arising based on *alaya* means that the karma that sentient beings create becomes the seeds for the karmic results of future lives. The good or evil karma that one creates in this life may be rewarded or paid back in this life, but mostly not in this lifetime. This is because karmic retribution (or rewards) is of three

kinds: fruit retribution, flower retribution, and remainder retribution. What we receive in this life for the karma we create in this life is the flower retribution, which can be said to be like the tip of an iceberg. Most of the retribution will be received in the future, and is the fruit retribution. The retribution that we cannot complete in one future lifetime or even many lifetimes is the remainder retribution.

As examples: to commit the five grave offences and fall into hell is called fruit retribution; to be despised in the human realm before falling into hell is called flower retribution; and to be poor and sick, or lowly, or handicapped physically after leaving hell and taking rebirth in the human realm, all belong to remainder retribution. When one has not received retribution in the present life after creating karma, all the karma one has created are the causes for one to receive results in the future. These causes are stored in the core of our life, namely, *alaya*, the eighth, or store consciousness.

Alaya in Sanskrit means "store." The *alaya* stores all the karmic causes we create, and when the causes and conditions ripen in the future, it will turn into the result of life and its environment. A karmic cause is also called a karmic seed, and the *alaya* is also called a consciousness of seeds, or a maturing consciousness. This means that the seeds of *alaya* mature at varied times and into varied results. "Varied times" means that one creates the karma in this lifetime and receives the result in some future lifetime. "Varied results" means one creates the karma when one is a human being, and may be receiving the retribution in the realm of animals or hells, or receiving the reward in heavens. "Variation" means that the karmic seeds may go from qualitative change to quantitative change. For example, if one kills nine people and saves one person, then, when one receives the retribution in the future, one may not end up with being killed nine times and killing another person once. Rather, because one has grave evilness and weak goodness, one will probably not be reborn as a human being when receiving the retribution, but will possibly receive the retribution of animals and hells, with both the quality and quantity change.

Nevertheless, having the virtuous cause of having saved one person, a person may possibly encounter good causes and conditions after receiving retribution for his evil. For instance, he may encounter a benefactor to help him, or hear a line of Buddhadharma that inspires him in some way, but it may not necessarily enable him to be rescued from the jaws of death. This is the meaning of maturing through variation. If you want to know in detail the principles of conditioned arising based on *alaya*, you may study the Consciousness-Only philosophy.

2. *Viewing the origin of life from the standpoint of sages*: Most people misunderstand Buddhism and think that Buddhism seeks to renounce the world. Even Buddhists think that the goal of Buddhadharma is to escape from reality, to leave the world in order to attain liberation and nirvana. This idea seems to mean that all the activities that sinful sentient beings display in this life are the results of karma they created in the past. They do not understand that if one practices successfully and achieves liberation, one will naturally depart from the world of sentient beings.

As a matter of fact, the correct Buddhadharma as understood by orthodox Buddhism is not like this. Indeed, it is the Buddhist concept that the sages of the Theravada tradition will not return to the human realm when they achieve the third fruit. And when they achieve the fourth fruit of arhatship, they will have gone beyond the three realms, and may enter into the state of quiescent cessation—which is called nirvana—and no longer have anything to do with the world of sentient beings. In fact, from the time when Shakyamuni Buddha founded Buddhism until the present day, there indeed existed the Hinayana ideals, and the Hinayana practices may also have appeared, but they are not the purpose for which the Buddha founded the Buddhist faith, and they remain problems for people who practice this way.

Why? Because in the monastic community at the time of Shakyamuni, the World-Honored One, there were over one thousand great arhats, and the majority of them were bhikshus engaging in the world; that is, they were the fourth-fruit sages who taught the Dharma in the world. If we say that one who attains arhatship should depart from the human world, then it is inconsistent with the historical and the general facts. Suppose there really were monastic communities following Hinayana principles. Such monastic communities would not associate with people in society, so it follows that they would not be able to acquire space for their survival. But since the various early schools did spread among many parts of the world, it shows that there has never been truly a Hinayana tradition in Buddhism. No matter what their thoughts were, they would never depart from the human world. Before attaining enlightenment, they practiced in the human community; after enlightenment, they would still remain among humans to teach and transform people. Only then is it the original intention of Buddhism.

This gives rise to another question: some people practice Buddhadharma to resolve the sufferings and vexations of samsara, with the aim of attaining sagehood. When they achieve sagehood through spiritual practice, there will be no more personal problems, so why remain in the human world? What is their purpose? If a sage still lived with ordinary beings, wouldn't this sage encounter the same problems as ordinary beings—food, medicine, clothing, housing, transportation, and so on? All this does not go beyond walking, standing, sitting, and lying down, and matters related to livelihood. So, if they still have the same problems as ordinary people, why are they called a sage? For what purpose did they self-cultivate to become a sage? The answer is that ordinary people with a selfish perspective and egocentric mind create a variety of physical and mental conducts that cause vexations. The sages, on the other hand, help sentient beings with selfless compassion, and though they live among ordinary people, they perceive life in a completely different way. Being selfless, they do not have vexations such as craving, anger, low self-esteem, and arrogance. Precisely because they are liberated, they treat all sentient beings with equal mind, and offer timely help and relief in appropriate measure.

After attaining supreme enlightenment, Shakyamuni still lived among humans, taught them the Dharma, and delivered sentient beings universally. He did this for more than forty years, until his physical body died naturally. Just like him, those who achieved sagehood in this lifetime not only did not depart from the human community, but would also take rebirth in the world of ordinary beings one lifetime after another, giving them teaching and relief unceasingly. So, how do the lives of such sages come about? Generally, ordinary beings receive result of births and deaths according to their karma, and bodhisattvas come and go amidst births and deaths because of the power of their vows. But buddhas appear due to the conditioned arising of pure mind and true suchness, neither according to karmic forces nor due to the power of vows.

(1) The conditioned arising of pure mind is also called the

conditioned arising of *dharmadhatu* (dharma realm). The pure mind of the buddhas is such because they have no attachment. Since they have no attachment, they do not discriminate between "self and others." In terms of time, they share the same mind with all buddhas of the past, present, and future; in terms of space, they share the same body with all sentient beings in *dharmadhatu*. They do not think of themselves as buddhas, nor do they think there are sentient beings to be delivered—because they have no self, they also do not have the notion of others either; however, as long as sentient beings generate good intention, and have karmic affinity with a buddha, the buddha will accord with and appear before them. A buddha may appear in the status and form of a buddha because many sentient beings of a certain area, event, and time commonly require the manifestation of a buddha. Likewise, a buddha may appear as a bodhisattva, an arhat, or even a sentient being at a certain time and place, among people or other sentient beings. This is because sentient beings are not left out from the buddhas' pure mind, which, being beyond time and space, is free of worry, concern, and obstruction.

(2) In the true suchness of the conditioned arising, true suchness is the "original face" that sentient beings and buddhas have in common. If true suchness follows impure causes and conditions, namely, greed, anger, ignorance, and other vexations, then it becomes the state of selfish ordinary beings with attachments. If it follows pure causes and conditions, namely, upholding the precepts, concentration, and wisdom, etc., then it accords with the world-transcending sages, and one will eventually achieve buddhahood, becoming one and the same with all buddhas of the past, present, and future. The true suchness of sages should be undefiled, yet not attached to purity; in other words, it is neither pure nor impure. Whether one is impure or pure, true

suchness is immovable, unchanging, permanent, and universal; only then can it be called true suchness. Since it is neither pure nor impure, and is permanent and universal, in the eyes of sentient beings it is the true suchness of all buddhas.

Moreover, buddhas see the worlds of sentient beings as being all states of true suchness—neither pure nor impure, neither increasing nor decreasing, yet permanent and universal. Therefore, sentient beings who follow pure conditions can become buddhas, while the buddhas who follow impure conditions can remain in the world to deliver sentient beings. Why is this so? Because, only when one is neither pure nor impure, neither increasing nor decreasing, and neither coming nor going can one be *tathagata*. Since they are *tathagata*, buddhas do not need to depart from the world of ordinary people, nor do they need to vow to deliver sentient beings. They are present in all places and at all times, constituting the phenomena of life in which the sages forever dwell in, and transform the world.

(3) There is another kind of conditioned arising, that of the *tathagatagarbha* (womb of the *tathagata*). From the position of ordinary beings, this means that all sentient beings have the possibility of becoming *tathagata*, or buddhas. If one solely creates various kinds of good and bad karma with outflows, then one's karmic seeds for another rebirth are stored in the alaya. But if one practices the three studies of precepts, concentration, and wisdom, while cultivating giving and other good deeds with a selfless mind, then one will be practicing virtuous Dharma without outflows; then, what are stored are the karmic seeds for becoming a buddha. When storing the karmic seeds of ordinary beings with outflows, the eighth consciousness is called alaya, and when storing seeds without outflows, it is called *tathagatagarbha*. Therefore the saying, "The *tathagatagarbha* stores a

tathagata."

From the standpoint of a buddha, all sentient beings are the same as buddhas; the mind of each and every sentient being is the treasury of *tathagata*, which stores [the seed of] *tathagata*. After attaining buddhahood, *tathagata* also possess *tathagatagarbha*, as do sentient beings. So the chapter, "The Underlying Truth in the Meaning of Emptiness" of the *Sutra of Queen Shrimala of the Lion's Roar*, says that *tathagatagarbha* has the two meanings of emptiness and non-emptiness. The *tathagatagarbha* that is empty is separate, free, and different from the store of all vexations. The *tathagatagarbha* that is not empty is not separate, not free, and different from the inconceivable Buddhadharmas, which are more numerous than the sands of the Ganges. That is to say, for the buddhas themselves, *tathagatagarbha* is empty because buddhas do not accord with vexations; from the perspective of the buddhas' compassion and wisdom for transforming the world, the *tathagatagarbha* is not empty because the buddhas live among the multitude of sentient beings, and possess countless kinds of inconceivable merit.

The chapter on "Dharmakaya and the Meaning of Emptiness" from the *Sutra of Queen Shrimala of the Lion's Roar*, says that although the *tathagata* "has eradicated all vexations…the *dharmakaya* (Dharma Body) is not separate from the store of vexations, and is called the *tathagatagarbha*." This means that the *tathagata* has cut off all vexations, but the Dharma Body of the *tathagata* is not separate from vexations, so that the *tathagata* can complete infinite inconceivable Buddhadharma. Since sages possess *tathagatagarbha* just like ordinary beings, except with attachment, after buddhahood, they are neither sentient beings, nor do they need to leave the world of sentient beings. If, after buddhahood, they leave the world of sentient beings, or they appear as buddhas to show they are different from sentient beings, then they cannot be called *tathagata*. Therefore, it is not surprising that sages manifest in the world of ordinary beings, and possess the life of ordinary beings. What is different is that one is liberated, and the other has attachment.

Transcending Time and Space

To transcend time and space means to transcend life itself—one goes from being a sentient being trapped in self, attachments, samsara, and vexations, to being a sage who has no self or vexations, and who has realized the oneness and sameness of birth-and-death; this is called being liberated, free, and at ease. This must be achieved through the guidance of concepts and the application of the methods of practice. Let me explain this from three points of view.

Point of View of the Four Noble Truths

The Four Noble Truths are the four mutually related truths that Shakyamuni Buddha first spoke after he attained enlightenment. These are the four truths of suffering, the cause of suffering, the cessation of suffering, and the path out of suffering. The first two noble truths—suffering and cause of suffering—are the results received by ordinary beings through their creation of karma; receiving the result is called suffering and creating the karma is the cause of suffering. Suffering includes birth, aging, sickness, and death, separation from loved ones, association with enemies, inability to obtain what one desires, and the flourishing of the five *skandhas*—eight kinds in all.

The trials and afflictions that one endures and undergoes are consequences from a variety of karma created in past lives. What karma did one create in the past? Whether they are virtuous or evil karma, so long as they are related to the ego, selfishness, and attachment, they are the causes of suffering, and will gather and amass as karmic causes into "the accumulation of suffering." Therefore, creating karma and receiving the results are the interminable cycle of the two phases of suffering and cause of suffering, as well as the cycle of birth and death in the three realms. In order to go beyond such phenomena, one has to follow the principles and methods of practice that the Buddha spoke of, putting them into action accordingly.

"Path" has the connotation of principle, road, and method. If we keep practicing in accordance with it, we will certainly reach the goal of transcending birth and death. What is the content of Path? [It is precisely the fourth noble truths, consisting of] eight individual paths of practice called the Noble Eightfold Path:

1. *Right View*: To have the correct understanding, such as knowing that birth and death is suffering, and suffering arises from karma.

2. *Right Thought*: To practice the correct methods of contemplation. For instance, one has already experienced that life is the bitter consequence of karma, so one applies the methods for freeing oneself from suffering, mainly through meditative contemplation.

3. *Right Speech*: To not speak the words that are useless to practice, but to speak only the words that are useful.

4. *Right Action*: To not do the bodily actions that are useless to practice, but only those that are useful to the practice.

5. *Right Livelihood*: To not earn one's livelihood by means of the tricks of charlatans or quacks but with proper means, so as not to contradict with the goal of spiritual practice.

6. *Right Effort*: To put one's effort into the Dharma practice of precepts, concentration, and wisdom. For example, one should do the

good deeds that one has not done yet, and enhance the good deeds that one has done; one should stop the evil deeds that one has done, and prevent oneself from doing the evil deeds that one has not done yet.

7. *Right Mindfulness*: To always collect and restrain one's mind, practicing the methods such as contemplation on impurity.

8. *Right Concentration*: To practice different kinds of contemplation to achieve the eight kinds of meditative concentration attained in the four dhyana heavens and the four formless heavens, and eventually achieve the concentration of extinguishing feeling and perception, so as to reach the goal of liberating oneself from samsara.

The truth of the cessation of suffering is actually the result of the truth of the Path—one eliminates the burden of samsara by cultivating the Path, and thereby transcends time and space where one is no longer bound to arising and perishing. This is called nirvana. This shows that the first two truths of suffering and the cause of suffering are one level of cause and effect for those in the stage of ordinary beings, whereas the cessation of suffering and the Path out of suffering are the other level of cause and effect for those who go beyond ordinary beings and reach the stage of sagehood.

The stage of ordinary beings belongs to causality with outflows, which generates karma; while that of sages belongs to the causality without outflows, which generates no karma. Causality with outflows reflects the phenomena of life in time and space while causality without outflows represents the phenomena of life that transcends time and space. However, according to the *Agamas*, there are no phenomena to be perceived for a life that has transcended time and space, and this is called the quiescence of nirvana.

Point of View of the Teaching on the Five Skandhas in the Heart Sutra
In Buddhism, the five *skandhas* are the phenomenal aggregates that together make up a person. They are the five kinds of physiological and psychological phenomena, namely, form, sensation, perception, volition, and consciousness.

1. *The skandha of form*: this refers to the material aspect of our body, which are generally called the four elements of earth, water, fire, and wind. Among them, the bones, skins, muscles, nerves, etc. are called the earth element; the blood, fat, and water are the water element; the body temperature is the fire element; and the breath is the wind element.

2. *The skandha of sensation*: this refers to the feelings of suffering, happiness, sorrow, joy, equanimity, etc.

3. *The skandha of perception*: this refers to making distinctions of good, bad, virtue, evil, etc.

4. *The skandha of volition*: this activates the bodily, verbal, and mental behavior.

5. *The skandha of consciousness*: this is the overall name for discrimination and attachment, as well as the creation of karma and the seeds of karma.

From the above, we can see that the last four *skandhas* belong to the scope of mental phenomena and spiritual activities, and the phenomena of life of sentient (human) beings do not go beyond the boundary of these five conditions. If we cannot experience or realize that the five *skandhas* are empty, then we will always remain in the state of ordinary people, going through infinite vexations and an endless cycle of birth and death. The five *skandhas* are empty and selfless. In terms of time, all phenomena come and go in an endless flow, changing again and again; thus, they are impermanent. Similarly, in terms of location in space, all phenomena grow and decline interactively, constant changing, so there is no unchanging self. Since both material and mental phenomena are ceaselessly changing in time and space, we know that none of the five *skandhas* is permanent, and none of them has a self. As life is an aggregation of the five *skandhas*, and the five *skandhas* are impermanent as well as selfless, what is there for us to attach to? Since there are no objects to attach to, nor a self that can attach, it is then liberation.

Impermanence and no-self are emptiness. Emptiness means that although spirit and matter have temporary characteristics that we can perceive, they do not have unchanging substance to be found. Although there is no unchanging substance, it does not hinder the changing of phenomena. Therefore, the emptiness as expounded by Buddhist teachings does not deny the existence of the phenomenal world. Because there is no substance and no obstruction, it is called emptiness, yet it does not hinder existence. One does not attach to permanent existence, nor does one deny the existence that varies; this is called the emptiness without a self-nature. Being without self-nature means that phenomena are empty, without permanent substance. If there is a substance, it is not empty of nature. So, if one can realize that all five *skandhas* are empty, as the *Heart Sutra* says, that is transcendence.

The Point of View of the Sudden Enlightenment of Chan

The Chan School originated in India and matured during the peak of the Chinese Tang Dynasty (618-907). The Chan masters advocated teachings not established on words or language, aiming at attaining buddhahood through "sudden enlightenment." "Not established on words" means that the mind of *tathagata*, which has no notion of a self, cannot be realized through knowledge, study, words, language, or all varieties of symbols. Therefore, to awaken to one's inherent nature is to realize directly that all dharmas are empty of self-nature, without resorting to any special methods or graduated approaches. One's intrinsic nature is buddha-nature, which is the nature of emptiness. This empty nature is also the nature of *tathagata*. In his *Platform Sutra*, Sixth Patriarch Huineng wrote this verse:

> *Bodhi is fundamentally not a tree,*
> *Nor is the clear mirror a stand.*
> *Fundamentally there is not a single thing,*
> *Where could any dust collect?*

Buddhists generally think that all sentient beings have an inherent buddha-nature to become a buddha, and some liken this buddha-nature to a tree that can bear the fruit of the bodhi. Some people think that the mind of a buddha is like a clear mirror, which can "show a Chinese when a Chinese comes and show a foreigner when a foreigner comes." No matter what scenery or things appear in front of it, the mind of a buddha can reflect them without the slightest error, just like a clear mirror. Then again, other people think that when one becomes a buddha, there will surely be the fruit of buddhahood to be obtained, so they practice desperately in hopes of getting results.

However, Master Huineng said very clearly that bodhi is not a tree, the clear mirror is without a stand, and fundamentally, not a single thing exists, so there is no need to seek to attain buddhahood. Thus he said, "Where could any dust collect?" These insights show that the inherent substance is without substance, the fundamental nature is without nature, and an illuminated mind is no-mind.

How can one suddenly awaken to no-self and the inherent nature of emptiness? To do so, one should apply the attitude and methods that many generations of lineage masters of the Chan School taught us. For example, we should "always maintain an ordinary mind" as taught by Master Mazu (709-788), and should "always maintain a straightforward mind" as taught by Huineng. An ordinary mind does not make self-centered judgments on advantages and disadvantages, gain and loss, right and wrong, or good and bad; a straightforward mind does not impose intellectual judgment on the self and others, subject and object, long and short, round and square, and the like. Actually "ordinary mind" and "straightforward mind" have the same meaning. If we remove self-centered discrimination and attachment, then each and every thought that arises in our mind is ordinary and straightforward without exception, and will accord, here and now, with the selfless nature of emptiness.

If Chan practitioners do not have sharp karmic capacity or deep virtuous roots, they will need to rely on some methods, so the accomplished Chan masters would use the methods such as investigating the *huatou* to help them. If practitioners can persist in working on their *huatou*, they would eventually generate the doubt sensation, which would turn into a "doubt mass." When they break through the doubt mass, like a chick pecking its way out of its shell, they would see their "original face before they emerged from their mother's womb," and the life that transcends time and space would manifest before them. What is all this about? To find this out and realize it personally, you will have to make effort in practice.

Author's note: This text was based on a lecture I gave at the University of Massachusetts at Lowell, on November 11, 1988. However, at that time, to meet the needs of the audience and the time limit, I did not make a deeper elaboration, and was not able to present the whole outline that I had prepared. After returning to the Chan Meditation Center in New York, with the help of Ms. Ye Cuiping, who spent 2 ½ days transcribing the talk, I added more content to the text according to the outline I drew up previously. The result is that this current text contains more detail and a deeper elaboration than the actual talk.

Chan and Daily Life

Washington University, Washington, USA, April 17, 1990.

Everyone has innate buddha-nature; therefore, anyone can become a buddha. However, most people do not know that Bodhidharma, the First Patriarch of Chan, said that "making the mind like a wall" is the very method to become a buddha. There is no need to talk about doctrines, no need to practice any special method. All one needs is to train one's mind to be as stable and unmoving as a wall.

Transparent and Unmoving, yet Useful

This wall is transparent and immovable; yet, you may use it as you wish— hang something on it, or paint on it. But however you choose to use it, the wall itself does not change. I have often said, "Don't keep anything in your mind." For example, you should save your money in the bank, or keep it in your pocket, but do not keep it in your mind. This does not mean that you do not need to retain your knowledge, learning, or experience. What you have is what you have, but have it for the sake of sentient beings, not for yourself. For yourself, you should have nothing.

The mind should be like a storeroom with everything in its proper place. There would be chaos if the objects in a storeroom kept moving about. But when we need something from the storeroom, we should get it and use it; when we don't need it let it stay where it is. The mind behaves very strangely: thoughts pop up in it when we don't need them. On the other hand, when we want to use our mind, nothing seems to come out of it. Once I was talking to a lady who could not find her words, so she tapped her head impatiently: "Come out quickly!" In fact, when our mind is calm, the things we need from it come out naturally and without effort.

Because the mind fluctuates a lot, when we don't want to be distracted, outside thoughts barge in; but when we want to think usefully, the right thoughts are not there. Therefore, I wish that all of you will train your mind to be clear and stable like Bodhidharma's wall. In that way you will be training to become a buddha. Can you train your mind so that it becomes like a wall? Can you manage to achieve that? Put everything that you have learned and experienced from the past into your storeroom, and just let them be. Can you do that? If you can't, what should you do?

When someone is rude and we find that irritating, we can ask them to shut up. However, when your mind is in such chaos that you cannot command yourself to perform ordinary tasks, can you tell it to shut up? This is indeed no easy matter.

The Two Entrances and Four Practices

The path to enlightenment that Bodhidharma taught is called the Two Entrances and Four Practices. The first entrance is the entrance through principle; the second entrance is the entrance through practice. The entrance through principle is to directly train one's mind to be unmoving, like a wall. The entrance through practice consists of accepting karmic retribution, adapting to conditions, seeking nothing, and acting in accord with the Dharma. These four practices advance in levels, one higher than the other.

Accepting Karmic Retribution

All the current consequences in our life definitely have their causes, but we cannot know each and every one of them. According to Buddhism, the reason is that these consequences are brought along to the present life from previous lifetimes, since time without beginning. However, we know nothing about our past lives, nor can we prove anything about them. Even in the current life from birth till now, there is much of which we have no memory. Therefore, when we meet misfortune, frustration, and unhappiness, how can we think, "There must be some cause for this suffering"? While we may not fully know the related causes for these things, there is also no need to pay attention to them. We just need to recognize that everything has its causes and therefore we can only accept that. On the other hand, wouldn't it be too submissive if we simply accepted all adversity? In the past there were contributing causes, so adding new causes in this life will definitely change matters. Therefore, our attitude should be first, to accept the fact of past karma and next, to seek solutions in this life.

First of all, when you have a problem, don't get so troubled that you cannot respond appropriately. Here's an analogy: if a fire breaks out in your house, do you first try to put out the fire? Or, should you sit there trying to figure out what caused the fire? Something did cause the fire, but for now, you should put that aside; it is more critical right now to put out the fire. With this principle, many frustrating problems will get resolved. We should assume such attitude in our acceptance and dealings with any difficulties.

Adapting to Conditions

Good fortune and good things have their causes, so it is normal to feel afflicted when misfortune strikes. However, some people suffer a lot even though they enjoy good fortune. We often see people who are wealthy, powerful, and influential, but are they always happy? Many people think that having these things, one will be happy, but that is not necessarily so. Is it definitely a lucky thing when a boy wins the love of a girl? It is not necessarily so. But being in love is also not necessarily an unhappy thing. But while a romance is developing, something unpleasant may still happen. Therefore, when you find success and luck in life, do not get too excited, nor do you need to be proud. When people indulge in pride, they tend to forget who they really are.

Dr. Sun Yat-sen, the founder of the Republic of China, told this story: A beggar just learned that he won the grand prize in a lottery. All he owned was a bamboo cane, and to avoid losing the ticket, he had hidden it in the cane. He was so happy about becoming rich! He thought, "I am not a beggar any more! I don't need this beggar's stick anymore!" In his elation, he threw the bamboo cane into the river. It then dawned on him that the lottery ticket was still in the cane. So, not only could he not collect the winnings, but he also lost his walking stick. Originally, he was so poor that he only owned a bamboo stick, and now what? Being so pleased and proud of himself made this beggar lose everything he owned.

For those practicing Chan in daily life, such incidents would be ordinary matters. When money comes, it just comes; when it goes, it just goes. There must be causes for it to come and for it to go. It amounts to withdrawing savings from one's own bank account and taking it home. So what is there worthy of the excitement?

Seeking Nothing

Regardless of Eastern or Western perspectives, if people should not seek anything, then what is the point of living? Whatever mankind seeks, they seek it because they harbor hope. As there is hope, we work hard in our pursuits and that is only normal; it is also normal to want to achieve something. However, most of the goals that people pursue may not be achievable. As a proverb has it, "Follow love, and it will flee; flee love, and it will follow thee."

The majority of you here are young. As a child, did you ever say, "When I grow up, I want to be so-and-so?" In high school or university did you change your mind again and again about what you want to do? A disciple of mine was originally a professor of philosophy. Later he studied music, and now he teaches Buddhism and works as a part-time masseur. He was never clear as to what kind of career he truly wanted. Nor did he know what he wanted to learn after all. Although he learned a lot, this was not the issue.

Imagine a large house with many doors. Everyone wants to get into this house. One can enter from the east, from the west, from the basement, or you could also come down from the roof. If you thought that entering through one door was not enjoyable enough and wanted to explore more options, that's fine. Most important is that as long as you can reach the center of the house, no matter which entrance you took, you would see the same things. However, if at the beginning you already made up your mind to enter through a specific door, then that could be a problem. There might be some doors that you wanted to enter but couldn't, even though others used it. As a matter of fact, it doesn't matter. If you can't go through one door, just take a different door. The people inside would then say, "How did you manage to get in here through *that* door?"

Therefore, the non-seeking attitude teaches us not to pursue a goal that would make us desperate if we failed to achieve it. Nevertheless, we should make sincere endeavors in whatever we do, because life itself is about making endeavors. If one practices Buddhism in order to achieve a preconceived goal, then the practice will be in vain. It would be an attachment, a hindrance to achieving the goal. What is this hindrance? It is precisely seeking something. Ordinary goals can be reached while doing ordinary things. However, enlightenment is different: one can vow to attain enlightenment and also attain it, but the realization of enlightenment itself recedes farther if one seeks to attain it through constant practice. Enlightenment means being liberated from the fetters of the self and the external environment. But if you go after it with a seeking attitude, then what you seek becomes an attachment, and of course, it will bind you; it will become your hindrance towards actually attaining liberation.

Acting in Accord with the Dharma

Acting in accord with the Dharma teaches us to do everything the way it should be done and however it needs to be done, I will do it. If we take "seek nothing" too literally, we may get caught up in a passive mindset. We may think, "If I am supposed to seek nothing, why do anything?" However, acting in accord with the Dharma requires that we be actively engaged, and that we strive in our endeavors.

I met a young man who aspired to become a lawyer. After high school, he failed three times the exams to enter law school. In the end he was admitted to the school of library management. Even so, he was very disappointed and frustrated. Many years later, he went to France for advanced studies in library management and earned a doctorate. At that time in Taiwan, this expertise was difficult to find. Before he returned home, he already got a job offer from the largest and newest library in Taiwan. When he decided to study library management someone told him, "Once you get on board a pirate ship, you have to go where the pirates go. Since you will be majoring in library management, be committed to studying it well." In other words, do your best within the permitted scope, in any position, at any post, and under any circumstance.

So, acting in accord with Dharma also means that when confronted with a new environment and new conditions, and you find yourself in what seems a totally different situation, keep a steady attitude and work hard. You will have smooth sailing in life and not be troubled so often.

Chan and Modern Life

University of Massachusetts at Lowell, Massachusetts, June 5, 1987

The Problems of Modern Life

It is a rare honor for me to lecture at Lowell. I once lectured on Chan in modern life in Taiwan, but life there is not entirely the same as the United States, so the angle presented in this lecture will not be identical either. What are the problems in modern life for which we need Chan, and what can Chan offer to people today?

Generally speaking, the problems of people nowadays can be seen in four aspects: First, life today is marked by frequent changes and fast movements, unlike the more stable lifestyles in the past. Second, today people live more and more distant from each other; there is less and less interaction, mutual care, and concern among people. Third, since people in modern societies today enjoy abundant material comforts, sustaining life is no longer difficult. Nevertheless, people's desires are endless. Because people pursue more and more pleasure and excitement, many strange and eccentric lifestyles have emerged. Fourth, not confident and secure about future prospects, people live under constant stress and uncertainty.

If we look deeper, however, we find that although their living environments are different, the psychological problems of people today and in the past are actually similar. The roots of the problem lie in the pain of being alive, or of feeling forlorn, small, and helpless. This very problem had already been discovered in Shakyamuni Buddha's time. In fact, the pain of being alive has never changed and is never going to change. Nonetheless, I would still like to raise some major issues. For example, people today face ever more family, marital, and parenting problems. Also, career and environmental problems are much more complex. This is because, despite the advantages of modern life, it is not that easy to live and survive.

Using Chan to Solve Problems

Today, social interactions are more frequent, and personal contacts have expanded. However, everyone is working hard, fighting or planning, mainly in the interests of themselves and their group. As a result, there is personal as well as social conflict. These conflicts are more explicit than that seen in societies in the past. How can these problems be solved? From the perspective of modern people, it is through overcoming difficulties, changing the environment, and changing the other party. With this approach, we may be able to overcome some problems and change the other party a little bit; however, in the process, we may create even more problems. That is why we need to talk about Chan, and realize how Chan can help address these problems.

What is Chan Buddhism? The origins of Chan are in India, where meditation represented an approach and effort to teach people to reflect on oneself. It required one to examine one's inner mind rather than seeking external solutions. When a problem occurs, don't just look at the problem itself; instead, turn around and reflect: "Why would this problem and difficulty happen to me?" With this approach, one would eventually realize that the problem starts with ourselves, and its solution also starts with ourselves.

Traditionally, religions in India practiced meditative concentration to resolve afflictions and relieve pain and suffering. At times you may be in agony and feel vexation, and don't have anyone to talk to. At such times, you may think the best way to feel better was to just go to bed, get under the blanket, and sleep until morning. When you wake up the problem may still be there, but your suffering may have been alleviated, at least temporarily.

First, by practicing meditative concentration we can achieve what some people only try to achieve by going to bed. We can put aside our problems and use meditation to settle the body and mind, thus achieving some peace of mind. As a further step, by practicing Chan with a peaceful mind, we can generate the wisdom to deal with problems, facing them, and then solving them. Traditionally, the concentration methods practiced in India were, first, to put aside the problem, and next, to solve the problem smoothly. That is, through meditative concentration we generate wisdom, which helps us solve our problem, thus alleviating affliction.

Family and Marital Problems

Regarding family problems, if married couples bicker over having a divorce, do they actually get a divorce? In the US, many states allow uncontested divorce. And, of course, after divorce, people are allowed to remarry. Once, a couple told me that they could not live together anymore and were about to get a divorce. I asked them if they got divorced, would they want to marry again. They said, "Sure, as soon as we find another suitable person, because we are still young." Then I asked, "If you had similar problems again, what would you do?" They simply said, "Then we'll get a divorce again and remarry again." Then I said to them, "This way, you would conceivably end up getting married a dozen times! What a pain and hassle! If you can solve the problem once and for all, wouldn't you be free of breaking up a marriage?" Then they asked me how to solve the problem all at once. I said, "Come learn sitting meditation with me. Come learn Chan with me. Then you will gradually know how to solve the problem between you two."

Troubles between husband and wife happen not just because they don't understand each other, but because fundamentally they don't understand themselves. As a result they blame the other person, whom they deem problematic. By practicing Chan, one will get to know oneself and be clearer about oneself. By understanding oneself, one already solves half of the problem, even though the issues of the other party may still remain unsolved. If a couple can come and learn sitting meditation together, then things will be much easier. When both parties get to understand themselves, the problem will be solved altogether. Even with only one party learning meditation, very often most of the problem would be solved. Because as long as one of them knows him or herself well, and realizes how important it is to treat the other party sincerely, the other will change as well. In the United States and Taiwan, there have been around dozens of married couples who came learn sitting meditation with me and therefore, didn't resort to divorce in the end.

Physical and Psychological Problems

In modern society, actually few people are one hundred percent psychologically stable; almost everyone has some kind of problem, although not necessarily needing professional treatment. Nonetheless, psychological problems have become an important issue for modern people. However, when people come and learn sitting meditation with me for a week, most of them will realize that they do have psychological problems, because they understand themselves better.

Also, modern people suffer from many kinds of physical illness, such as high blood pressure, heart diseases, and diabetes. These diseases were rarely seen in ancient times, but happen to modern people frequently. From recent newspapers we have read reports about cancer and AIDS, and that the latter is in some ways even more dreadful than the former. These diseases are only seen in modern society. But whether it is mental or physical illness, it all has something to do with the four kinds of societal problems we have raised in the beginning. Because people in modern society live a stressful life and tend to pursue excitement, if we can adjust ourselves both physically and mentally, these problems can actually be solved.

For the past two years, a British psychology professor has participated in seven-day meditation retreats at our Chan Meditation Center in New York. He leads a group in England for treating mental illness by applying Chan methods and the curative effects are positive. Nevertheless, he felt that his expertise was not good enough, so he came to participate in our retreats. Every time he returned to England, he felt that he had taken home with him some better methods. It was not his original idea to use Chan methods to treat mental problems, but when he was in California, he met an American who had learned Zen in Japan for a few years. The American started to use Zen as an aid in his psychotherapy practice when he returned to the United States. So this British professor adopted and modified the methods by the American and applied them in his own practice.

The people he helped with his therapy were not mental hospital patients, but those who regarded themselves as having some mental issue or imbalance. They suffered from psychological problems, lacked confidence or determination, including those who were uncertain and depressed about their own future. In addition, two Japanese medical doctors found that Zen meditation can help people lose weight, reduce high blood pressure or raise low blood pressure, as well as keep diabetes symptoms under control.

I have taught pregnant women to do sitting meditation, and almost always, they got beneficial results. Pregnant women can practice sitting meditation up until one month before delivery, or up to the time of delivery. Of course, they would not sit in a lotus position but on a chair instead. Children who are birthed by women who meditate during pregnancy usually have stable personality, a healthy body, a clear head, and are well behaved, and intelligent. This certainly has something to do with the state of mind of the mother during her pregnancy. This tells us that sitting meditation benefits greatly for its function of adjusting our bodies. Children, who are very active, can meditate, but not for long, at most 15 minutes. However, meditation works for them too.

How Chan Practice Can Benefit Modern People

In the past, Chan was practiced by monastics in the mountains, where they spent much time meditating. This is the source of the saying, "A senior monk absorbed in meditation." But nowadays, Chan meditation is increasingly popular among lay people. In today's commercial and industrial society, people live a hectic life—busy with working, rushing home, watching TV, going to movies, going out for fun, looking after their children, looking after their spouse, and so on. Busy with everything in their lives! Even playing can be something to be busy with. Therefore, I say that busy people are the ones that need Chan the most.

I often come across very busy people, and encourage them to practice sitting meditation and learn Chan. But they would say,

"Master, look how busy we are. How can we ever find time and leisure to learn sitting meditation? Meditation, that's only for monks!" I said, "Monks nowadays are different from those in the past; they are busy too. But, it is exactly because one is busy that one needs meditation. Meditating helps you regulate your body and mind so you can find more time for the things you need to do." Believe it or not, busy people often have moments when they will make mistakes. When one is busy, one will not be as meticulous or stable and thus, one's efficiency will be compromised.

Studies show that people are less likely to lose their temper when they have meditated in the morning. When you start the day with meditation, you tend to have a more stable mood for the rest of the day. Therefore, if busy people can spare some time during the day to meditate, they would enhance their work efficiency, and save working time. As a result, they will have more spare time. That is why today in Japan and Taiwan busy people in corporate and political circles practice meditation. When you are troubled and occupied with work, taking time to meditate is the best way to help yourself. So, meditation is not something for monks to entertain themselves when they have nothing else better to do.

Phases of Chan Meditation

The first phase of Chan practice is learning how to sit in meditation. The next level is to practice meditative concentration. The third phase is the actual experience of Chan. The effects and functions I just mentioned can be all achieved in the phases of sitting meditation.

Sitting Meditation

Would you all like to know how to do sitting meditation? I will now teach you a very simple method. Just relax your whole body, sit upright and straight; do not lean your back against the chair. Close your eyes, and place the hands on the knees. It is very important to relax the body, and the mind needs to be relaxed too. It is best not to think about anything, and if you are unable to stop thinking, just focus on one thing. If you think about your cute baby, focus on that one thought. But only focus on this particular thought and do not think about what your baby is doing. You can also focus on a sensation, like the feeling of your feet touching the floor. Sit that way for five minutes and your body will become relaxed and comfortable, and the pressure in your mind will lessen. After you've got it, please practice this back home. If you use this method in your sitting meditation practice, it will work for sure.

Meditative Concentration

Now, let's talk about meditative concentration. Modern people seek excitement—for their eyes, ears, nose, tongue, body, and mind—the more the better. For example, King Kong in the movie was portrayed as a huge gorilla, and there are those enormous balloon characters such as Donald Duck and others in Macy's Thanksgiving Day parade in New York City. Many people go to these events for excitement. What is there to excite? These are excitements for our eyes. Normally, only older people or those with ear problems have hearing loss. But a few months ago, I learned that young people also have hearing loss. I asked some of these young people what caused their hearing loss, and they said it was rock and roll music. The high volume, long duration, and frequency of listening to rock and roll music caused their hearing loss. Why do people listen to it? For excitement! Moreover, this music is only satisfying if the volume was loud. If one practices sitting meditation and attains meditative concentration, one can easily satisfy the senses of eyes and ears, which are much more subtle compared with those excitements.

The first level of meditative concentration is called "infinite light and infinite sound." That light is not the simple, coarse light commonly seen in this world but rather, an inner light. It is not the light that can be seen with the eyes. Regardless of how beautiful things may appear in this world, they cannot compare with what we experience in meditative concentration. One time a young person participated in a seven-day Chan retreat. From the second day, he often remained sitting after the meditation period was over. After he got up, I asked him, "Were you sitting well?" He said, "Very well." I asked, "Did you find anything?" He said, "Wow! After I started to sit the wall revealed another world. Then I walked into it. That world was so peaceful, so refreshing, and so beautiful. Nowhere in this world could be that beautiful. So I liked it very much and every time I meditated I looked forward going into it." However, I told him, "What you saw was an illusion; it is not meaningful. Do not dwell there." Illusory as it may be, if seeking excitements or aesthetics were the intent, the beauties of this world could not even compare with those in the state of meditative concentration.

There are five tones in Chinese music and seven tones in Western music, and there are not any more subtle tones. The music in the state of infinite light and infinite sound cannot be found in the ordinary human world. As the saying puts it, "The melody only exists in the heaven, and it is hardly heard in the human world." Such music has more than seven tones and it sounds utterly tender, comforting, and seems capable of melting the entire body. Every pore is so filled with ease and tenderness, that one forgets one's body's existence.

I have met young people including some of my disciples, who have used mind-altering drugs. I asked some of them what the benefits of using hallucinogens were. They said it was marvelous and the real world became totally different, and temporarily forgotten as they entered another time and space. I said there was nothing special about it. Through meditation, when one attains unity of mind, body, and the environment, one would have the feeling of transcending the real world.

Among physical pleasures, sex is the strongest form of all. However, in meditation, when one has attained some serenity, without even reaching meditative concentration, one can already feel a bliss that exceeds that of sexual pleasure by many times. Once experiencing this serenity, one's interest in sexual pleasure will lessen. This is also a good way to avoid sexually transmitted diseases.

People who meditate often experience heightened sensitivity of the palate. It is called the "wonderful offering from the celestial chef," meaning food will taste like nothing else in the world. Why do people who meditate have such experiences? It is because after meditation, the flow of saliva increases, appetite and digestion improve, but more important, the food is not eaten with greed, but delivered into the mouth in a natural and mindful manner. Therefore, eating becomes a more heightened sensation. Once during a seven-day Chan retreat, a woman had a fairly good experience of meditation. At a supper I asked her, "How was the supper tonight?" She said, "Wonderful! I've never had a better supper before."

These experiences tell us that exciting the senses is not as satisfying as meditating. Indeed, it is not easy to find truly satisfying pleasures in the world of the senses. In fact, the pursuit of excitement is often harmful to the body and mind—the more excitement, the more harm, the easier to get sick. Whereas, meditation is more beneficial to body and mind, and is ultimately more satisfying.

Realizing Chan

After learning meditation and cultivating meditative concentration, one should practice to realize Chan itself. Chan means wisdom, meaning it is devoid of self-centeredness. Only by leaving behind self-centeredness can one develop genuine wisdom. When self-centeredness is present, any wisdom would be subjective and there are conflicts of interest; therefore, it can't be genuine wisdom. We can say, then, that Chan is absolutely objective wisdom. The purpose of Buddhadharma is to give rise to wisdom. Therefore, the practice methods taught in Buddhist scriptures are meant to develop wisdom and dissolve self-centeredness. One way to achieve these goals is to cultivate concentration; another is to "investigate" Chan, to directly shatter one's delusions and self-centeredness, without needing any other practice methods. Cultivating concentration is the more common approach, and is the way of "gradual enlightenment." The second way is not easy to accomplish, and is the way of "sudden enlightenment."

The gradual approach can be likened to wiping a dusty mirror bit by bit, until the mirror is so clear that one doesn't even realize its existence. Images are reflected in it, but one doesn't notice the mirror itself. Imagine yourself in a hall with mirrors on the walls. The space may be small originally, but the mirrors on its walls make the room seem much more spacious. Wiping a mirror represents a gradual approach to enlightenment, as it uses the methods of concentration to gradually lessen our issues of ego and selfishness, so that in the end these issues disappear naturally.

Let me use the mirror analogy again to explain the sudden approach to enlightenment. If a mirror is very dusty, instead of gradually wiping it, we shatter it with a rock, or just blow it up, and the wall along with it; when this happens, we can see farther into vast openness and spacious emptiness. There is no longer the need to wipe the mirror, as it is completely gone. Therefore, the power of wisdom realized from the sudden approach to enlightenment is huge and vast.

The methods for cultivating concentration are called "Chan contemplation." There are many different methods of contemplation, but Chan methods are the simplest. This includes Chan dialogues and actions, as well as "investigating" Chan. Chan dialogues and actions are employed by the master to help the students' practice, while investigating Chan is employed when the student practices on their own.

The Culture of Chan

Chan Meditation Center, New York, April 28, 1990

Today I will talk about the culture of Chan Buddhism from three aspects: Chan philosophy, the morality of Chan, and Chan Art.

Chan Philosophy

The philosophy of Chan originated in India and flourished in China. The roots of Chan grew from the concept of the emptiness that characterizes the law of causes and conditions, in which constant change is a fact of existence. When the idea of emptiness was transmitted to China, it was compatible with the concept of "non-being." In Chan, emptiness does not signify empty space or voidness but rather, the process of ceaseless change—that all things in the world comprise the phenomenon of arising and perishing—of transforming from being to non-being, and from non-being to being. Due to their nature of undergoing constant change and cycling between being and non-being, all phenomena are impermanent; therefore, they are said to be "empty." The *Middle Treatise* (Skt. *Madhyamaka Shastra* or *Mulamadhyamaka-karika*), says, "All dharmas derive from various causes and conditions, and as I say, are non-existent." This says that phenomena result from the arising and perishing of causes and conditions, and are innately void of self-nature; in other words, they are "empty."

Sometime during the late fifth and early sixth centuries (C.E.), the First Patriarch Bodhidharma introduced Chan teaching to China. In the *Two Entrances and Four Practices*, he expounded on both emptiness and non-being. Regarding emptiness he said, "All things that exist are empty of self-nature." When discussing "non-being," he associated it with the "emptiness," saying, "Based on this principle, all forms (phenomena) are empty and are free of contamination, attachment, and this or that." He said this so as to expound on non-attachment and non-discrimination.

After Bodhidharma's time, the Sixth Patriarch Huineng, in his *Platform Sutra*, put special emphasis on the teaching on "no-form," which was also derived from the meaning of emptiness in the *Prajnaparamita Sutra*. The no-form mentioned in the *Platform Sutra* was based on the *Diamond Sutra*. "No-form" signifies that all mundane and supramundane phenomena are false and illusory. Whether they are material objects, thoughts, language, or words, they are all forms. None of these forms perceived by the senses or conceived by the mind are real, so they are considered "no-form." No-form does not mean that there is a transcendental world of truth that is separate from mundane phenomena. In fact, the truth is here and now, amidst the world of illusion, and all phenomena are, in themselves, the truth.

Ordinary people think that things in the world are real so they develop attachments to this and that, to gains and losses, to good and bad, to virtue and evil, etc., and thus, create troubles for themselves. For philosophers and religious figures, the world is unreal and the truth transcends the world. Philosophers believe that there is a metaphysical realm of ideas, and religious figures think that there is a heavenly kingdom of god(s) beyond the actual world; they distinctly separate the reality from the ideal, and human beings from holy beings.

However, from the perspective of Chan Buddhism there is no need to separate them, and it is impossible to separate them.

It is impossible to go beyond the real world to seek the truth. For Chan, to go beyond the world is no different from abiding in the world; the world of truth is inseparable from the real world. When one is deluded, one is in the realm of ordinary people; when one is enlightened, one transcends the mundane realm. The difference between delusion and enlightenment is that in the latter case, one realizes that mundane phenomena per se are no other than the truth, and that the intrinsic nature of all dharmas is empty.

Viewing the world through the eyes of Chan is like entering a forest and seeing it as a panorama, rather than just as trees, branches and leaves, and all their details; thus, the phenomenal world is in good order and has its natural changes, but not that intricate. On the other hand, ordinary people tend to see things in detail, seeing twigs, knots in tree trunks, even the minute details of each leaf. Therefore, they are unable to unravel what they see to find the leads and clues to the big picture, so they think it is complicated. In the Chan perspective, falling leaves and jostling branches are naturally unfolding phenomena replete with harmony and unity. If the causes and conditions require that we dispose of them we do it accordingly; if the causes and conditions do not allow that, we simply leave them alone. However, ordinary people let mere trifles draw them into eating and sleeping problems, and unnecessary worries and troubles. Rather, in our daily life, we should also apply Chan concepts and a relaxed attitude in everything we encounter. Not to worry about petty or trifling things to the extent that we miss the complete picture, and live with burdens and unwanted afflictions. Moreover, we should further understand that the panorama itself also does not exist and is a transient phenomenon as well.

Therefore, in the view of Chan, the world both exists and does not exist. It exists insofar as life continues, so we need to actively engage the actual world and assist in its operation. We ought to adapt to causes and conditions in all things, act according to our abilities and resources, and commit to doing our best in everything we do. On the other hand, we should not pursue things so forcefully that we cause ourselves more trouble. If we hold overly high expectations about people and things, and fame and fortune, we will surely also fret about gains and losses; we will harm others and ourselves and suffer tremendously. Therefore, Chan requires that we view phenomena as constantly changing, and also understand that even viewed in its wholeness the world is temporary and illusory.

Morality of Chan

Chan is Buddhism; therefore Chan morals are founded in the spirit of the Buddhist precepts. The precepts were established in accordance with the core of Buddhist thought, and in reference to the laws and morality of Indian society at that time: one must do what should be done, need not do what does not need to be done, and should not do what must not be done. There are different precepts depending on a person's status. There are precepts instituted for the laity and for monastics, and precepts in the Hinayana (Theravada) tradition and Mahayana tradition.

The precepts for the laity and the monastics are called the shravaka precepts of the Hinayana, and they lay a foundation for the bodhisattva precepts of the Mahayana. The Mahayana precepts take the generation of thoughts as the criteria for judgment, whereas the Hinayana precepts take the bodily activities and verbal expressions as their domain for observation. Therefore, the Mahayana precepts have stricter requirements and guidelines than the Hinayana precepts.

In the observance of Hinayana precepts, as long as one's verbal and bodily actions do not violate the rules or commit wrong doings, one is considered keeping precepts in purity. Whereas, in Mahayana precepts, if one arouses impure thoughts then one is considered breaking the precepts.

The precepts were transmitted from India to China with many rules that were minute and intricate. In the Hinayana precepts there were the vinaya texts transmitted to and upheld by different traditions and sects, and in the Mahayana precepts there were the contents expounded by different sutras and treatises. Passing over times and through different places, those Buddhist teachings were spread to China, and the Chinese found them difficult to comply with all of the rules of precepts of Indian Buddhism.

When Venerable Master Baizhang Huaihai (720-814 or 749-814), (the fourth generation descendant after Huineng) established the *Rules of Purity for Chan Monasteries*, some people complained that he did not abide by the vinaya of the Hinayana and the Mahayana. The explanation he provided was: "What I uphold as the standards are not restricted to Mahayana and Hinayana and are not different from Mahayana and Hinayana precepts. We should balance the comprehensive and the simplified precepts to set the standard of rules and make sure that they are feasible."

This means that he did not rigidly adhere to the text of the Mahayana and Hinayana precepts, nor did he go against the spirit of the Mahayana and Hinayana precepts. To stipulate the rules for living in a Chan monastery, he also considered their relevance to Chinese customs, and to the living conditions of his time. For instance, his monastery had no hall where Buddha images were enshrined and worshipped, but only had a Dharma hall for expounding the Dharma, and the monastics' halls for sitting meditation and taking a nap. Again, for instance, according to the Hinayana precepts, bhikshus are not allowed to dig the land and plough the field, whereas Baizhang advocated the principle of "a day without work is a day without meals," a life that combined farming and Chan practice.

According to the Hinayana vinaya, one must not cook in the monks' quarters and must beg for food with an alms bowl. As for Chan, in a life that combined farming and practice, the monks lived together in groups in the mountains; furthermore, begging for alms was inconvenient and not respected by Chinese customs. Therefore, the monks cooked for themselves in the monastery. In addition, according to the vinaya, bhikshus are not allowed to take meals after noontime. However, once in the time of Zhu Daosheng (360?-434), Emperor Wendi of the Song Dynasty made offerings to the monastics, though it was past noontime, saying, "The noontime just begins now." Daosheng then said, "The sun shines brightly in the sky, and the emperor says that it is just about noontime now, so how can we say it is not noontime?" Because of the emperor's words, Baizhang abandoned the observance of the precept of not eating after noontime.

Nevertheless, the pure rules of Chan monasteries still followed the precepts of vinaya in principle, yet they did not emphasize observing the texts of precepts in a very rigid and inflexible way. This is undeniably influenced by the Chan idea of perceiving with a comprehensive view of the whole, without rigidly sticking to the details or trivialities. Basically it is fine as long as rules do not go against the spirit of the Buddha's founding the precepts to help disciples live contently in a simple life, have few desires, and harbor a sense of shame. The behaviors that the Chan tradition displayed were not passive, but rather, were very active amidst a simple and frugal life. For the monastery's organization where people live together in a community, *Baizhang's Rules for Purity* stipulates that "a monastery establishes ten departments [for monastery operation] and are named quarters, in which a leader is appointed to take charge of a team of several people, and each individual is assigned their own tasks respectively." With regard to his teachings for cultivating the mind, Master Baizhang said, "Don't memorize anything, don't be conditioned by your thoughts, and let go of the body and mind, so you will be at ease."

Chan perceives things with a holistic view of the totality; therefore, our every thought is identical to and not separate from the pure and true wisdom, the quiescent nirvana; our every bodily act, each movement of our limbs, is not separate from the ten dharma realms—the four realms of the sages and the six realms of ordinary beings. Therefore, the Chan attitude towards life is naturally peaceful, harmonious, and positive. This is why the life in Chan monasteries is always simple, tidy, solid and tranquil.

Chan Art

The arts of Chan can be concretely expressed through architecture, paintings, literature, and other forms. With regard to architecture, I will give examples from Japan, Mainland China, and Taiwan, where I have stayed or visited, to explain the artistic spirit of Chan found in them. The architecture of monasteries in Kyoto was basically meant to imitate the style of Tang Dynasty (618-907), but in essence, their features were closer to those between the Five Dynasties (707-960) and Song Dynasty with Daitokuji Temple and Shokokuji Temple as being representative. The architectural style of Nara imitated that of

Tang Dynasty with Horyuji Temple, Todaiji Temple, and Toshodaiji Temple as the representatives. Of the two places, the monasteries of Kyoto inclined more to the simple unadorned spirit of Chan, while the style of those in Nara was basically more magnificent and adorned. Again, the Eiheiji Temple in Fukui Prefecture was imitative of Song style, so it had a strong feature of Chan.

Regarding Chinese temples and monasteries, there are still some in the architectural style of the Ming Dynasty (1368-1644) in Beijing in Mainland China. There are also the architectural styles of the late Ming Dynasty and early Qing Dynasty (1644-1912) at Mount Jiao in Zhenjiang of Jiangsu Province which still show the simple unadorned characteristics. As for the palatial architecture found at the Imperial Palace in Beijing with its rich carvings, colorful paintings, and upturned cornices, as well as at the Martyrs' Shrine in Taiwan with its vivid colors, they are not of the Chan style. If they were of the Chan style, they would exhibit the features of unadorned simplicity, applying original wood and color, and being natural and practical.

Regarding paintings, the history of Chinese art can be traced back several thousand years. However, after the emergence of landscape paintings, the most famous of all such painters was Wang Wei (701-761), a scholar and a poet at the time of Emperor Xuanzong of the Tang Dynasty. His style exemplifies simple presentation with concise meaning. For example, houses are partly hidden behind trees, human figures appear as simple strokes, and the elements of nature are set off by contrasts which imply a reality beyond the painting itself. Different viewers will interpret such paintings differently, but such expressions of artistic charm resonate with the spirit of Chan.

With regard to figurative painting, early Chinese art also emphasized realistic drawing, which happened to coincide with the style of Western painting in ancient times. We can tell from the story of *Marrying Zhaojun to the Huns beyond the Great Wall* that the way of painting with fine, meticulous brushwork was valued back then, but with the later evolution people tended to paint in exaggerated and unrealistic ways, which differed greatly from the realistic paintings. Take the paintings of the figures of arhats as examples: Legend has it that Wang Wei at the time of Emperor Xuanzong of the Tang Dynasty painted forty-eight pictures of sixteen arhats, and Lu Lengjia, a contemporary of his, also loved to paint the picture of the sixteen arhats. Afterward, those who painted the arhats include Tao Shouli and Wang Qihan of the Southern Tang State, Li Sheng, Zhang Xuan, and Guan Xiu (832-912) of the Anterior Shu State, and Wang Daoqiu of the Wuyue State, and down to the Venerable Master Lingyuan of modern times. The figures of the arhats were painted with individual imagination in an exaggerated way, often with weird appearances. The arhat paintings can be said to have a unique style of their own. On top of the sixteen arhats of the earlier period, two more arhats were added in Song Dynasty to form a total of eighteen pictures and sculptures of arhats.

The Qian royalty of the Wuyue State in the Five Dynasties had five hundred bronze statues made at Mount Wutai. No two figures were identical in the paintings and sculptures of arhats as to their countenances, dresses, and postures. The figures of arhats mostly came in weird appearances such as baring the upper body, taking a leisurely posture, playing merrily, being sloppily dressed and shod, picking the ears, resting the chin on the hand, knitting the brows, protruding the eyes, crossing the legs, reclining sideways, differing greatly from the proper, dignified deportments of typical monastics. Why did the painters adopt such a method of expression? They did it to express a charming flavor of openness, magnanimity, breadth of mind, freedom, ease, and spontaneity, while showing the inner ease and boundless naturalness that come with liberation. This has to do with the spirit of Chan that does not stick to anything rigidly or inflexibly. One does not need to behave with affectation or effort, and the natural deportment [of an enlightened arhat] is in itself, venerable.

Finally, I will discuss the arts of Chan from the angle of literature. Among the literary works in China there are many styles, topics, and artistic visions (conceptions) that are derived from the inspirations and revelations of Chan. In the Tang and Song dynasties many poets expressed the spirit of Chan in their poems, with Wang Wei, Bai Juyi, and Su Dongpo being the great masters among them. I will give three examples.

First, here is "A Visit to the Temple of Gathered Fragrance," by Wang Wei (701-761) of the Tang Dynasty, which reads:

I do not know the Temple of Gathered Fragrance,
For several miles entering cloudy peaks.
Ancient trees, paths without people;
Deep in the mountains, where is the bell?

This poem does not directly describe the scenery of the Temple of Gathered Fragrance, but uses the technique of setting off something by contrast, writing only about towering old trees, peaks that reach high into the clouds, and the faint sounds of bell from the Temple of Gathered Fragrance. This gives the reader free play to evoke their own images of the temple. This accords with the spirit of Chan, in which one practices diligently, and awakening happens naturally.

Next, "Failing to Meet the Hermit," by Jia Dao of the Tang

Dynasty (779-843).

> *I asked the boy under the pine tree, who told me:*
> *"The master is away collecting medicinal herbs.*
> *He's right in the mountain, but I don't know*
> *His whereabouts in the mist of the heavy clouds."*

The artistic flavor of this poem lies in implicitly depicting the tranquility in motion and the reality in the void. It describes how an enlightened person gives guidance to a beginning practitioner who is groping to find the entry; that is, who asks where the pure buddha-nature is. If only you practice in accordance with the Dharma by yourself, then though you have not witnessed or realized it personally, you still need to have faith. Buddha-nature is right there; when the enlightened state appears as if the clouds and mist have dispersed, you will then know.

Third and last, "A Village at Sunset," by Lei Zhen of the Song Dynasty.

> *Grass and water fill the hillside pond*
> *Drifting with cold ripples reflecting the sun setting behind the hill.*
> *The young cowherd, going home, sits on the back of an ox*
> *Randomly playing a short flute without melody."*

This poem expresses a leisurely mindset of being contented and perfect, as if depicting the state after attaining enlightenment. The self-contented, leisurely, free mental state does not necessarily need to have a purpose or to do something. In addition, both doing something and not doing anything are good and complete. "Randomly playing a short flute without melody," means the boy does not mind whether he plays the flute well or not, nor does he consider whether things are good or bad. This implies that one has removed all discriminations, vexations, and attachments. Therefore, we may regard this poem as one that describes the enlightened state of Chan.

The Meaning of Chan Is Beyond Words
Commentary on Master Hongzhi's Inscription on Silent Illumination

Chan Meditation Center, Elmhurst, New York, June 30, 1990

Prominent in the Chinese Chan School during the Southern Song Dynasty (1127-1279), there was Master Dahui Zonggao (1089-1163) of the Linji sect (Jpn. *Rinzai*) who advocated the *huatou* method, and Master Hongzhi Zhengjue (1091-1157) of the Caodong sect (Jpn. *Soto*), who was the first to promote the Silent Illumination method. These two masters were known as "the peerless duo of the Gate of Chan" in the Song period. Today *huatou* (Jpn. *wato*) is still a good method that is used energetically in China and Japan. The Silent Illumination method did not circulate for long in China, and in Japan, it became the *shikantaza* ("just sitting") method of the Soto Sect.

Huatou (along with its counterpart, *gong'an*) is a very familiar method of Chan practice in the Chinese Buddhist community in Taiwan. On the other hand, the Silent Illumination method is not well known even in the monasteries of the Caodong sect. Actually, in the late Ming Dynasty (1368-1644), the Caodong masters mostly used the methods of reciting the Buddha's name and *huatou*, so the sect almost became indistinguishable from the Linji. This [general unfamiliarity with Silent Illumination] is my motive for using the *Inscription on Silent Illumination* of Master Hongzhi Zhengjue as the text for my commentary.

From November 27 to December 2, 1980, I held a Chan retreat at the Chan Meditation Center in New York. For five evenings I lectured on the first 58 of the 72 lines of Master Hongzhi's *Inscription on Silent Illumination*. The English translations of the verse and the lectures were later edited and published as a chapter in my book, *Getting the Buddha Mind*.

At the time of the lectures, I tried to avoid using obscure quotations from the sutras, and did not pay close attention to formality in my choice of terms. However, after reading the Chinese transcript of these lectures recorded by lay Buddhist Wu Lihuan, even I was not sure what I meant! Ten years had passed since then, and Ms. Wu again suggested that I revise the transcript. Due to her sincerity and respect, as well as my wish to take responsibility, I spent a week reworking the transcript word by word, line by line.

The Chan of Silent Illumination

> *Silently and serenely one forgets all words,*
> *Clearly and vividly it appears before you.*

"*Silently and serenely*" refers to a state of mind that is peaceful and serene; "*one forgets all words*" means that in one's mind, there is neither language nor concepts. The ordinary mind is silent only to the extent that one is not speaking, but it is not necessarily free of wandering thoughts; that is not really forgetting all words. "*Clearly and vividly*" refers to a mind that is bright and pure; "*it appears before you*" means one reflects without making distinctions, truthfully contemplating all phenomena that one faces as they really are. If you add subjective judgment, then what you perceive differs from the facts before you.

Thus, these two lines summarize both the method and experience of Chan.

"*Silently and serenely one forgets all words*" means that the mind is presently empty of language, objects, and mental activities. One first isolates oneself from the environment, then isolates the present self from the past and future; lastly one isolates the present thought from the previous and next thoughts. "*Clearly and vividly it appears before you*" means that after forgetting all words, one attains clarity and luminosity; one begins with being aware of the rise and fall of thoughts; next, one becomes aware of thoughts as soon as they arise; finally, what remains is a mind that is clear and vivid, illuminating like a vast, bright mirror without defilement.

Silent Illumination can be practiced using a taut approach or a more relaxed approach. In the taut method, the practitioner uses will power to suppress wandering thoughts so that they will not arise, inducing oneself to give rise to mindfulness in order to prevent drowsiness. One sits with correct posture, the lower back and neck in a straight line, guarding one's body and mind, abiding in one state, so that one gradually reaches the state of forgetting all words. For others, the relaxed approach may be more suitable; this means using the conscious mind to deliberately, as well as naturally, relax the muscles and nerves of the whole body. Neither controlling nor following wandering thoughts, yet not fearing their arising; not worrying about being distracted, just relaxing both body and mind; not intending to think of the past or the future, not suppressing thoughts nor raising one's mindfulness; just letting oneself be serene, contented, and pure. This way, one will gradually enter the wonderful state of Silent Illumination.

When one realizes it, time has no limits.
When experienced, your surroundings come to life.

If you work hard at Silent Illumination yet still sense the passing of time, then you have not reached the level of silence and serenity. In silence, you would not sense the passing or even the existence of time. Having no sense of time means time is infinite, which is saying that the infinitely fast is the same as the infinitely slow. If you think you are in the state of silence and serenity, but still have the concept of time, then that is not the real silence; you are aware of time because your thoughts are still rising and falling; otherwise, you would not have a sense of time.

Venerable Master Taixu was a contemporary Chan monk. One night, he heard the evening bell indicating time to retire for the night [but he continued meditating]. Right after that, he heard the bell again, indicating the time to wake up. In between the two bells a whole night had passed, yet he sensed no passage of time. This example shows that when one has practiced to the state where there are no thoughts in the mind, for you time no longer exists.

"*When experienced, your surroundings come to life*" refers to the infinite space described in "*clearly and vividly it appears before you.*" This infinite space includes every thing that rises and falls and within this space, everything is lively and active, free, and at ease. In this situation, thought is not abiding and not moving. If thoughts were abiding or moving, then they would lack the liberation of "*surroundings come to life,*" and they would surely be restricted by a definite space. If thoughts are neither abiding nor moving, then the space experienced would be infinite vastness. However, if thoughts follow the movements in the surroundings, then the scope of the six sense organs and the six consciousnesses is definitely limited. As an example, if your thoughts were not abiding and not moving, then you would see a lot more with your naked eyes. They would function like a camera; since the negative is not abiding, not attached, and not moving, it could instantly capture everything within the range of the lens. If the negative is originally abiding and moving, would it be able to take a clear and vivid photograph?

In Chan retreats, I sometimes teach people to just look and listen without thinking. At such time, what do you see and hear? However, in the first two days, this method cannot be used successfully because people's mind has not yet settled, so it is nearly impossible not to think with the brain. Even after the fourth day, not many people are able to give up using the brain to think. But if one can reach the state of unmoving mind, then one is able to experience a similar infinite space.

Regarding the experience of infinite space, there are three situations: First is the buddhas' supramundane state of infinite space; whereas, ordinary and sagely sentient beings do not. Second is the ability to see infinity within a miniscule point. The *Shurangama Sutra* says that the buddhas of the past, present, and future are turning the great Dharma wheel at the tip of a hair; that is to say, they are speaking limitless Dharma and delivering innumerable sentient beings within the point of a hair. That which is infinitesimally small— being nothing—is also infinitely large. Third is the experience of illuminating the mind and seeing the nature, when one experiences that one's true nature is really no-nature.

> *Lively and animated, it simply illumines,*
> *Full of wonder is this pure illumination.*

"*Lively and animated*" says that what is illuminated is not void, but vast spaciousness—neither within nor without, but in the mind. Only the experience of the unmoving mind is infinite space. Therefore, that which is lively and animated is very clear, bright, real, and lively. Only contemplation and awareness can simply illumine. In silence there are no scattered thoughts, and in illumination one is not scattered; in silence the mind is serene, and in illumination the mind is bright. This experience can only occur when silence and illumination compensate each other. Otherwise, it could only be said to be "in darkness, solely ambiguous," and that is why sentient beings see others as sentient beings. If one were able to turn dimness into brightness, one would be able to transform the ambiguous into illumination. Therefore, in the eyes of a buddha all sentient beings are buddhas.

Once during a retreat interview a practitioner told me: "I seem to be fighting with someone!" I said: "No, you are fighting with yourself." He asked: "How could there be two of me?" I said: "Not just two of you; there are many of you. The scattered and wandering thoughts are like countless threads of silk and flax. Due to the contradictions between the previous and later thoughts, we feel like there are two people in the mind, fighting. This is ambiguous darkness, not Silent Illumination." I later taught him the sentence: "Seek no truth and suppress no wandering thoughts." There is no need to reject wandering thoughts; as long as one ignores them, they will quiet down by themselves. The water in the pond is originally pure, and it is only due to the disruption from outside forces that make it muddled. If one is able to let the water naturally settle, then it would return to purity. To experience the bright awareness of the simply illuminating, one must first practice to attain the skill of silence and serenity.

"*Full of wonder is this pure illumination*" illustrates that this clarity encompasses everything. When one practices Silent Illumination well, one can get countless insights from various angles and aspects in regards to issues great or small. One can even say that the world is contained in a grain of sand, and in each flower there is a buddha. That is the inconceivable state beyond the expression of words and language and beyond the scope of symbols and thoughts. All this wonder is encompassed within this pure illumination.

> *The moon's appearance, a river of stars,*
> *Snow-clad pines, clouds hovering on mountain peaks.*

These two lines describe the state of mind of Silent Illumination. "*The moon's appearance*" means that there is neither cloud nor fog, only the full bright moon, which is the state of mind of silent illumination. The "*river of stars*" is the Milky Way. When the moon is out, it is very clear; when it is not out, we can clearly see a sky filled with stars. Shakyamuni Buddha was enlightened when he saw a very bright and clear star. This river of stars, where we can see multitudes of bright stars at a glance, represents the state when we practice Silent Illumination very well. As for the minds of ordinary people, there is no moon or river of stars; instead, there is a sky filled with dark clouds of vexations.

"*Snow-clad pines*" describes a mind that has made good progress in practicing Silent Illumination. Each pine is covered by a mantle of snow which hides the tree itself. After a winter storm, the pines look as if they were sculpted from crystal and decorated with jade; the snowy scene is one of vast clarity and brightness. A mind in this state is open, bright, calm, and serene. "*Clouds hovering on mountain peaks*" likens this mind to clouds rising at mountain peaks; it is a mind free and at ease, with no restraints. Unlike clouds in a clear sky that freely drift, here we see clouds hovering over the mountain despite the obstruction of the peaks. This is a mind that is liberated, free of obstructions. Even a "beauty sitting on one's lap" would not scatter this mind; it is not moved by threats, rewards, or temptations; it is without fear, even if one's body was being amputated. Because this mind is liberated, it is not affected by circumstances.

> *In darkness, it glows with increasing brightness,*
> *In shadows, it shines with a splendid light.*

"*Darkness*" and "*increasing brightness*" describe a mind that glows brighter in darkness, meaning that wisdom is enhanced amidst vexation. "*Increasing*" means the glowing is frequent and ongoing. To outward appearances, one may seem confused, but inwardly there is depth and profound wisdom. Wise ones may look ordinary and dull, but their mind is open and honest, and they will not deceive themselves or others.

"*Shadows*" implies concealing and "*shine*" implies revealing. "*Darkness*" and "*shadows*" correspond to silence, while "*brightness*" and "*shines*" correspond to illumination. A silent person may look like an imbecile who is in darkness and shadows, but when there is illumination, wisdom manifests in a lively and animated manner; so it shines like a splendid light. When silence and illumination function together, the mind is unmoving yet shining with everlasting brightness. This state expresses the form and power of the mind of wisdom.

> *Like the dreaming of a crane flying in empty space,*
> *Like the clear, still water of an autumn pool.*

In Silent Illumination the mind can be likened to *"dreaming of a crane"* flying in a boundless expanse of clear blue sky. This *"empty space"* is vast, without limits, and within it there is no obstruction and no separation. Whether this mind moves or is utterly still, it is without boundaries. This is the state of mind when silence and illumination function simultaneously.

"Like the clear, still water of an autumn pool" describes a mind that is pure as a lucid autumn pool, deep and bottomless; so serene and distant that it seems unreachable. Looking into this pool, one sees everything in a single glance, under and on the surface. Still, one cannot see its depths to the bottom. The autumn pool, clear and still as a mirror, reflects a boundless sky. With thin clouds and little fog, the autumn weather is soothing and refreshing; the sky is wide, high, and boundless. This is the sense of limitless space in Silent Illumination, where, simultaneously, there is utter stillness, deep and profound.

> *Endless eons dissolve into emptiness,*
> *Each indistinguishable from the other.*

"Endless eons" means that time is infinitely long and some believe it to be eternal; but regardless of its duration, time does not exist for a mind in Silent Illumination. An eon can be shorter or longer, but "endless eons" is surely infinity and therefore empty, just as a fleeting moment in the present is empty. *"Indistinguishable"* means one makes no distinction between previous and following thoughts—the

previous thought is silent and illuminated, and so is the following thought. And through this the mind remains clear and discerning. "*From the other*" refers to the changing relations between past, present, and future. In Silent Illumination there is no mind [that cogitates], but there is a mind [of awareness] which does not attach to time; therefore, past, present, and future are indistinguishable. Our ordinary sense of time derives from the coming and going of thoughts, and since our mind in Silent Illumination is without thoughts, time has no duration and is at each moment, "empty."

> *This wonder exists in a place of silence.*
> *In this illumination all striving is forgotten.*

"*This wonder exists in a place of silence*" says that the mind's wonderful functions are contained in silence. The Western saying, "Silence is golden," cannot adequately describe the profundity of this silence. But when the mind still has an object to cling to, it is scattered, and any silence and brightness would be lost; of course, the wisdom eye would also be obscured, and there would be no wonder to speak of. "*In this illumination, all striving is forgotten.*" While illuminating, one does not think, "I am illuminating." Indeed, one has forgotten all sense of striving. Only then is one truly illuminating in constant silence. *The Stanza of Samatha* by Chan Master Yongjia Xuanjue (665-713) states: "When one is using the mind, there is no mind that can be used." To connect these two states amidst silence is the infinite function of wisdom. When wisdom is used to illuminate all states, at that time, one would not be aware of a mind that is illuminating, or that objects are being illuminated.

Where does this wonder exist?
Brightness and clarity dispel confusion.

Hongzhi said earlier that within the silence there is wonder. However, please do not misconstrue and think that wonder can be achieved through silence alone; if there were silence without illumination, then one may fall into drowsiness and dullness. Indeed, the verse reminds us that there must also be brightness and clarity, a clear and alert mind to deal with such obstructions. When there is clarity and wakefulness, the mind remains peaceful and serene as still water. The phrase "brightness and clarity" is seen in *The Stanza of Samatha* by Master Yongjia: "Silence and serenity to calm the thinking mind, brightness and clarity to clear the drowsy mind."

Silent illumination is the path
And the root of the subtleties of li.

Practicing Silent Illumination, one is able to cut off vexations and even the most subtle roots of ignorance. Within vexations there are coarse and fine, and within ignorance there are roots and branches. In practice, one starts with coarse vexations, gradually alleviating them, until one reaches the silent state of "in silence, constantly illuminating; in illumination, constantly silent." At such time, the roots of the subtlest vexations will be severed. When the mind is moved by and attached to what it perceives, its scope becomes infinitesimal; when the mind is not attached to things—when there is illumination within the silence—then the mind becomes infinitely expansive. Thus, wisdom is inversely proportional to vexation—the bigger the vexation the smaller the wisdom. When wisdom expands so as to be without limits, vexation shrinks until it is infinitesimal. Ultimately, wisdom itself can no longer be perceived, and so with the most subtle of vexations. That is to say, the vexations of ignorance become so small that they vanish, and wisdom grows so large that it also cannot be perceived. For these reasons, sentient beings practice in order to enhance wisdom and sever vexations. For buddhas there is no vexation and no wisdom.

In his *Song of the Precious Mirror Samadhi*, Chan Master Dongshan Liangjie (807-869) has the lines: "Doubling the *li* ("fire") trigram (☲) makes six lines, the outer and inner lines mutually interacting…the exact center subtly harmonizing, drumming and singing simultaneously." This passage uses the wondrous subtle changes expressed in the *li* trigram from the *Book of Changes* (Chn. *Yi Jing*) to describe the mind of wisdom. Hongzhi was a great and virtuous master in the lineage of Master Dongshan, so it was natural for him to use the subtle wonders expressed in the *li* trigram to describe Silent Illumination.

> *Thoroughly perceiving li and its subtleties*
> *Like weaving with the gold shuttle on a loom of jade.*

In the mind of silence, wandering and scattered thoughts do not arise, and one has already had a thorough insight that buddha-nature is like the emptiness of space. This silence is not a dull stillness, so it follows that the deeper one's silence, the stronger one's illumination. Within the silence is concealed the wondrous subtle functions like that of the *li* trigram. The "*gold shuttle*" and "*loom of jade*" describe the mutual functioning of silence as host, and illumination as guest. A weaver's loom remains stationary while the [threaded] shuttle is moved back and forth to create the woven cloth. Thus, the loom of jade and golden shuttle can be likened to the method of Silent Illumination—the best tool for practicing Chan and attaining enlightenment.

> *Center and off-center interchange with each other.*
> *Light and darkness are mutually dependent.*

"*Center and off-center*" corresponds to the line (quoted previously) from the *Precious Mirror Samadhi* which says, "The outer (off-center) and inner (center) lines [of the *li* trigam] mutually interact." The phrase "*mutually interchange*" comes from Master Dongshan's *Preface to the Inscription within the Wondrous*, which refers to "the interchange between the circle and the slant." "*Light and darkness*" is from the *Inquiry into Matching Halves* by Chan Master Shitou Xiqian (700-790), which says: "In the midst of brightness there is darkness; don't take darkness as darkness. In the midst of darkness there is brightness; don't take brightness as brightness." Yongjia Xuanjue's *Stanza of Upeksha* also says: "The origin of brightness and darkness is not different…as one who can illumine in darkness, it is the wise who is transformed from ignorance."

In the Caodong School, "off-center" and "center" are used to describe vexation and wisdom respectively; while the two correspond to each other, they are not in opposition. To reflect levels of cultivation and realization, the terms were used to describe five levels of Chan attainment:

1. *Seeing one's nature*, called "the off-center within the center"
2. *Reducing vexations*, called "the center within the off-center"
3. *Vexations tamed*, called "coming in the center," or "manifesting within the essence"

4. *Vexations severed*, called "arrival in dual aspects"

5. *Vexations are precisely wisdom*, called "perfection in both aspects."

These five relations between off-center (vexation) and center (wisdom) are what the verse means by "interchanging with each other." These ideas allow us to express the relations between the diminishing of vexations and the growing of wisdom. However, though we talk of diminishing and growing, in actuality there is no movement—this is just the active functioning of silence and illumination.

"Light and darkness" here symbolize wisdom and vexation. [Just as without darkness, there would be no light,] if vexation did not exist, there would be no way wisdom can manifest. Wisdom exists in the midst of vexation, and in giving rise to wisdom, we take vexation as its source. However, one should rely on wisdom and not on vexation. In the midst of vexation, if one is aware of this, that is already wisdom. But we should not take wisdom to be vexation itself; light and darkness depend on each other for their existence, but we must clearly recognize light and darkness for what they are.

[Although we can say that wisdom exists amidst vexation,] we should not see vexation and bodhi—or for that matter, samsara and nirvana—as separate. We should still be clear about how [vexation and wisdom] are influenced by causes and effects [in our activities]. This is the truth of Silent illumination: do not mistake phenomena for the underlying principle; do not confuse between cause and effect.

> *There is neither subject nor object to rely on,*
> *Yet, at this time, there is mutual interaction.*

The phrases used above, "mutually dependent" and "mutual interaction," express the interdependency between subject and object. From a common sense point of view, the relationship between two things can be seen as "host" and "guest"—the host being that which is depended on, the guest being one who depends on the host. In this distinction, host and guest are related but not identical. The line "*There is neither subject nor object to rely on,*" says that we cannot speak of [silence and illumination] in terms of guest and host, or subject and object; they are two facets of the same totality—mutually existing and mutually dependent. "Within sameness, there is difference; amidst difference, there is sameness." Sameness and difference are clearly distinct, yet they are mutually embracing and not contradictory.

"*Yet, at this time, there is mutual interaction*" means that silence and illumination function simultaneously. This is the same as Master Dongshan's "center and off-center interchange with each other." It is also the same as the Master Shitou Xiquan's interdependence of "brightness and darkness." Thus, between silence and illumination there is no guest-and-host distinction; however, they interchange as substance and function.

> *Drink the medicine of correct views.*
> *Beat the poison-smeared drum.*

If one practices Silent Illumination, its efficacy is like drinking "*the medicine of correct views*" which can cure the vexations of birth and death. It is also like beating "*the poison-smeared drum*" that can destroy a whole army of vexations connected with the birth-and-death.

The analogy of drinking "*the medicine of correct views*" comes from the 60-chapter version of the *Flower Ornament Scripture* (Skt. *Avatamsaka Sutra*) translated from Sanskrit in the Jin Dynasty (1115-

1234). Chapter 37, "The Wholesome Appearing Medicine King," says: "Legend has it that in the Snow Mountain there is a great medicine king named Wholesome Appearance. Whoever sees him, their eyes are purified; whoever hears him, their ears are purified; whoever smells his fragrance, their nose is purified; whoever tastes his flavor, their tongue is purified; whoever touches him, their body is purified. If one obtains the soil from his kingdom, one will be cured of countless illnesses and attain peacefulness, stability and happiness."

References to beating "*the poison-smeared drum*" are found in many sutras, and they liken the power of Buddhadharma to poison smeared on the face of a drum; when this drum is beaten—and its power enhanced by incantation—sentient beings near and far, great and small—whoever hears it—their greed, hatred, and ignorance would be "killed," that is to say, extinguished. The *Nirvana Sutra* uses two drum analogies that epitomize Buddhadharma: in the first, the teaching of the Five Vehicles is likened to the beating of the divine drum of the heavens. In the second, the Mahayana teaching of buddha-nature as constantly abiding is likened to a poison-smeared drum. Hongzhi's verse says that the method and function of Silent Illumination, is the teaching of the Supreme Vehicle that extinguishes all illness and eradicates all confusion.

> *When Silence and Illumination complement,*
> *Killing and bringing to life are up to me.*

These lines say that when silence and illumination mutually respond, then one is like a sovereign who holds the power of life and death. Silent Illumination is actually [the method of] *shamatha-vipashyana*, in which *shamatha* and *vipashyana* complement each other. When there is silence in illumination, and illumination in silence—each complementing the other—that is precisely the dual functioning of *shamatha-vipashyana*. "*Killing*" here recalls the sayings, "When demon Mara appears, kill him," or "If you see the buddha, kill him." Killing means cutting off the attachments of mind, thought, and consciousness to attain a mind that is not grasping at conditions, where thoughts are not bound to objects of perception. "*Bringing to life*" reminds us that the mind is like a mirror: "When a northerner appears [before it], a northerner is reflected; when a southerner appears, a southerner is reflected." A mind like this is a great and bright mirror that, despite myriads of states appearing in front of it, clearly reveals and reflects all things while remaining perfectly undisturbed.

When one should kill [attachments], then do so; when one should bring [wisdom] to life, then do so; there is no need to rely on outside forces. So we say, "*Killing and bringing to life are up to me.*" Only when one is immersed in silence may one illuminate well; therefore, the deeper one's silence, the stronger the illumination. Only in illumination can one attain silence, and the stronger the illumination, the deeper the silence—the two complement each other, growing mutually. When silence and illumination function together, it is not the ordinary state of meditative concentration in which there is no contemplation; and it is definitely not the drowsiness and scattering of the ordinary state of mind.

> *At last, through the door, one emerges.*
> *The fruit has ripened on the branch.*

In traditional Chinese culture, "emerges" has two meanings: The first is to offer oneself [to others]; the second is to pay gratitude to one's country by becoming a public official. No matter which, one must leave home in order to devote oneself to express gratitude, or become a public official. From the Song Dynasty to the Qing Dynasty, someone who wanted to enter civil service needed to pass the county, prefecture, and capital exams. When one finally became an imperial official, one was said to have "emerged." In this passage, *"through the door, one emerges"* refers to the silence which is quiescent and still, so it is likened to being "inside the door." This is not passive escapism, but rather, it serves as an ally to the function of outward observation. If there is no true silence, then there is also no true illumination. Although silence does not manifest outwardly, its function is devoted to, and expressed by, illumination.

"The fruit has ripened on the branch" refers to something an ordinary person can see with their eyes, but in Silent Illumination it refers to the [ripening of] illuminating awareness which enables one to see through vexations and cut them off. While not yet through the door, one already has the foundation of giving oneself to the Dharma. This potential may be hidden and not yet revealed, but it is indeed an extremely important condition. It is like a fruit tree with its roots and trunk behind one side of a wall, with branches hanging over the other side. People outside the wall can see ripened fruit on the overhanging branches, and of course, they would guess that the trunk is behind the wall. The unseen trunk on one side and its visible branches on the other side are interdependent and inseparable; they may appear to be separate phenomena, but actually are two aspects of the same thing.

> *Only this Silence is the supreme speech.*
> *Only this Illumination, the universal response.*

"*Silence is the supreme speech*" says that words cannot express the ultimate truth. After teaching the Dharma and delivering sentient beings for over forty years, Shakyamuni Buddha said that he had not spoken a single word. When there is no other choice, we use language as a tool to express our thoughts, but we must use our mind directly to experience our intention. Therefore, the more the mind is imbued with silence and stillness, the deeper, vaster, stronger, and clearer our experience will be. Therefore, the real truth need not be expressed with words; as with the truest of languages, there's no need to talk. Silence is the supreme language, while illumination is all-pervasive and responds to sentient beings universally. Someone asked me, "Does illumination mean having clear awareness of one's environment?" My answer was that in daily life one may be clearly aware of one's environment, but that is not enough; the mind's illuminated wisdom needs to be infinitely profound, infinitely pervasive.

> *The response is without effort.*
> *The teaching, not heard with the ears.*

Here, "*response*" means according with, echoing, or interacting, with one's environment. "*Without effort*" means spontaneity in action, without leaving traces afterwards. Before the event there is vast emptiness; afterwards, it is like a bird flying through the air leaving no traces; the mind maintains a pure, silent, and lively spaciousness. Universally responding to external conditions, the mind is serene. Effort implies intention and attachment, but after one attains Silent Illumination, one's mind would not be attached to form, so there would be no virtue and benefit to speak of.

Language is a means for transmitting information using symbols.

Since the illuminated mind clearly perceives all dharmas, it is able to receive information from all directions; however, this information is not necessarily perceived through hearing. The six sense organs—eyes, ear, nose, tongue, body, and mind—are all capable of receiving information. However, the best mode of expression is wordless. In China during the reign of Emperor Wudi of the Liang Dynasty, there was a Chan Master called Fu Dashi, the Distinguished One (497-569 CE). One time the emperor invited Master Fu Dashi to his palace to speak the Dharma. After ascending the platform, without speaking a word, the master just banged the platform with the wooden clapper, stepped down, and walked away. The emperor found this quite strange, wondering why the master walked off without speaking the Dharma. Actually, the highest Buddhadharma cannot be spoken. The *Diamond Sutra* says: "To say that the Tathagatha, the Buddha, has Dharma to expound, would be slandering the Buddha." The sutra also says, "The Dharma has no Dharma to speak of; this is called "Speaking the Dharma."

> *All the myriad things in the universe*
> *Emit light and speak the Dharma.*

It is said that emerald-green bamboo and yellow flowers are the Buddha speaking the Dharma. Is there any single thing or any single place that does not manifest the Buddha expounding the Dharma? Chan Master Niutou Huizhong (682-769) said that wall and rubble are not different from the mind of the Buddha, and that all non-sentient beings also speak the Dharma. The *Flower Ornament Scripture*, Chapter 31 on "The Vows of Bodhisattva Samantabhadra" says: "The earth speaks, sentient beings speak; everything in the three periods of time speaks the Dharma." The *Amitabha Sutra* clearly states that "Birds expound the thirty-seven aids to enlightenment; trees resonate with myriad kinds of music that give rise—in those who hear it—to mindfulness of the Buddha, Dharma, and Sangha.

When the mind is free of obstructions and it is bright and illuminating, the myriad phenomena in the universe are seen as the Buddha's Dharma body (Skt. *Dharmakaya*). The Buddha is often depicted as having a body of radiant gold, and before expounding the Dharma, he would auspiciously emit rays of light. If one could experience the pervasiveness of the Buddha's Dharma body, one would also see that all places and all things are radiant with light and speaking the Dharma.

> *They testify to each other,*
> *And correspond in dialogue.*

If one were able to experience all phenomena in the universe as emitting light and expounding Dharma, it would not be so difficult to see each and every thing in relation to everything else, all in mutual affirmation, all using wordless speech to respond to each other. It's as if one were in the Pure Land of the buddha realms, and all beings that one encounters—sentient or otherwise—are sages who have transcended the samsara, and all manifest buddha-nature. Whether or not they speak, all are expressions of the Dharma dialogue between the myriad phenomena.

> *Corresponding in dialogue and testifying,*
> *They respond in perfect harmony.*
> *When illumination is without silence,*

Then distinctions will be perceived.

The ordinary mind likes to make distinctions—things are seen as wholesome or unwholesome, good or bad, beneficial or harmful, beautiful or ugly, and so on. Sunshine and gentle breezes are good; pouring rain and blustery winds are bad; material abundance is good, deprivation is bad. However, seen by the illuminated mind of wisdom, events follow their natural course according with conditions, and everything corresponds in harmony, without conflict or contradiction. One receives wholesome results from planting wholesome causes, and unwholesome results from planting unwholesome causes; one receives present results from causes planted in the past, and causes planted in the present will yield future results. When one acts, the other responds; everything is of one's own doing and receiving. This is harmonious, so there is nothing to be joyful about, nor anything to fear; since there is nothing to blame, there is nothing to worry about.

Only when silence and illumination work simultaneously is there perfect harmony; if there is only illumination and no silence, there will be disharmony in the mind; one lacks serenity and purity of mind, seeing oneself as opposing and conflicting with the environment. One would also discover that among phenomena there is competing with, fighting, destroying, and subduing each other. This would generate vexations, and any active wisdom that was there would be lost.

Attesting and corresponding in dialogue,
Perfectly they respond to each other.
When silence is without illumination,
Then all will be in waste.

These four lines emphasize the meaning of the previous four lines, thus clarifying the inseparable nature between silence and illumination. When there is lack of one of them or partiality towards the other, both will be deficient in power. One who sits in silence without illumination is like a dead log or cold ashes, and would be just idling in drowsiness and torpor. Neither of these practices is the Chan approach that upholds concentration and wisdom in equal measure.

> *When the principle is realized through silent illumination,*
> *The lotus will blossom and the dreamer will awaken.*

When Silent Illumination is thorough and perfected, one will completely realize the principle, awakening the mind and seeing one's nature. One will personally open to enlightenment like the blossoming of a lotus, or waking from the dream of birth-and-death. Buddhadharma often describes birth-and-death as illusory, not true reality, and when one awakens to bodhi, one sees that the buddha-nature—one's "original face"—is in fact, emptiness. At that time, one can say one has finally awakened from the dream. In Chan Master Yongjia Xuanjue's *Song of Enlightenment* there is the line, "In dreams there are clearly six paths of existence; upon awakening the universe is empty throughout."

> *The hundred rivers flow to the ocean,*
> *The thousand peaks face the loftiest mountain.*

The mind of Silent Illumination is vast and open. "*The hundred rivers flow to the ocean*" is a figure of speech saying that, although sentient beings differ in their karmic capacities all can become buddhas; as each river flows to the ocean, its individual flavor merges with that of the ocean. In the *Lotus Sutra*, the chapter on "Expedient Means" says: "There is only the teaching of one vehicle, not two or three." "*The thousand peaks*" describes the countless vexations of sentient beings that "*face the loftiest mountain.*" These images say that the mind of Silent Illumination is completely unified.

Within the simultaneity of silence and illumination, the hundred rivers and the thousand peaks are clearly distinct; this clarity is illumination. The hundred rivers merging with the ocean and the thousand peaks facing the lofty mountain are like the functions of silence. A hundred rivers rush ahead, a thousand streams contend towards the ocean to become united; a thousand peaks rise and fall, and ten thousand ridges overlay in stacks, all together returning to the one mountain. Whether or not one makes distinctions does not matter, for these images express the mutual enrichment between motion and stillness that is characteristic of Silent Illumination. They speak of the wondrous and limitless functioning of compassion and wisdom.

> *Like geese preferring milk;*
> *Like bees gathering pollen.*

"*Geese preferring milk*" and "*bees gathering pollen*" are like accomplished Chan practitioners whose cultivation in Silent Illumination gives them the ability to discriminate and make choices. In the *Sutra on the Basis of Contemplation of True Dharma* (Skt. *Saddharmasmrity Upasthana Sutra*), there is this legend: "If you mix milk and water in a bowl and let the King of the Geese drink it, he is able to drink only the milk and leave the water behind." In the *Sutra of Buddha's Bequeathed Teaching*, it says: "Bees gathering pollen extract the essence of the flower without damaging its fragrance and hue." Both of these analogies express the deep cultivation of one who is well practiced in the Chan of Silent Illumination, of one who has attained the Dharma principle of non-discrimination. This practitioner is no longer troubled by vexation, discrimination, attachment, and the agony of not getting what one seeks, or not letting go what one should. Such a person would uphold ethics, laws, social customs, and the Buddhist precepts; they would not contradict these norms. As well, they practice restraint in the appropriate manner, according to time and place, taking only what they should and letting go what they must. This is the spirit of "speaking according to one's position, and fulfilling the duties of a monastic tolling the bell." At this level of cultivation, one contributes while being very clear of one's role.

> *When reaching the ultimate in Silent Illumination,*
> *I will embody the tradition of my lineage.*

If one has diligently cultivated Silent Illumination, one will be able to realize the Dharma of the supreme vehicle, called "the ultimate attainment," which is actually, no attainment. The *Diamond Sutra* says: "If there is a Dharma called *anuttara-samyak-sambodhi* that can be attained, then the Dipamkara Buddha would not have foretold my being the future Buddha." This is similar to the concept in the *Heart Sutra*: "There is no wisdom and no attainment; therefore with nothing to attain…" This is because in Silent Illumination, if there still is a self-center whose value is based on attainment and realization, this self is far from true liberation. Only by practicing

Silent Illumination to dissolve self-attachment and the view of self, may one truly "breathe through the same nostrils as the buddhas of the past, present, and future." Only then can one turn the great wheel of Dharma and spread the Buddha's tradition.

> *This tradition of Silent Illumination*
> *Penetrates from the highest to the deepest.*

The Caodong Sect [in which Silent Illumination originated] is in the tradition of Chan Buddhism, and Chan is in the tradition of the Buddha. Buddhadharma's deliverance of the world is the dual functioning of wisdom and compassion; and to cultivate wisdom and compassion, we engage in the dual practice of calming and contemplation.

The essence of Silent Illumination advocated by Master Hongzhi is the dual practice of calming (*shamatha*) and contemplation (*vipashyana*). In Sanskrit, *shamatha* means "calming" and *vipashyana* means "contemplation." Practiced together, *shamatha-vipashyana* has the meanings of calming-contemplation, concentration-wisdom, silence-illumination, serenity-clarity. It is the method used by the Three Vehicles: [the *shravaka* and *pratyekabuddha* vehicles of Hinayana, and the bodhisattva vehicle of Mahayana]. In Chinese Buddhism, the words "calming" and "contemplation" seemingly give some people the impression that the method almost solely belongs to the Tiantai School. In the Tiantai School, calming-contemplation is divided into four practices: Lesser Calming and Contemplation, Sequential Calming and Contemplation, Indefinite Calming and Contemplation, and Complete and Sudden Calming and Contemplation. Of these, Complete and Sudden Calming and Contemplation is actually similar to the method of sudden enlightenment in the Chan School. Also, the expedient means of entering the Chan gate usually adopts calming-contemplation as the most practical. Volume One of the Tiantai classic, *The Great Calming and Contemplation* says: "The quiescent Dharma nature is called 'calming,' the constant illumination in quiescence is called 'contemplation'." This is extremely similar to the opening lines of Hongzhi's *Silent Illumination* verse:

> *Silently and serenely one forgets all words*
> *clearly and vividly it appears before you.*

Master Hongzhi evidently adopted the basic method of calming and contemplation, and coordinated it with the theory of mutuality and interdependence of the Caodong School, and invented the new term "Silent Illumination."

"*Silent Illumination penetrates from the highest to the deepest*" has three meanings: First, Silent Illumination Chan is the highest teaching in Buddhadharma that encompasses the three karmic capacities of high, middle, and low. Second, Silent Illumination Chan enables the practitioner to gain ultimate enlightenment of the true nature of the Dharma, once and for all. Third, Silent Illumination Chan is the practice inherited by the buddhas and transmitted to all ages.

Afterword

I have always believed that to write books and produce literature is not easy, and especially difficult is it to comment on the Buddhist sutras and shastras. This is because we ourselves are not the Buddha, nor are we even the lineage masters. This being the case, how can we truly know the meanings of the sutras and shastras they bequeathed to us? How can we appropriately comment on these profound works? Therefore, although this essay is presented as an explanation, in reality it is merely my personal thoughts about Master Hongzhi's *Inscription on Silent Illumination*, which itself is based on the Buddhist sutras and words of the ancestral masters.

Bibliography

The Platform Sutra（T48，no. 2008）

《六祖壇經》。《大正藏》冊48，第2008號。

Diamond Sutra（T8，no. 239）

《金剛經》。《大正藏》冊8，第239號。

Kindred Sayings（T2，no. 99）

《雜阿含經》。《大正藏》冊2，第99號。

Long Sayings（T1，no. 1）

《長阿含經》。《大正藏》冊1，第1號。

Middle Length Sayings（T1，no. 26）

《中阿含經》。《大正藏》冊1，第26號。

Sutra of the Past and Present Cause and Effect（T3，no. 189）

《過去現在因果經》。《大正藏》冊3，第189號。

Shurangama Samadhi Sutra（T15，no. 642）

《首楞嚴三昧經》。《大正藏》冊15，第642號。

Pratyutpanna Samadhi Sutra（T13，no. 417）

《般舟三昧經》。《大正藏》冊13，第417號。

Great Calming and Contemplation（T46，no. 1911）

《摩訶止觀》。《大正藏》冊46，第1911號。

Mahaprajnaparamita Sutra（T21，no. 1339）

《大方等陀羅尼經》。《大正藏》冊21，第1339號。

Lotus Sutra（T9，no. 262）

《妙法蓮華經》。《大正藏》冊9，第262號。

Akshayamati Sutra（T54，no. 2128）

《阿差末經》《大正藏》冊54，第2128號。

Vimalakirti Sutra（T54，no. 475）

《維摩詰經》。《大正藏》冊14，第475號。

Bhadrakalpa Sutra（T54，no. 425）

《賢劫經》。《大正藏》冊14，第425號。

Sutra of Akshobhya Buddha's Land（T11，no. 313）

《阿閦佛國經》。《大正藏》冊11，第313號。

Sutra of Contemplating on the Amitayus Buddha（T12，no. 365）

《觀無量壽經》。《大正藏》冊12，第365號。

Record of the Transmission of the Lamp Composed in the Jingde Era（T51，no. 365）

《景德傳燈錄》。《大正藏》冊51，第2076號。

Shurangama Sutra（T19，no. 945）

《楞嚴經》。《大正藏》冊19，第945號。

Lokasthanabhidharma Treatise（T32，no. 1644）

《立世阿毘曇論》。《大正藏》冊32，第1644號。

Mahaparinirvana Sutra（T12，no. 374）

《大涅槃經》。《大正藏》冊12，第374號。

Sutra of the Buddha Speaking to Suka the Elder about Different Karmic Retributions（T1，no. 80）

《佛為首迦長者說業報差別經》。《大正藏》冊1，第80號。

Commentary on the Ullambana Sutra（T39，no. 1792）

《于蘭盆經疏》。《大正藏》冊39，第1792號。

Heart Sutra（T8，no. 253）

《心經》。《大正藏》冊8，第253號。

Faith in Mind（T51，no. 2076）

《信心銘》。《大正藏》冊51，第2076號。

Song of Mind（T51，no. 2076）

《心銘》。《大正藏》冊51，第2076號。

Reply to the Crown Prince's Question about the Essence of the Mind（T51，no. 2076）

《答皇太子問心要》。《大正藏》冊51，第2076號。

Two Entrances and Four Practices of Bodhidharma（T51，no. 2076）

《略辯大乘入道四行》。《大正藏》冊51，第2076號。

Song of Enlightenment by Yongjia（T48，no. 2014）

《永嘉證道歌》。《大正藏》冊48，第2014號。

Great Treatise on the Perfection of Wisdom（T25，no. 1509）

《大智度論》。《大正藏》冊25，第1509號。

Abhidharma Treatise（T29，no. 1588）

《阿毘達磨俱舍論》。《大正藏》冊29，第1588號。

Abhidharma-mahavibhasa-shastra（T27，no. 1545）

《大毘婆沙論》。《大正藏》冊27，第1545號。

Nyayanusara shastra（T29，no. 1562）

《阿毘達磨順正理論》。《大正藏》冊29，第1562號。

Madhyamika Shastra（T42，no. 1824）

《中觀論疏》。《大正藏》冊42，第1824號。

Vimshatika-vijnapti-matrata-siddhi-shastra（T31，no. 1588）

《唯識論》。《大正藏》冊31，第1588號。

Sutra of Queen Shrimala of the Lion's（T85，no. 2761）

《勝鬘經》。《大正藏》冊85，第2761號。

Inscription on Silent Illumination（T48，no. 2001）

《默照銘》。《大正藏》冊48，第2001號。

Song of the Precious Mirror Samadhi（T47，no. 1986）

《寶鏡三昧歌》。《大正藏》冊47，第1986號。

Inquiry into Matching Halves（T51，no. 2076）

《參同契》。《大正藏》冊51，第2076號。

Stanza of Upeksha（T48，no. 2013）

《優必叉頌》。《大正藏》冊48，第2013號。

Flower Ornament Scripture（T10，no. 279）

《華嚴經》。《大正藏》冊10，第279號。

Nirvana Sutra（T12，no. 374）

《涅槃經》。《大正藏》冊12，第374號。

Shih, Yinshun. 1981. *Origin and Development of Early Mahayana Buddhis*, Taipei: Zhengwen Publisher.

釋印順（1981）。《初期大乘佛教之起源與開展》。（臺北：正聞出版社，1981年初版）

Shih, Yinshun. 2009. First printed in 1949. *Introduction to the Buddhadharma*, Taipei: Zhengwen Publisher.

釋印順（2009）。《佛法概論》。（臺北：正聞出版社，1949年初版，2009年修訂版）

Shih, Sheng Yen. 1995. *Essentials for Cultivation and Realization in the Chan Tradition*, Taipei: Dharma Drum Publication.

釋聖嚴（1995）。《禪門修正指要》。（臺北：法鼓文化出版社，1995年初版）

Shi, Sheng Yen. 1989. *Gettig the Buddha Mind*, Taipei: Dharma Drum Publication.

釋聖嚴（1989）。《佛心眾生心》。（臺北：法鼓文化出版社，1989年初版）

Shi, Sheng Yen. 1982. *Gettig the Buddha Mind*, New York: Dharma Drum Publication.

Shi, Sheng Yen. 2005. *Gettig the Buddha Mind, On the Practice of Chan Retreat*, New York: North Atlantic Books.

Williams, Monier. 1899. *A Sanskrit-English Dictionary: Etymologically and Philologically Arranged with special reference to Cognate Indo-European Languages*, Oxford: Oxford University Press.

McRae, John. 2000. *The Platform Sutra of the Sixth Patriarch. Translated from the Chinese of Zongbao.* Berkeley: Numata Center for Buddhist Translation and Research.